Portland Community College

WITHDRAWN

Counseling Lesbian, Gay, Bisexual, and Transgender Substance Abusers
Dual Identities

Dana G. Finnegan, PhD, CAC
Emily B. McNally, PhD, CAC

D0223052

Routledge
Taylor & Francis Group
New York   London

Routledge is an imprint of the
Taylor & Francis Group, an informa business

Portland Community College

© 2002 by The Haworth Press, Inc All rights reserved. No part of this work may be reproduced or utilized in any form or by any means, electronic or mechanical, including photocopying, microfilm, and recording, or by any information storage and retrieval system, without permission in writing from the publisher. Printed in the United States of America Reprint - 2007

Reprinted 2009 by Routledge

Permission for Elsa Gidlow's work courtesy of Celeste West and Booklegger Publishing. P O. Box 460654, San Francisco, CA 94146. (415) 642-7569. <BookleggerPubl@aol com>

The Moon Is Always Female by Marge Piercy, copyright © 1980 by Marge Piercy. Used by permission of Alfred A. Knopf, a division of Random House, Inc

Excerpts from Anne Wilchins, *Read My Lips. Sexual Subversion and the End of Gender* © 1997. Reprinted by permission of Firebrand Books.

Excerpts © 1996 from *Psychology and Sexual Orientation* by Janis S Bohan. Reproduced by permission of Routledge, Inc., part of The Taylor & Francis Group.

Excerpts from *Trans Liberation* by Leslie Feinberg. Copyright © 1998 by Leslie Feinberg. Reprinted by permission of Beacon Press, Boston.

Cover design by Jennifer M Gaska

Library of Congress Cataloging-in-Publication Data

Finnegan, Dana G., 1932-
Counseling lesbian, gay, bisexual, and transgender substance abusers · dual identities / Dana G. Finnegan, Emily B. McNally.
p. cm.
Rev. ed. of: Dual identities. 1987.
Includes bibliographical references and index.
ISBN 0-7890-0403-8—ISBN 1-56023-925-5 (alk paper)
1. Gay men—Alcohol use—United States 2. Gay men—Drug use—United States. 3. Lesbians—Alcohol use—United States. 4 Lesbians—Drug use—United States. 5 Alcoholism counseling—United States. I. McNally, Emily B. II. Finnegan, Dana G., 1932- Dual identities. III. Title.

HV5139 .F56 2002
362.29'186'08664— dc21

2001051588

For all those lesbians, gay men, bisexuals, and transgendered
people who struggle daily to overcome the dual oppressions
of substance abuse and homo/bi/transphobia

and for all those families, friends, partners, co-workers,
educators, and counselors who care about them

and for all those pioneers who have gone before us,
some of whom have lost their lives along the way.

ABOUT THE AUTHORS

Dana G. Finnegan, PhD, CAC, has been an alcoholism counselor for many years and was a faculty member of the Rutgers Summer School of Alcohol and Drug Studies. She also served as Senior Editor of the *Journal of Chemical Dependency Treatment.*

Emily B. McNally, PhD, CAC, has been a psychologist and alcoholism counselor for many years. She was a faculty member of the Rutgers Summer School of Alcohol and Drug Studies, teaching courses on women and addiction, sexual identity, and supervision.

Both Dr. Finnegan and Dr. McNally are consultants specializing in the areas of substance abuse, sexual abuse, sexual identity issues, relationships, and trauma. Since 1979, they have presented at many national conferences and have conducted many workshops on these issues. They are co-founders and current board members of the National Association of Lesbian and Gay Addiction Professionals (NALGAP). In 1987, they wrote *Dual Identities,* the first book on the subject of counseling chemically dependent lesbians and gay men. This current book is a completely revised version of the earlier edition.

Dr. Finnegan and Dr. McNally are life partners who have been together for over 25 years.

CONTENTS

Foreword

In 1987 when the Lesbian and Gay Community Services Center of New York City started Project Connect, its alcoholism outreach, education and counseling program for the lesbian and gay community, it encompassed several firsts: the first time the state of New York funded a lesbian and gay-specific health promotion, disease prevention effort to be implemented by an openly gay and lesbian organization; the first alcoholism prevention program for the lesbian and gay community; the Center's first alcohol intervention effort. As the inaugural director of Project Connect, I was both exhilarated and challenged by all of these firsts. It soon became apparent as we got Project Connect off the ground that there was a pervasive lack of alcoholism and substance abuse programming and treatment in the greater metropolitan area that was sensitive to, relevant to, or affirmative of the lives and concerns of lesbians and gay men. One of the initial tasks we undertook, in addition to setting up counseling and support for the community at the Center, was to try to reach and educate mainstream providers on how to better serve their lesbian and gay clients.

Needless to say, we encountered resistance. Some programs did not understand or see a need to offer lesbians and gay men "special treatment" and others claimed not to have any lesbian or gay clients. The programs that were responsive to our contact were eager to have training and support. Although some research was available on lesbian and gay alcoholism, there was very little written that was supportive of lesbian and gay affirmative addiction treatment. Then I found *Dual Identities: Counseling Chemically Dependent Gay Men and Lesbians,* which had recently been published.

The book itself was an important first: the first comprehensive guide to understanding and treating lesbians and gay men with substance abuse issues. The book became our handbook, our resource, and our major reference. Whenever we encountered resistance to the notion that lesbian and gay affirmative substance abuse counseling was a valid and critical area of practice, we were able to brandish this credible and useful tool; whenever folks we trained were hungry for more information and knowledge, we had an actual and impressive textbook to hand them. Shortly afterward I had the good fortune to meet Dana Finnegan and Emily McNally for the first time and they have been invaluable colleagues and friends ever since!

Much has changed in the past fifteen years. Today, Project Connect is one of many such programs around the country, and since 1987, Project Connect and others have offered thousands of hours of training to hundreds of prevention and treatment providers, locally, regionally, and nationally. We have seen the inclusion of both the bisexual and transgender communities in our mission and our work, we have been able to document the needs of our communities more thoroughly as well as establish standards of care that other providers can utilize. This year we saw the U.S. Department of Health and Human Services publish two historic documents on LGBT health care, including alcoholism and substance abuse, *Healthy People 2010*, the LGBT Companion Document, and *A Provider's Introduction to Substance Abuse Treatment for Lesbian, Gay, Bisexual, and Transgender Individuals*. Both documents were prepared with important contributions from Dana Finnegan and Emily McNally.

However, much still needs to be done. Too many programs both here in New York City and elsewhere are not yet able, and even some are still unwilling, to treat LGBT persons with sensitivity and affirmation. There is still a paucity of public and private funding to support these lifesaving efforts in our communities. Dana Finnegan and Emily McNally remain active in their advocacy and education efforts to achieve these objectives.

Back in 1987, the book *Dual Identities* filled so many gaps. Dana and Emily articulated the needs, issues, and concerns of lesbian and gay consumers; helped nongay and gay providers alike to understand and apply appropriate counseling skills to these communities; addressed so clearly and profoundly the direct relationship between homophobia and discrimination against LGBT people and other forms of oppression—racism, sexism, classism—which enabled non-LGBT people to identify with the gay and lesbian experience, and opened the door to building allies.

It is with great excitement and with an enormous debt of gratitude that I help to introduce the updated version of this groundbreaking and important work by Dana Finnegan and Emily McNally, which now has added information about bisexual and transgender substance abusers. I look forward to working with them using the new edition of *Counseling Lesbian, Gay, Bisexual, and Transgender Substance Abusers: Dual Identities* for many more years to come as we, together, continue to work for the health and well-being of all of us.

Barbara Warren, PsyD, CASAC, CPP
Lesbian, Gay, Bisexual,
and Transgender Community Center,
New York City

Foreword

The revision of this book provides an important milestone in the advances in substance abuse treatment for lesbian, gay, bisexual, and transgender (LGBT) individuals. Until the latter part of the twentieth century, most of society misunderstood addiction as well as sexual orientation and gender identity. As a result, we spent much time educating society about the need for addiction treatment as well as providing accurate information about LGBT people. Though there are still many prejudices and biases that need to be confronted, since the first edition (titled *Dual Identities*) in 1987, some significant steps forward have been taken in the provision of culturally competent substance abuse treatment for the LGBT communities. More clinicians and treatment programs are recognizing the importance of providing culturally competent services to all their clients. For LGBT individuals seeking substance abuse treatment, more options are now available for treatment that is safe, accepting, and attuned to the needs of a diverse LGBT community.

In 1995, NAADAC (National Association of Alcoholism and Drug Abuse Counselors) published their first monograph focusing on the significant treatment issues for LGBT persons titled *Counseling Lesbian, Gay, and Bisexual Persons with Alcohol and Drug Abuse Problems.* In 2001, CSAT (Center for Substance Abuse Treatment) published a landmark federal government document titled *A Provider's Introduction to Substance Abuse Treatment for Lesbian, Gay, Bisexual, and Transgender Individuals.* In addition, since 1979 the National Association of Lesbian and Gay Addiction Professionals (NALGAP) has consistently advocated for quality treatment for LGBT substance abusers and has provided training and information to clinicians. These are just three examples of national agencies addressing the importance of clinicians and treatment providers improving their cultural competencies regarding LGBT clients.

In addition, the cultural milieu has improved for LGBT people. Nowadays, individuals grow up in a society encompassing much more understanding, tolerance, and acceptance of LGBT persons. The previous generation grew up with few images or articles in the media about LGBT people. Today, the media includes many images of LGBT persons, and their experiences are readily presented in television, newspapers, magazines, the Internet, etc. All of this points to the increasing understanding of LGBT by society, which parallels treatment providers' improved cultural competencies in service delivery.

Even with all these advances, however, there is still an enormous amount of prejudice against and oppression of lesbians, gays, bisexuals and transgender individuals, especially those who are substance abusers. Much work remains to be done in educating treatment professionals. *Counseling Lesbian, Gay, Bisexual, and Transgender Substance Abusers* provides that education. In addition, the book provides hope and support for those LGBT individuals seeking help with their substance abuse by addressing their issues, their concerns, and most important, their experiences. This book allows LGBT individuals the opportunity to see how cultural victimization such as heterosexism and homophobia have contributed to their abuse of alcohol and drugs. With this recognition, it offers a voice of hope for healing . . . a voice for people to say with LGBT pride, "I am clean and sober and proud!"

This is an excellent book for clients to validate their experiences and for clinicians to learn about the experiences of LGBT individuals and effective ways to counsel them. This book helps lead the way in the provision of treatment services for LGBT individuals so that their needs are met, and that ultimately they are able to achieve recovery from substance abuse and lead productive and fulfilling lives.

Joseph Neisen, PhD

Acknowledgments

We started out doing what we thought was a relatively small project, revising our 1987 book, *Dual Identities*. Many people helped and supported us during this process. To say that we could not have written this current book without their help may seem extreme, but the truth is that whatever book we would have written without their help would not be this book. Arlene Istar Lev very generously shared her material on transgender identity, even though she was working hard to finish her own book on the subject. When we were unable to find any books or articles that included material on transgender communities, Barbara Warren sent us studies and needs assessments that included a wealth of information and many rich descriptions of communities. Roz Blumenstein and Emilia Lombardi also shared information with us and pointed us in the right direction to find what we needed.

We are grateful to Karl White and Ed Craft for inviting us to participate in the SAMHSA:CSAT Workgroup in Washington, DC, which was the most rich, meaningful, and enjoyable work we have done in a long time, as well as being a consciousness-raising experience. We are grateful to all the people in the workgroup who were part of that powerful experience. Most especially, a number of people shared their experience and expertise about bisexuality and transgenderism, research about lesbians and gay men, and information about race and ethnic issues which were not our areas of expertise. Much of that material ultimately became a part of our book. For their contributions, we thank Alejandro Marcel, Tonda Hughes, Ron Fox, Marge Charmoli, Laurie Drabble, and Ednita Wright. In addition, we appreciate the help of the hardworking people at Johnson, Bassin, and Shaw, especially Cathy Crowley and Edna Davis-Brown.

One of our most rewarding ongoing experiences during the past years has been our involvement on the Board of the National Association of Lesbian and Gay Addiction Professionals (NALGAP). We thank Rodger Beatty, the President of NALGAP, for his excellent leadership and steady, solid support. We thank the other Board members who have dedicated themselves to helping LGBT substance abusers and their significant others. Many of the e-mails George Marcelle sent provided the latest information from CDC reports, the Gay Men's Health Summit, and other groups, and his accompanying good humor cheered us on. Nancy Kennedy's work has been invaluable on the CSAT workgroup, on the important LGBT companion document to the HP2010 document, and other projects which contribute to improving treatment for LGBT people. Sandi Armstrong, Rodger Beatty, and Irene Jillson helped NALGAP, especially by getting a grant from the Gill Foundation so the organization could continue its vital work. Our thanks go also to the other members of the Board, Joe Amico, Philip McCabe, Barbra Ann Perina, Michael Ralke, Candace Shelton, and Michael Browning for their hard work, dedication, and support.

In recent years, we have served as the co-chairs of the NALGAP Conference and have worked closely with NAADAC. One of the most positive parts of this experience has been working with Candace Baker, who never seems to run out of energy or good humor and who has helped us immeasurably.

Without the pioneering work of two people in particular, this book could not have been written. We thank William Cross for developing what he calls his "Afro-American model for self-actualization under conditions of oppression" (1971, p. 109). And we thank our friend, Vivienne Cass, for developing her model of homosexual identity formation in 1979.

We are grateful to Fritz Klein for generously allowing us to include his Klein Sexual Orientation Grid in our book. We also appreciate Tony Silvestre's generosity in sharing his organization audit and agency checklist on diversity with us.

We acknowledge and thank all those people who have supported us over the years and who have helped make the world a better place for LGBT people, especially Cody Barrett, Le Clair Bissell, Roxanne Kibben, Gail Milgram, Joe Neisen, Jack Ryan, and Michael Shernoff.

Finally, many special people helped in deep and profound ways: Madelyn Miller, Sue Elkind, Joyce Lerner, Michael Eigen, Sandy

Feinblum, Janet Linder, Judy Rowley, Janel Carino, and Nancy Grace. Our families have stood by us for many years with acceptance and love. especially Sylvia Bush, Emily's mother, who is in her nineties. She continues to be as interested in and accepting of our lives and our work today as she was when we met twenty-eight years ago. We should all have such a mother.

Every form of addiction is bad, no matter whether the narcotic be alcohol or morphine or idealism.

C. G. Jung, *Memories, Dreams, Reflections*, 1962

Thus far, I have learned that everybody is somebody's Other.

Armand Cerbone

As long as you are trying to be something other than what you actually are, your mind merely wears itself out. But, if you say, "This is what I am, it is a fact that I am going to investigate and understand," then you can go beyond.

J. Krishnamurti, *Talks and Dialogues*, 1968

To be nobody-but-myself—in a world which is doing its best, night and day, to make you everybody else—means to fight the hardest battle which any human being can fight, and never stop fighting.

e.e. cummings, *Collected Poems*, 1938

You say I am mysterious.
Let me explain myself:
In a land of oranges
I am faithful to apples.

Elsa Gidlow, "You Say I Am Mysterious,"
from *I Come with My Songs*, 1985

Praise the lives you did not choose. . . .
Freedom
Is our real abundance.

Marge Piercy, "The Sabbath of Mutual Respect,"
from *The Moon Is Always Female*, 1980

Chapter 1

Introductory Material

Where language and naming are power, silence is oppression, is violence.

Adrienne Rich
On Lies, Secrets, and Silence, 1979

INTRODUCTION

In the twenty-five years since we started working in the substance abuse treatment field, we have seen many changes both in the field and in society. Some of these changes have been phenomenal. In 1973, the American Psychiatric Association voted to no longer consider homosexuality as a mental disorder and it was removed from the *Diagnostic and Statistical Manual of Mental Disorders* (DSM-III) (1980); in the past five years, lesbians and gay men have appeared on the covers of and been featured in national magazines such as *Newsweek;* popular television and music stars have come out publicly; lesbians and gay men are characters in soaps and popular prime time sit-coms (though the men are often presented in very stereo-typed ways); and an openly gay man recently won a million dollars on the television show *Survivor.*

In addition, *M Butterfly,* the story of the love between a man and a male-to-female transgendered person was very popular both as a Broadway play and as a movie; mainstream culture seems fascinated by RuPaul's transgender drag and Dennis Rodman's "gender-bending" outfits and behaviors; Sandra Bernhard's bisexuality is an integral part of her comedy act; Renee Richards, an open male-to-female transgendered person, was active in U.S. tennis tournaments and long served as Martina Navratilova's coach.

But even though there is far more openness about and acceptance of different sexual orientations and gender identities than there once was, all is not well. The fact is, homophobia, biphobia, transphobia, hetero-sexism, and virulent hatred for those who are "Other" are alive and thriving in America. Even now, in the new century, the current *Diagnostic and Statistical Manual of Mental Disorders* (DSM-IV) categorizes gender dysphoria (discomfort, unease with one's gender) as a mental disorder, a classification which ignores the fact that one could be content with one's gender but experience dysphoria because of transphobic oppression.

The current political climate in this country is threatening, as evidenced by the current president who openly stated during his campaign that, if elected, he would not hire *any* lesbian or gay person to work in his administration. Other evidences of the harsh political climate are the many states that have created laws preventing the legalization of gay marriages and the numerous school boards that have voted to exclude sexual orientation from their antidiscrimination policies. In effect, these school boards have given tacit support to harassment of LGBT teachers and kids.

In many places in this country it is not safe to be out as a lesbian, gay male, bisexual, or transgendered person. Matthew Shepard was beaten to death because he was gay. Brandon Teena was beaten to death because he was transgendered. "Gay-bashing" and other hate crimes against lesbian, gay, bisexual, and transgendered (LGBT) people happen at an alarmingly high rate. Laws ensuring civil rights protections for LGBTs are extremely rare, and it is not uncommon for people to lose their jobs, family, friends, or places to live because they are lesbian, gay, bisexual, or transgendered.

Homophobia, biphobia, transphobia, and heterosexism are still such powerful forces that lesbian, gay, bisexual, and transgendered people (LGBT) who seek (or need) substance abuse treatment now face many of the problems that existed over twenty-five years ago— problems fueled by attitudes that LGBT people are abnormal or sick or sinful and deserve to be regarded (and treated) as second-class citizens, unworthy of compassion and care. In addition, many counselors who do provide care to these groups face problems created by a homo/bi/transphobic atmosphere—inadequate referral, training, and supervision resources and administrative policies that hamper their efforts to provide good treatment (see Neisen, 1994a).

We decided to revise this book now because of our deep concern about the plight of LGBT substance abusers who are still caught in the oppressive chains of homophobia, biphobia, transphobia, and heterosexism. As board members of the National Association of Lesbian and Gay Addiction Professionals (NALGAP), we see and hear of the problems LGBT substance abusers face. We are in contact with professionals from all over the country so we hear the latest about treatment conditions and the latest about advances and findings in the field.

Information about and understanding of LGBT issues have increased tremendously in these past years, and some research has begun to provide important facts about the LGBT communities and substance abuse. There is more information, broadened perspectives, and greater understanding of such matters as sexual orientation, gender identity, the formation of gender, the traumatic effects of oppression, the process of recovery when coupled with such trauma, and effective ways to help LGBT substance abusers recover. We are revising this book in order to present this material and to discuss effective ways to use it. We have updated the information, clarified terms and ideas, and broadened our perspectives.

Focus of This Book

The primary focus of this book is on substance abusers whose sexual orientation is toward people of the same sex. This population includes (1) substance abusers who are lesbian or gay identified; (2) substance abusers who are bisexual and have been or may be involved with a same-sex partner; (3) substance abusers who are transgendered and who have or have had same-sex partners or who self-identify as lesbian, gay, or bisexual.

In addition, the book will take into account two other groups of substance abusers: (1) those men who have sex with men (MSM) and women who have sex with women (WSW) but who do not identify themselves as being lesbian, gay, or bisexual; and (2) those who, for whatever reason, are confused and conflicted about their gender identity, sexuality, or sexual orientation or are questioning who they are and where they fit on the continuums of gender, sex, and sexual orientation.

Because all of these people, to some extent, belong in the category of the despised or discounted "Other," the category of "Queer" because they are different from the mainstream, they are vulnerable to and often subject to the oppressive and destructive forces of homophobia, biphobia, transphobia, and heterosexism. Thus this book will focus on the destructive effects and consequences of these oppressions (e.g., shame, self-hatred) and on ways to help people who are burdened by *two* stigmatized identities (substance abuser and sexual and/or gender minority member). All who are subjected to these oppressions must ultimately deal in some way with who they are and hopefully learn to accept themselves in an unaccepting world. This book, then, is offered as a guide for helping counselors help their clients accomplish these tasks.

Basic Premises

At the outset, it is important to establish the basic assumptions and premises that underlie what is said in this book.

- Throughout the book, we use the term "substance abuse" to refer to the abuse of alcohol and other mood-altering drugs (including such drugs as cocaine and crystal meth, designer drugs such as GHB or Special K, and prescription drugs such as Valium or Seconal).
- Throughout the book, we use the term "LGBT" to refer to lesbian, gay, bisexual, and transgendered people. We have chosen to group them together because they are "Queer-identified"; i.e., diverse as they may be, they share the stigma of being different from the mainstream and therefore unacceptable. They are also extremely vulnerable to abuse, rejection, and oppression.
- This matter of terminology reflects a problem basic to discussing different groups of people as though they were the same because they belong to a larger grouping. For example, in some ways lesbians are more like all women than they are like gay

men. Some bisexual men identify more as gay than as bisexual. Yet for the purposes of this book, we discuss lesbians, gay men, bisexuals, and transgendered people together because they share some similar issues and problems as a result of both their gender identity and sexual orientation and their substance abuse. Other books remain to be written on the specific issues and problems of each particular group.

- It is important to keep in mind the tremendous diversity among lesbians, gay men, bisexuals, and transgendered people. The range of diversity is as great as it is among the non-LGBT population. Therefore, it is inaccurate to refer to or view someone as *the* lesbian or *the* gay man or *the* bisexual or *the* transgendered person. Each person must be regarded as a unique individual, distinct from all others in his or her group.

- This book is not intended as a primer on substance abuse treatment, but rather as a guide to the issues specific to the treatment of lesbian, gay, bisexual, and transgendered substance abusers.

- It is our view that addiction to alcohol and other drugs is a physical/emotional/spiritual disease. In the past ten or fifteen years, what constitutes successful treatment has become controversial. In some areas of the substance abuse field, abstinence is no longer viewed as the primary goal for successfully treating addictions. Instead, there are now many proponents of harm or risk reduction as a viable form of treatment, especially with particular populations such as adolescents and those who are HIV positive. We believe that harm or risk reduction is a valid and helpful form of treatment for many people. For many others, however, if they use alcohol and/or other drugs addictively in ways that are harmful to themselves and/or others, then full recovery ultimately requires abstinence.

- LGBT substance abusers are frequently unrecognized and *underserved* populations with issues that are specific to them and that need to be understood and addressed by helping professionals.

- There are no easy answers or formulas of the "Always do X; but if the client is LGBT, do Z" variety. There *are* many questions and some helpful suggestions and guidelines. But much of what is said must be tempered by the qualification that, "It depends. . . ."

- The treatment of LGBT substance abusers is an extremely complex subject which, of necessity, is presented in a somewhat simplified manner. It is important to remember that any consideration of LGBT substance abuse issues needs to involve an awareness of interactions among many factors such as sexuality, addiction, trauma, psychology, physiology, social and religious mores, and cultural attitudes.
- Because of this complexity, this book can serve only as a beginning, a guide, and cannot replace experiential training, reading, interacting with people who are LGBT, direct counseling experience, and good supervision. This book can, however, provide helpful information, practical suggestions, guidelines, techniques, and resources for further exploration of the subject.
- This book is primarily directed to and written for counselors and other helping professionals, the majority of whom are not lesbian, gay, bisexual, or transgendered. These are the people who are on the "front lines," helping LGBT substance abusers in their struggles to recover. As Markowitz (1997) so powerfully notes:

Straight allies are a great and often unacknowledged gift to the queer community. . . . I feel safer and less isolated when I consider that there are straight teachers, religious leaders, politicians, family members, friends and neighbors out there who are willing to put themselves on the line because of my inalienable right to dignity and respect. (p. 2)

Design of the Book

The book is divided into three major parts.

- Chapters 1 through 5 supply information basic to understanding the issues and problems specific to lesbian, gay, bisexual, and transgendered people. These chapters also examine how these issues and problems affect LGBT people who are substance abusers and the treatment they receive. In other words, before an LGBT substance abuser even walks through the door, counselors should know these things.
- Chapters 6 through 9 present information and discuss skills counselors will use directly in treatment.

- The Appendixes give information about the resources counselors will need in order to assist their clients.

The Counselor's Part

Although you may spend only a short time with each lesbian, gay, bisexual, or transgendered client and although you may play only a small part in the long process of recovery, whatever support and respectful treatment you provide has an impact far beyond the act itself. Your humane treatment in a frequently hostile, heterosexist, homo/bi/ transphobic society can tip the balance toward recovery.

LANGUAGE PROBLEMS

Language is slow to catch up with reality. There simply aren't enough words to describe everyone who reads the pages of our magazine because we cross into new territory of sexual identity, multiple genders and relationships.

L. Markowitz (2000, p. 2)

It is sometimes said that whoever has the right words, whoever has the power to name things, rules the world. The power of wizards and charismatic leaders rests in great part on two powers: their ability to communicate, to say the right words at the right time so they stir people's passions and get them to act; and their ability to name things and thereby control them. Conversely, when people do not have the right words or control over the naming process, they lack power because others label them and their reality and use words as weapons to oppress.

Greene (2000) agrees. As she points out,

In both the psychology and politics of oppression we acknowledge that those who have the power to define experiences also have the power to confer or deny legitimacy to experiences selectively. (p. 34)

Greene (2000) goes on to note the power of the other side of language—"the violent and oppressive effect of silencing."

Exclusive attention to the most explicit, blatant, or outrageous incidents of heterosexism fails to capture the oppressiveness of omission and invisibility for many diverse groups of lesbians, gay men, and bisexual men and women. (p. 34)

Unclear Language

For the length of its history, the lesbian, gay, bisexual, and transgendered population has been plagued by the problem of not having the right words and of being negatively named or labeled. The task of communicating clearly about lesbian, gay, bisexual, and transgendered people is made extremely difficult because many of the words available for thinking about and discussing concepts, thoughts, and ideas about LGBTs frequently do not have clear meanings and understandings although they often convey distinctly negative values.

Many words used to describe experiences that are relevant to the treatment of LGBT substance abusers do not have common, agreed-upon meanings and are fraught with controversy and confusion. In addition, the processes by which people come to know about and manage their stigmatized identities, the identities that LGBT people claim, and the destructive oppressions they face, are all in need of clearer words and definitions and neutral, value-free language. Unfortunately, many of the words that are currently available do not communicate clear or value-free understandings about the complex experiences and lives of LGBT people.

Shedding some light on the problems, issues, and lives of LGBT substance abusers is no small task, given the limitations in the quantity and quality of existing words. The language now available for describing very powerful and complex experiences is a nightmare. It is impossible to find clear, meaningful words to define or even fit all the various experiences, identities, behaviors, and feelings of LGBT people. Precise language just doesn't exist at this point. Many of the words that do exist are so overused or misused that they do not clarify the subject, but rather add more confusion to an already complex topic.

For example, what does the word *lesbian* mean? Is a lesbian a woman who has sex with other women? What if a woman is attracted to other women, but has never had sex with a woman? Is she a lesbian? Does she have to label herself a lesbian to be one? Does she have to take on the identity of a lesbian in order to be one? Does she have to be labeled a lesbian by others in order to be a lesbian or is her identity dependent on what she calls herself? What if she has sex with other women, but does not consider herself a lesbian? Is she one? What if a woman lives with another woman for thirty years and the two women live their lives as heterosexual couples do—sharing a household, raising children, taking vacations together, working for the good of their relationship, and sleeping in the same bed—but never label themselves or declare themselves to be lesbians. What label fits them? What if a woman has a husband and children and considers herself heterosexual, but has sex with another woman. Is she a lesbian? Is she bisexual? What should she be called?

The confusion about words, labels, and language becomes even more problematic when the concept of *gender* is introduced. A transgender person can be a lesbian, a gay man, a bisexual, or a heterosexual. What name should be given to the fear, hatred, and hostility expressed toward transgender people? Is it homophobia if the transgender individual is heterosexual? Is it heterosexism? Transsexism? Transphobia? No specific and explicit words exist to describe the variety of identities and oppressions experienced by people who are outside the mainstream of society. This is another form of prejudice—the lack of language to name and describe the depth, richness, and creativity of different identities and experiences and the cruelty of the oppressions that keep them hidden and unnamed.

Another problem is that there are no adequate words to name and describe the many varieties of complex sexual and relationship behaviors and experiences that occur. For example, many men who have sex with men do not identify as "gay" or as "homosexual." What should they be called? Are they gay or homosexual if they don't consider themselves to have that identity? Some people now prefer the term "MSM" to refer to men who have sex with men. Are there female counterparts for this male experience? If so, are they women who have sex with women (WSW)? Or should they be called women who love women (WLW)? Some women refer to themselves and others who love more than one woman as "polyamorous," rather than non-monogamous.

Who makes the decisions about what words fit which experiences and what the words really mean? It is difficult to discuss the experiences of people who are different from the mainstream of heterosexuality and gender conformity when there are not clear, agreed-upon words with which to communicate. It seems as though there are many more questions than answers at this point.

Some people have begun to use the term *Queer* to refer to people who live their lives outside the mainstream of heterosexuality and traditional gender rolès and scripts. *Queer* would include all of the varieties of sexual orientations and gender identities (LGBT) as well as all the behaviors (e.g., MSM) imaginable. As Markowitz (2000) comments,

> There is a word that invites us all into the big tent together, that is broad and expansive and plastic enough to encompass all our diversity and permutations we have yet to invent. But that word is deeply controversial, and is associated, for some, with the pain of harassment and ridicule. The word is "Queer." (p. 2)

Although many people are uncomfortable with the word and associate it with oppression and homophobia, many LGBT people are claiming it as a political term and a rallying cry to express their identity as marginalized outsiders who neither want nor intend to become part of the traditional mainstream. As Markowitz (1997) notes, the word "has also been reclaimed by many urban and younger 'queers' who like identifying that way because they feel it represents their fluid sexual identity" (p. 2). Similar to the ways that African Americans claimed the word *black* and the experience of Black Power and "Black is Beautiful" to assert their pride and individual and social identity, many LGBT people are calling themselves and each other "Queer" to express their positive feelings about being different from the mainstream and about being who they are.

The Term "Homophobia"

It is important here to consider a powerful term that is central to any examination of the oppression of LGBT people. The word *homophobia* has been used to describe the experience of society's oppression of homosexual people and has been compared to sexism, racism, and classism. Yet, homophobia is not an "ism." It is a "phobia," as in *fear of;* the rest of the word is "homo," as in *same.* Thus "homophobia" means *fear of the same*—"homophobia." When we consider other "phobias," we think of strong fears of such things as snakes, bugs, elevators, or flying. Phobia is an intense, irrational fear of something. But certainly irrational fear is not the only—and often not the primary—feeling that fuels oppression of LGBT people. Yet the term homo*phobia* is expected to capture the power of that oppression, to refer not only to fear, but also to rage, hatred, revulsion, disgust, and derision. The word homophobia just does not adequately convey the full range of ugly and cruel feelings.

Other words to describe prejudices against hated people or groups carry meanings associated with irrational fears *and* rage, hatred, and violence. For example, racism raises the specter of not only fear, but also hatred, violence, and anger toward blacks or other ethnic minorities. It is not difficult to see some of the consequences of racism when a group of white men tie a black man to the back of a pickup truck and drag him to his death. When we think of racism, we can see and feel the cruel and evil power that resides in the word and in the images the word conjures up. The word and the experience have a history. We have seen pictures of the results of the racism of slavery and the violence done to blacks, Native Americans, Asians, and other ethnic groups in this country, and we know how destructive racism is to people every day.

Racism has a geography, too. In our newspapers, magazines, and on television, we can see the consequences of it both in this country and in many other countries throughout the world. For example, beatings of black men occur from California to New York. In the Middle East and in Europe, we witness the violence that takes place when one race of people considers itself superior to another race of people and attempts to wipe them out. Both historically and geographically, we have powerful, violent images of people and places to associate with the word and the concept of racism.

It is not difficult to see the consequences of sexism, either, when women are victims of domestic violence, rapes, and other abuses. These crimes are visible on TV, in newspapers and magazines, in our everyday lives. Like racism, sexism has a history. Early in the twentieth century, women in our country had to fight to get the vote. Statistics continue to show that women do not get equal pay for equal jobs, and women are still fighting for protections against sexual harassment and domestic violence.

Sexism has a geography, too. Frequently, reports and articles circulate in the media about violence against women in this and other countries. In many other countries, it is acceptable for women to be oppressed, attacked, mutilated, or killed. For example, in Afghanistan, crowds of men have stoned women to death for exposing their faces or even their arms in public. In Bangladesh, young men whose attentions are rejected throw acid in the young women's faces—and do so with impunity.

What about homophobia? Does it have a history? Does it have a geography? Historically, most lesbians and gays in this society have been invisible and most of the hatred and violence against them has been hidden from view. People in the heterosexual mainstream want LGBTs to stay in the closet and the violence against them to stay hidden, as it has for so long. For years, most of the aggression and brutality against LGBT people was reported only in underground newspapers, in the "Gay Press," or was spoken about by LGBT people as part of an oral tradition. So, homophobia does not have a visible history. Only in the past thirty-some years have LGBTs even begun to receive any kind of coverage in mainstream media.

Homophobia does not have a geography, either. Very few people know what goes on in this country and in other countries to oppress LGBT people. Only recently have stories begun to find their way into the mainstream media. For example, one can certainly see the consequences of homophobia when gay men are beaten and left to die in a field in Oklahoma or on some dark road in Alabama or lesbians are raped outside a lesbian bar in California or transgender sex workers are murdered in New York City, often with apparent impunity. In addition, even to this day little is reported or known about the status (or plight) of LGBT people in other countries. In much, if not most, of the media, LGBTs do not exist—they are non-news, therefore, nonentities.

When violence against LGBT people *is* covered by the media, the only word available to describe it is "homophobia." But this word does not seem to carry the same meanings and images that racism and sexism do. Were the men who killed Matthew Shepard afraid of him?

Or did they hate him and want to rid the world of him? Perhaps these feelings should be called "homohatred" rather than "homophobia." Maybe other words can be found that convey more intensely rageful feelings, words such as "genocide" or "homicide." There is a need for words that can capture the intensity of the hatred and violence directed at LGBT people. Perhaps a better word would be something like "homo-cide" or "homo-cidalism."

Instead of homophobia, a number of people prefer the word *heterosexism* because it puts the onus of negative feelings and actions on the heterosexual persons who are doing the hating, rather than on those who are the object of that hatred (LGBT people). In addition, "heterosexism" is a parallel word with sexism and racism. It means that the people in the heterosexual majority have rights and privileges not accorded to those who do not belong to that majority. It also describes ideas and feelings of some people in the mainstream, such as a belief they are superior to those in the oppressed minority. Herek (1995) provides a succinct definition of heterosexism: "the ideological system that denies, denigrates, and stigmatizes any nonheterosexual form of behavior, identity, relationship, or community" (p. 321).

However, the word *heterosexism* does not have a history or a geography of hatred, cruelty, and oppression associated with it. Thus it cannot really be classed with sexism and racism as a term powerful enough to accurately describe destructive societal forces directed against LGBT people. In effect, heterosexism does not adequately convey the same images of cruelty, hatred, and violence as do racism and sexism.

The Language of Oppressions

These words—heterosexism, homophobia—are not sufficient to capture the terrible power and effects of cruel and deadly oppression. Unfortunately, they are what currently exists. In addition, there are no adequate words to specifically describe the oppressions visited upon bisexuals and transgendered people. There are only the terms *biphobia* and *transphobia* which suffer from the same inadequacies and problems that beset *homophobia*.

No single word captures the thousands of ways that LGBT people are oppressed every day of their lives. Racism, sexism, classism, and heterosexism (and bisexism and transsexism) keep people oppressed every day in ways that range from less dramatic and visible, but no less destructive acts to overt physical violence. Many people in society are kept "in their place" by the less visible forms of these powerful and oppressive forces.

These "isms" and "phobias" can be viewed on a continuum, ranging from subtle, quiet, invisible, but relentless and ubiquitous forces to the opposite end of the continuum of loud, overt, dangerous, violent, open, and blatant destructive forces. When we talk about heterosexism or homophobia or biphobia or transphobia in this book, we mean negative attitudes, feelings, and experiences that may fall anywhere on the continuum from negative looks to verbal slurs to physical assaults to murder.

Because the available words describing LGBT oppression are limited, we have had to choose words that hopefully can best convey the destructive effects of that oppression. Therefore, we have made the following choice. From time to time, we will use the terms *heterosexism* and *transsexism* as ways to refer to the institutional and institutionalized prejudice and oppression visited on lesbians, gay men, bisexuals, and transgendered people.

Furthermore, flawed as it is, because it is so widely used and is so familiar, we have chosen *homophobia* as the primary term to describe the oppression of people whose sexual orientation is lesbian or gay and people who are even suspected of such orientation. We use the term *biphobia* to describe the particular oppression visited upon bisexual people by both heterosexuals and homosexuals. We use the term *transphobia* to describe the prejudice against and oppression of transgender people for "transgressing" society's codes of gender conformity, prejudice directed at them from both the heterosexual and the gay and lesbian communities.

Perhaps the simplest way to approach these issues is to recognize that, whatever terms we use, people who are lesbian, gay, bisexual, and transgendered are affronted, mistreated, scorned, abused, injured, sometimes murdered. Many LGBT people are in danger every day of their lives. Those truths lie at the heart of all our considerations, all our actions, all our attitudes—no matter what the words, no matter what the language.

IDENTITY

Who is it that can tell me who I am?

W. Shakespeare
King Lear, II.iv.226

Every person has multiple identities—for instance, *racial* (e.g., African American, Latino/a); *religious* (e.g., Christian, Jew, atheist; Episcopal, Methodist, Sephardic, Reformed); *gender* (e.g., male, female, androgynous). In the best of circumstances, these multiple identities are forged into an integrated, overall identity in which the various "smaller" identities operate and relate to one another in a coherent manner.

Identity: A Basic Definition

Since so many definitions of identity abound in the psychological and sociological literature, it becomes necessary to choose one that can accurately represent basic thinking about this concept. Josselson (1987) provides such a definition. She states, "Identity is the stable, consistent, and reliable sense of who one is and what one stands for in the world" (p. 10) and goes on to note that identity is "a property of the ego that organizes experience" (p. 12).

Perhaps the clearest statement is that,

> Identity . . . is a dynamic fitting together of parts of the personality with the realities of the social world so that a person has *a sense both of internal coherence* and *meaningful relatedness to the real world* [our italics]. (Josselson, 1987, pp. 12-13)

Breakwell (1986) discusses how people develop their identity structure through the processes of: (1) *assimilation:* incorporating new elements into their identity structure; (2) *accommodation:* adjusting to make room for the new elements; and (3) *evaluation:* ascribing meaning to the old and new identity contents. These processes operate in relation to three principles—*continuity, distinctiveness,* and *self-esteem*—which describe the fundamental attributes of identity.

A threat to identity occurs when the ongoing processes of identity are challenged by outer or inner events and cannot support or sustain continuity, distinctiveness, or self-esteem. As Breakwell (1986) notes, threats to identity can only be meaningfully studied in a social context. . . . the structure of identity, the nature of the threat and the coping strategies deployed to deal with it, only achieve meaning when related to dominant social beliefs and cultural expectations. (p. 7)

For example, when people become addicted, their value systems often change radically. They may lie, cheat, and steal in order to maintain their addiction. Such behaviors seriously threaten the continuity of their original identity as a law-abiding, ethical person. Another example might be that of a man who discovers that he is attracted to both women and other men. Seeing himself (and fearing that others may see him) as bisexual may threaten his self-esteem if he has a strong investment in his identity as a heterosexual.

When people's identities are threatened, they develop *coping strategies* which consist of any activity that eliminates or alters the threat. Examples of some strategies are denial, passing, compliance, and getting involved in a support group. This concept of coping with threats to identity will be discussed later in more detail. (See section on Defenses Chapter 5, pp. 97-100.)

Social Constructionism and Essentialism

There are two basic views about the structure of identity. The *social constructionist* view argues that identity is not made up of traits or attributes that already exist in reality; rather, it is a socially constructed concept in which particular meanings are ascribed to the various components (e.g., actions and experiences). For example, depending on the context, different meanings will be ascribed to a man wearing women's clothing—he might be viewed as a homosexual or as a seeker after spiritual knowledge or as an entertainer. Thus an identity that was defined, at least in part, by a man wearing women's clothing would be a different identity in different contexts.

Because it depends on the interaction of social and psychological processes in a particular historical context, this social constructionist view obviously provides a freer, less rigid, more fluid emotional and cultural climate. It provides a climate in which people can develop their identities without the constraints of narrow, limited notions of identity.

The opposite view is the *essentialist* one. It asserts that identity has distinct, intrinsic, definitive traits and attributes. People living in a culture that views identity as basic and immutable would therefore experience particular identities as "set in stone" (See Bohan, 1996). An example of this view might be the belief that people who deviate from gender role expectations are homosexual. This is an essentialist belief that a person's experiences (gender role deviation) *are* that person (Bohan, 1996). In other words, in this example, the essentialist belief is that this person's identity is homosexual.

Bohan (1996) comments on how this perspective relates to sexual orientation:

> At present . . . the culture we live in . . . [regards] sexual orientation as a core, nuclear, essential defining attribute of identity, which can be defined by membership in one of two (or at best, three) discrete categories [heterosexual, homosexual, bisexual]. (p. 9)

In effect, such an essentialist view leaves people no room to simply experience life without having a label thrust upon them. For example, a woman who loves another woman but also loves her husband will be seen as lesbian or perhaps bisexual. There is no room for a broader, less restrictive description of her sexual orientation and sexual identity. Another example is that of a young person who has male genitalia but *knows* that "he" is really a female. A strict essentialist view marks this child as male, arguing that maleness is the core, defining attribute of this person's identity.

This view reassures those who need a rigid, either-or way to see the world and describe others, but it is restrictive and limiting—and often inaccurate. Certainly it does not help capture the tremendous, very real diversity of life.

Stigmatized Identity

Any discussion of lesbian, gay, bisexual, or transgender identity or of substance abuser identity must always attend to questions of stigma. Both identities are marked by *stigma*—what Goffman (1963) defines as "an attribute that is deeply discrediting" (p. 3), "an undesired differentness from what" others anticipate (p. 5).

Goffman (1963) goes on to differentiate between two types of stigma. A *discredited* identity is one that is devalued and is readily evident to others and that "immediately elicits prejudice" (Bohan, 1996, p. 124). Some examples are a person of a racial minority or a person who is blind or obese. A *discreditable* identity is one that is devalued but is not visible, not evident to others, and therefore does not elicit prejudice unless it is revealed or becomes known. Examples are LGBT people who are closeted and whose sexual orientation and/or gender identity are not known. Other examples are recovering addicts/alcoholics. Only if these people are found out or choose to reveal their identity can they be discredited, stigmatized.

Managing a discreditable, stigmatized identity carries a high price, as Bohan (1996) notes:

> A discreditable identity can be hidden, and therefore demands continuous decisions regarding whether to conceal the identity. The choice to remain invisible or "closeted," in turn, requires techniques not for managing prejudice and discrimination, but for controlling information about one's identity, and for coping with acceptance that one knows to be contingent on deception. (p. 125)

Managing *two* stigmatized identities increases the pressure exponentially. Either people are coping with concealing their stigmatized identities and the concomitant stress of being discreditable or are dealing with the usually negative reactions elicited by being "out" and therefore discredited.

Dual Identities, Dual Traumas

An examination of the effects of having two stigmatized identities—that of being an LGBT person and that of being a substance abuser—requires careful consideration of trauma. McCann and Pearlman (1990a) define psychological trauma in this way:

> An experience is traumatic if it (1) is sudden, unexpected, or non-normative, (2) exceeds the individual's perceived ability to meet its demands, and (3) disrupts the individual's frame of reference and other central psychological needs and related schemas. (p. 10)

Herman (1992) adds that "Traumatic events overwhelm the ordinary systems of care that give people a sense of control, connection, and meaning" (p. 33).

The devastating, traumatic effects of heterosexism and homophobia/biphobia/transphobia are discussed by various people. Alvarez (1994) contends that gay people are frequently victims of emotional, and often physical, abuse from this culture and likens them to Holocaust and sexual abuse survivors. Dillon (1993) speaks of "the malevolent influence of homophobia so evident in national life today . . ." (p. 1). Bohan (1996) notes how relentless hatred directed at LGB people traumatizes them. Various writers discuss the emotional cruelty and physical abuse visited upon transgendered people (Brown and Rounsley, 1996; Clements, 1999; Israel and Tarver, 1997; Lombardi et al., 1998; Marcel, 1998). Such abuse traumatizes.

In addition, addictions traumatize people. Bean (1981) describes alcoholism as a "catastrophic experience" (p. 90) that traumatizes alcoholics. Brown (1998) and Khantzian (1998) also contend that alcoholism and other drug addictions traumatize people caught in those addictions.

Trauma and Identity

> The only merciful thing about drug abuse is the speed with which it devastates you. Alcoholics can take decades to destroy themselves and everyone they touch. The drug addict can accomplish this in a year or two. Of course, suicide is even more efficient.
>
> Rita Mae Brown
> *Starting from Scratch*, 1988

It is important for counselors to have a clear sense of what their clients must struggle with as they seek to recover from the dual traumas inflicted by their substance abuse and by the oppression of heterosexism and homo/bi/transphobia.

The link between trauma and identity is a powerful one. As Herman (1992) explains, trauma shatters a person's sense of the self. She further describes the destructive power of trauma:

> Traumatized people suffer damage to the basic structures of the self. They lose their trust in themselves, in other people, and in

God. Their self-esteem is assaulted by experiences of humiliation, guilt, and helplessness. Their capacity for intimacy is compromised by intense and contradictory feelings of need and fear. The identity they have formed prior to the trauma is irrevocably destroyed. [There is a] . . . loss of self. (p. 56)

Although the traumatic effects of substance abuse and of the oppression of homo/bi/transphobia are different in some ways, they also share certain identifiable similarities. Thus it is feasible to group a discussion of some effects of both traumas. At the same time, it is important to remember that different people respond to these two traumas in very different ways, and the range of people's responses and experiences are as broad and varied as are the people themselves.

Trauma changes people's inner subjective world, and the resultant post-traumatic stress disorder (PTSD) involves a profound rearrangement in their ability to regulate their feelings (Khantzian, 1998)—for example, people may have difficulty regulating intolerable feelings (such as despair, guilt, terror); they may experience psychic numbing; they may become split off from their feelings and/or behavior (Herman, 1992; Krystal, 1988). Some other consequences of trauma may be failures in self-care (such as engaging in unsafe sex practices, putting oneself in harm's way); psychosomatic conditions; and shame and low self-esteem. Or, as Bean (1981) describes one of the effects of alcoholism, "the ruin of self-esteem" (p. 90).

The dual traumas of substance abuse and the oppression of homo/bi/transphobia can be devastating and far-reaching. As Herman (1992) notes, "The core experiences of psychological trauma are disempowerment and disconnection from others" (p. 133). The disjunctions created by trauma(s) disorganize, disorient, and disintegrate people's sense of self.

The boundaries of the self are violated by stigma, prejudice, and chemicals. For example, closeted LGBT people are assaulted daily by the casual cruelty of slurs and jokes. In addition, as people are "made deviant" by the culture and viewed as unacceptable and as people's abuse of chemicals separates them from the "normal" world, their connections with self and others are damaged or ruptured. Ultimately, they may end up feeling they are not worthy of connection.

It is important to note here that not all LGBT people are as traumatized by stigma and prejudice. D'Augelli's (1994) concept of "affirmative assumption" suggests that many LGBTs are strengthened by coming to terms with the challenges and stresses inherent in dealing with a stigmatized identity. Greene (2000) also discusses Jones' (1997) concept of "resilience," a

> form of psychological independence . . . characterized by an attitude that allows a person to structure their life so as to "ward off the malevolently controlling intentions of others. (p. 7)

And, certainly, not all substance abusers are traumatized in a major way. As Herman (1992) points out, the severity of the trauma and the basic resiliency of the individual determine the power and impact of the trauma.

On the other hand, counselors need to remember that many of the people they work with have been blasted by their substance abuse and injured by the violence and oppression of a homo/bi/transphobic society. They have been anesthetizing the pain of both traumas and now must deal with the effects of those traumas and with their stigmatized identities without the familiar "help" of chemicals.

The Counselor's Role

The counselor's role in this process is crucial. As Herman (1992) comments, "Recovery is based on empowerment of the survivor and the creation of new connections. Recovery can take place only within the context of relationships; it cannot occur in isolation" (p. 133). She goes on to explain that

> Because traumatic life events invariably cause damage to relationships, people in the survivor's social world have the power to influence the eventual outcome of the trauma. A supportive response from other people may mitigate the impact of the event[s], while a hostile or negative response may compound the damage and aggravate the traumatic syndrome. In the aftermath of traumatic life events, survivors are highly vulnerable. Their sense of self has been shattered. That sense can be rebuilt only as it was built initially, in connection with others. (p. 61)

Greene's (2000) explanation of Jones' (1997) ideas supports this view:

This form of psychological independence is nurtured in resilient individuals by loving and effective caregivers. Such caregivers need not be parents or biological relations. However, they are people whose entrance at critical developmental junctures in the course of the resilient individual's life has powerful remedial effects when they occur. (p. 7)

When counselors (among others) are supportive and empathic, LGBT substance abusers have their best chance to recover. If, however, counselors are homo/bi/transphobic or are prejudiced against substance abusers—or both—then they may well compound the damage already done by these dual traumas.

Counselors can play an integral role in people's recovery from the damage inflicted both by substance abuse and by a homo/bi/transphobic culture. They can do so by helping clients in their process of establishing or securing a positive identity both as a recovering substance abuser and as a lesbian, gay, bisexual, or transgendered individual. That is a privilege not accorded to many.

Positive Identities

Developing and expressing a positive identity, reaching a state of healthy balance, demands that people learn to manage stigmas and stigmatized identities, whether visible or not (Bohan, 1996). Much of this book, therefore, centers on (1) how LGBT people who are substance abusers manage two stigmatized identities and develop a positive sense of self and (2) how counselors and others can help them do so.

Chapter 2

Background Information

When we identify with our body, the condition of our body determines our feelings and attitudes—whether we are happy, peaceful, anxious, fearful, angry, or depressed. When we identify only with our body, we walk in a small, narrow world.

Tilleraas (1988)

INTRODUCTION

Our culture has great difficulty talking seriously about sexuality, and most people have trouble feeling at ease with the topic. Many people can joke about sex, tell and laugh at dirty jokes, enjoy sexual subjects behind the backs of "parent figures," or be involved in pornography. But a great number of people have difficulty talking openly, seriously, respectfully about sex. Because discussing sex is so difficult for some people, their resistance increases greatly when the specific topic is homosexuality or any other form of sexuality that differs from that of the mainstream.

Most people know very little about sexuality in general and bisexuality or homosexuality in particular. Many lesbian, gay, bisexual, and transgendered people know very little about bisexuality, homosexuality, or transgenderism. People's lack of knowledge creates discomfort and generates resistance to discussing or dealing with these subjects. Comments from LGBTs who are or were clients in treatment programs and from counselors who work in those programs about the attitudes expressed toward sexuality and bisexuality, homosexuality, and transgenderism are illuminating. For example, some substance abuse treatment programs still omit bisexuality, homosexuality, and transgender issues from their lectures on sexuality. Many programs do not routinely ask clients anything about their sexual orientation or their gender identity, even when taking a full-scale psychosocial history.

In order to be somewhat comfortable when trying to assist clients who are dealing with sexuality, sexual identity, gender identity, and/or sexual orientation issues, it helps to be familiar with the definitions, concepts, and terminology related to them. The following discussion is designed to provide some familiarity with these matters.

These definitions and explanations are nontechnical and are intended only as working definitions and concepts. Sex, sexuality, sexual identity, gender, gender identity, sexual orientation, and issues relating to them are extremely complex matters. This book, therefore, should be viewed as an introduction. Counselors need to go further— to read the materials on the suggested reading lists, to seek out information on the Internet, and to take specialized training courses to broaden and deepen their knowledge and understanding.

When considering and learning about these matters, the single most important action for counselors to take is to open their minds to difference and diversity and to expand their thinking (and feeling) in order to make room for the enormous variety, diversity, and richness of human sexual and gender experience. Counselors may encounter ideas and concepts that shake the beliefs and views they grew up with or have been comfortable with for many years. They may feel challenged or threatened. But if they can tolerate these feelings and remain open to the expanding perspectives on gender and sexuality, they will be rewarded with a much richer view and appreciation of what it is to be a human being. Also, they will be much better prepared to help *all* of their clients as those clients seek to find their way in recovery.

DEFINITIONS AND TERMINOLOGY

I wish I lived in a future time
Where it was accepted that each individual could choose their
    own sex.
Till then, it is much easier to change a body
than to change one's heart or soul.

"Transsexuals: In Their Own Words,"
quoted in Brown and Rounsley (1996, pp. 231-232)

Sex is a biological term used to describe a person's sexual anatomy—female, male, intersex. If a child is born with female sex organs (e.g., uterus, vagina), then she is female. If a child is born with male sex organs (e.g., penis, testes), he is male. As Stuart (1991) states, "Sex relates to . . . the genitals, the function the genitals perform, and how the genitals are used for reproduction or pleasure" (p. 5).

Some children are born with ambiguous or not clearly differentiated genitalia or "with medically established physical or hormonal attributes of both the male and female gender" (Israel and Tarver, 1997, p. 16). In some children, these conditions do not appear until puberty. Whatever the age, however, they are *intersex*. Traditionally, these children are assigned (either socially and psychologically or, sometimes, surgically) to the female or male sex by the medical profession on the basis of their physical attributes and are raised according to the gender roles of the designated sex. In recent years, this practice of assigning sex to babies and/or children has come under intense fire as some people discover that they were assigned to the wrong sex. That is, their anatomical sex is not congruent with who they know themselves to be—i.e., a person of the opposite sex.

The above definition of sex is solely a biological and anatomical classification. It is separate and distinct from the *feelings* a person (or other people) may have about his or her biological, anatomical sex.

Gender refers to what a culture determines (and dictates) are the behavioral, social, and psychological attributes of maleness and femaleness. "*Gender* is a social construct used to distinguish between male and female, masculine and feminine" (Brown and Rounsley, 1996, p. 20) and is based primarily on external genitalia. As Stuart (1991) notes, sex is a part of gender. *Gender roles* are society's "rules" that prescribe the appropriate behavior and ways of being that govern a person's presentation of self as a man or a woman. Gender roles consist of those characteristics, activities, and behaviors which society says are proper for someone of that sex and gender. Unfortunately, they often tend to be far-ranging and limiting generalizations that wield great power (e.g., real men do not cry; aggressive women are not feminine).

Gender identity refers to an individual's personal sense of how he or she experiences his or her sex and gender and the psychosocial and cultural factors that influence that personal sense (Marcel, 1998). "It is an individual's identification with maleness and femaleness, as well as how those feelings (and their subsequent needs) are internalized and possibly presented to others" (Israel and Tarver, 1997, p. 44). Gender identity "is our own deeply held conviction and deeply felt inner awareness that we belong to one gender or the other," an awareness that "is firmly in place by the time we are five years old" (Brown and Rounsley, 1996, p. 21). Traditionally, gender identity refers to how a person sees, expresses, and presents himself or herself as a man or a woman.

In recent years, however, there has been increasing controversy about the concept of just two genders. A number of people now argue that there are *many* genders and that to limit ourselves to just two genders (male and female) is to distort reality. Bornstein (1994) comments that

> Gender could be seen as a class system. By having gender around, there are always these two classes—male and female. As in any binary, one side will always have more power than the other. One will always oppress the other. The value of a two-gender system is nothing more than the value of keeping the power imbalance, and all that depends on it, intact. (p. 113)

Thus it becomes extremely important to recognize that *gender identity* refers most accurately to the way a person sees, expresses, and presents self as man, woman, or neither, or as a gender that falls on a continuum but is not either/or.

It is also important to remember that maleness and femaleness are not fixed opposites and "may graduate markedly, depending on individual and social interpretation" (Israel and Tarver, 1997, p. 6). In fact, *androgyny* is a gender identity in which people adopt both male and female characteristics or neither. They may exhibit mannerisms of both genders, they may wear gender-neutral clothes, and/or they may wish to be identified as neither gender or as both. Their reasons for identifying themselves as androgynous may be to meet their identity needs or to take a political stand challenging society's stereotypes (Israel and Tarver, 1997; Marcel, 1998).

For example, if a biological woman experiences herself as a woman—that is, her gender identity is that of a woman—she will tend to experience herself in relation to her gender role and will, to some extent, govern herself according to the dictates of the role. For example, she may temper any aggressiveness she might feel since that is stereotypically seen as a male attribute.

If a biological woman experiences herself as a man—that is, her gender identity is that of a man—she may well present herself as male. He may dress exclusively as a man, adhere to the attributes of masculine gender roles (e.g., not show his emotions openly), take a man's name, and basically live his life as a man.

Many people tend to evaluate themselves and construct their gender identity according to the strictures of sex and gender role stereotypes, and this often causes painful confusion and gender identity problems for those who cannot easily or simply do not match up with the stereotypes.

For example, suppose a man has what society might describe as a mincing way of walking and is distressed by how effeminate this makes him appear. He is comfortable in his gender identity, perfectly clear that he is a man. But he is unhappy because he feels his walk is unmanly and that others also see him as effeminate. From his and others' point of view, his walk does not match with the behavior of a "real man." This is a gender identity issue which is rooted in gender role stereotypes. It is *not* about sexual orientation.

Or suppose a woman is aggressive, dominating, independent, and tough and looks quite unlike the feminine stereotypes portrayed by the media. She may feel ill at ease and question her femininity and her desirability as a woman even though she is clear that she is a woman. This is more of a gender role stereotype problem but has links to gender identity issues.

For instance, this woman may worry that maybe she is a lesbian because that is how both she and others have been taught to interpret not fitting women's gender role stereotypes. Situations and feelings like these can lead to confusion and pain because gender role stereotypes and gender identity issues so often get misidentified as sexual orientation issues. It is extremely important for counselors to be aware of the differences between gender identity and sexual orientation so that they can accurately assess the information and situations presented by each client and offer appropriate assistance.

TRANSGENDERS

> I have begun speaking simply of gender as a name for that system that punishes bodies for how they look, who they love, or how they feel—for the size or color or shape of their skin. I do this not to collapse differences, but to emphasize our connection.
>
> R. A. Wilchins
> *Read My Lips* (1997, pp. 16-17)

Although our culture divides *gender* into just two possible categories—male and female—which match the two acknowledged sexes, *many gender identities* are actually possible (Bolin, 1997; Bornstein, 1994; Marcel, 1998; Wilchins, 1997). Although this culture tolerates some variations in the expression of maleness and femaleness, such as women wearing men's clothing or men dressing in drag for entertainment purposes, there are rather narrow restrictions on that expression.

Transgendered. When a person's gender expression is different from what our culture sees as appropriate for that gender, that person's identity is considered to be *transgendered.* When a person's culturally ascribed gender (which is assigned at birth according to the person's genital sex) conflicts with the person's internal, individual sense of his or her gender identity, then he or she identifies and expresses himself or herself as transgender (Brown and Rounsley, 1996; Israel and Tarver, 1997; Marcel, 1998). Because it is such an intensely personal, individual matter developed through a process of self-awareness and expression, gender identity must be viewed on a continuum which represents the enormous scope of identity and expression.

Transgender. This word is used as an umbrella term to refer to all people who in some way see and present themselves as the opposite gender. As Brown and Rounsley (1996) state, it is a "term used to describe the full range of individuals who have conflict with or question about their gender" (p. 18). Richards (1997) notes that,

> Transgender has come through common usage in our community to mean any type of behavior that challenges dichotomous societal roles. It is an umbrella term that covers the occasional cross-dresser, someone who has need for sex reassignment sur-

gery, a transgenderist, a post-operative transsexual, or any variation in between. (p. 504)

Boswell (1997) adds that

> The word "transgender" describes much more than crossing between the poles of masculinity and femininity. It more aptly refers to the transgressing of gender norms, or being freely gendered, or transcending gender altogether in order to become more fully human. (p. 54)

Or, as Denny and Green (1996) state, "The term *transgender* is commonly used to describe the global community of cross-dressing and transsexual persons" (p. 88).

It is important to note here that while the term transgender tends to be the most commonly accepted one to describe any gender-variant person, not everyone agrees about this or the other terms used to describe people who are gender variant. Ultimately, the best way to approach this subject is to *ask* clients what they call themselves, how they self-identify, and follow their lead.

The following groups fit under this umbrella of *transgender:*

Transvestites, or the more preferred term, *cross-dressers,* are those who dress in the clothing of the opposite gender. Cross-dressers ordinarily do not want to change their bodies, but wish to express masculine/feminine (or both together) aspects of themselves through their clothing. People cross-dress for a variety of reasons: to become sexually aroused, to make political statements, to entertain, to liberate repressed feelings, to play (known among GBT men as "camp" and dressing in drag). Most cross-dressers do not experience their gender as incongruent with their expression. Many male-to-female cross-dressers are heterosexual (Finke and Northway, 1997; Marcel, 1998) and "lead what are considered otherwise ordinary lives" (Marcel, 1998, p. 12). In addition, many lesbian, gay, and bisexual people cross-dress (Denny, 1994), as many transgendered people do.

Drag queens are considered cross-dressers. They are males who wear women's clothing but make no attempt to "pass" as women. *Drag kings* are females who dress as men but do not attempt to "pass" as men. Drag queens and drag kings generally cross dress to express their gender identity for political or entertainment purposes and for personal reasons as well (Marcel, 1998).

Transgenders or *transgendered people* (sometimes referred to as *transgenderists*) are those who make the choice to express themselves and live as members of the gender opposite to their anatomical sex. While some transgenderists may use hormones or other cosmetic procedures, they do not choose to alter their bodies via genital reassignment surgery (Brown and Rounsley, 1996; Prince, 1997; Richards, 1997). As Denny (1997) comments, transgenderists define themselves, "doing as little or as much as they wish to their physical bodies, but stopping short of genital surgery" (p. 39).

Transsexuals differ from transgenders in that their feelings about their sex, their gender, and their gender identity are often the consequence of physiological factors. Transsexualism is thought by a number of scientists to be a medical condition resulting from a discrepancy between the amounts of testosterone absorbed by both the brain and the body while in the womb (Brown and Rounsley, 1996; Marcel, 1998). Other scientists, however, argue that at least some influences are exerted by early social learning. As Brown and Rounsley (1996) note, "Many gender identity experts today believe that neither nature nor nurture alone is the cause but rather that transsexualism is most likely the result of an interaction of the two" (p. 25).

Transsexuals are people who are born with the biological characteristics of one sex but know themselves to be the opposite sex and gender. Some transsexuals are born *intersex* and grow up knowing they are not the sex they were assigned. Others grow up knowing that their bodies do not match their core gender identity. There are both female-to-male (FTM) and male-to-female (MTF) transsexuals, and many want to change their bodies to match their gender identity through hormones and, sometimes, through genital reassignment surgery. Transsexuals may be pre-op(erative) or post-op, but whatever stage they are in, once they make the transition they tend to live fully as the gender opposite their birth sex (Brown and Rounsley, 1996; Israel and Tarver, 1997; Marcel, 1998).

It is helpful to know other words and concepts related to transsexuals. The term "she-male" is sometimes used, but tends to have demeaning connotations. According to Brown and Rounsley (1996), "She-males are men, often involved in prostitution, pornography, or

the adult entertainment business, who have undergone breast augmentation but have maintained their genitalia" (p. 16). Another, less
pejorative term is "gender bender." Brown and Rounsley (1996) give
this definition: "Gender benders are males or females who challenge
and cross traditional gender boundaries, often in outrageous ways"
(p. 17).

More positive are ones like "new male," a term from within the
TG/TS community that gathers at the Gender Identity Project at
the Gay and Lesbian Community Center in New York City. This
term refers to and honors the experience a person is having of being
newly male. Two other terms are: male-to-male (MTM) which refers
to a male whose birth sex is female but who has always known that he
was male. female-to-female (FTF) refers to a female whose birth sex
is male but who has always known that she is female. These newer
terms are intended to celebrate each person's socialization and identity as their core gender identity. The perspective about this is that
calling someone MTF or FTM calls attention to their birth sex which
does not represent who they are and may remind them of the shame
they have suffered because of it. Thus MTM and FTF recognizes the
lifelong knowing of one's core gender identity (Blumenstein, 2001).

Although many of these terms are properly used only by those who
have lived the experience, some other terms to at least be aware of are:
femme queen, boy-chick, tranny-fag, two-spirit, stone butch. Terms
that may appropriately be applied by counselors and others not of
transgender experience are: *bigender, gender variant, of transgender
experience* (Perina, 2000).

TREATMENT ISSUES

> The problem with transsexual women is not that we are trapped
> in the wrong bodies. . . . The problem is that we are trapped in a
> society which alternates between hating and ignoring, or toler-
> ating and exploiting us and our experience.
>
> R. A. Wilchins (1997, p. 47)

The significance of counselors' understanding these distinctions is
that when transgendered people are in substance abuse treatment fa-

cilities, their differences may not only be confusing but also deeply disturbing to other clients and to staff as well. The more information and understanding a treatment center and staff have, the easier it will be for them to deal sensitively with the issues. This may involve helping clients and staff with their transphobic attitudes by challenging them and by educating them. It certainly will require counselors to make differential diagnoses—should treatment focus on issues relating to clients' transgender identity; to clients' drinking/drugging; or to a combination of both? The JSI Research and Training Institute report (2000) underscores this need:

> Mental health and substance abuse treatment providers need additional training in order to work cooperatively with TG/TS clients to identify when gender issues arc or are not relevant. . . . Sometimes gender issues are central to mental health or substance abuse treatment, sometimes they are peripheral, and sometimes they are unrelated. (p. 2)

Counselors will need to handle various issues in a sensitive manner. If bathrooms are specifically male or female, perhaps one bathroom can be designated unisex. Counselors need to advocate for TG/TS clients about appropriate housing. Clients who self-identify as women should *not* be housed on a male unit; clients who self-identify as men should *not* be housed on a female unit. These matters need to be handled properly, not sloughed off or ignored. If rooms are shared, the roommate's gender should be matched with the TG/TS's self-identified gender, or the TG/TS client should be placed in a single room. The client's self-identification should be the determining factor in what pronoun to use. If the client presents as a woman, she should be addressed as "she"; if as a man, he should be addressed as "he." And pronoun usage (or anything else) should not be a source of gossip or ridicule. A flexible, sensitive, accepting, and advocative approach will be most helpful in this situation.

Another matter that will need attention is whether or not clients are following the Standards of Care (SOC) developed and updated by the Harry Benjamin International Gender Dysphoria Association (HBIGDA). These SOC set minimum standards that must be met before a person can receive hormones or proceed with sex reassignment surgery. Is the client under a doctor's care and receiving hormones legally? Then the doctor needs to be contacted and involved in the treatment protocol. If the client has been getting hormones illegally, from the street, then the client needs a thorough, *sensitive* medical evaluation and assistance from the agency to adjust or maintain those hormones while in treatment. Hormones are powerful drugs which must not be ignored in treatment planning. Counselors should also guide clients to resources like books and the Internet for further information (see Appendix C).

New and different as these explanations and definitions of the concept of *transgender* may be, becoming familiar and comfortable with them is of critical importance. Transgendered people are among this culture's most reviled and oppressed minorities. Those who are plagued by substance abuse are subject to even worse oppression because of the added stigma of substance abuse. If counselors do not know enough about being transgendered and therefore are unable to help and support their TG clients, those clients are at great risk of destruction and death.

SEXUAL ORIENTATION

> To speak about sexual "orientation" makes it seem as if human beings are like compasses, continually pointing to some inner True North. Indeed, the reality . . . is much more complex, heterogeneous and paradoxical.

> L. Markowitz (1995, p. 7)

There is often much confusion about the distinction between gender identity issues and sexual orientation. All too often people think that gender identity and sexual orientation are the same because of the misguided notion that people who do not conform to gender roles are necessarily homosexual. That is simply not true.

Sexual orientation refers to a person's sexual and/or affectional attractions to another person, including fantasy, behavior, and emotional/affectional needs. Thus the sexual orientation of a *homosexual* involves an attraction to a person or persons of the same gender. The sexual orientation of a *heterosexual* involves an attraction to a person or persons of the opposite gender. A *bisexual* is one whose attractions are to persons of both genders.

Because people are complex and are not static, they do not always fit neatly into distinct categories of sexual/affectional orientation. Although sexual orientation is most commonly thought of as designating a person's sexual behavior, it has a wider, more comprehensive application—to human relationships and emotions. The more accurate term then is *sexual identity* which refers not just to people's sexual behavior, but to who they are as complete human beings.

The reality is that the world is not divisible into two separate camps of 90 percent "pure" heterosexuals and 10 percent "pure" homosexuals or even into three distinct camps of heterosexual, homosexual, and bisexual. Rather, there is a wide, wide range of experience, a very broad array of sexual/affectional orientations. The range can run from *asexual* (a person who is not attracted to anybody and not involved in any sexual behavior) all the way to *pansexual* (a person whose sexual feelings and behaviors are fluid, ranging from heterosexual to bisexual to homosexual) (Bohan, 1996; Kinsey et al., 1948, 1953; Klein, 1993).

Two other matters need to be discussed here. It should be noted that two terms—MSM (men who have sex with men) and WSW (women who have sex with women)—are applied to men and women whose behavior is *technically* homosexual (same-sex), but who do not see or identify themselves as homosexual. Ordinarily, these are people from cultures (e.g., Hispanic, Turkish) that allow for certain kinds of same-sex behaviors but do not ascribe sexual orientation meanings to them.

Bisexuality

> One of the original goals of the gay liberation movement was to gain acceptance for everyone's sexuality for what it was, but somehow for many people, this didn't extend to bisexuals—you were either gay/lesbian or straight.

> R. Fox (2000, p. 8)

Because it falls in the middle ground of the sexual orientation continuum, because it is little understood, and because it is central to understanding sexual orientation, it is important to discuss bisexuality in more detail.

First of all, bisexuality is much more common than is generally acknowledged (Klein, 1993). Blumstein and Schwartz (1977) note that

> a mix of homosexual and heterosexual behaviors in a person's erotic biography is a common occurrence, and that it is entirely possible to engage in anywhere from a little to a great deal of homosexual behavior without adopting a homosexual lifestyle. (p. 61)

Klein (1993) adds that "The ability to eroticize both genders is one dimension of bisexuality" (p. 128). He also notes that "*bisexuality is not disguised homosexuality, nor is it disguised heterosexuality*. It is another way of sexual expression" (p. 7).

The term *bisexuality,* the concept, the behaviors, the state of being, the identity—all are subject to great controversy. Does it exist? Is it legitimate? Is it the ultimate perversion? Some people consider it "as a set of acts" (Hemmings, 1995, p. 198), others as an identity.

What is bisexuality? Markowitz (1995) states that it is "the recognition that the capacity for intimacy and passion is not limited to those of a certain biological makeup" (p. 11). Valverde (1985) comments that

> Bisexuality is best seen not as a completely separate Third Option that removes itself from all the problems of both hetero- and homosexuality, but rather as a choice to combine the two lifestyles, the two erotic preferences, in one way or another. (p. 116)

Or as Hemmings (1995) notes, bisexuality is "the presence in one body of same-sex and opposite-sex desire . . ." (p. 195). Bisexuals represent the *both/and* rather than the *either/or* of the sexual orientation continuum (Pramaggiore, 1996).

George (1993) explains further that " 'bisexual' does not describe a specific sexual activity" nor is it an identity that can be limited by gender or "altered by a partner—whoever they are, whatever the type or length of the relationship" (p. 105). A person can be bisexual whether the partner is of the opposite or the same gender or if there is no partner. This is one of the factors that can confuse counselors—that identity and behavior are not necessarily congruent (Markowitz, 1995).

Weinberg, Williams, and Pryor, in their book *Dual Attraction: Understanding Bisexuality* (1994) explored the complexities of bisexuality via the responses of self-identified bisexuals in regard to three dimensions—sexual attraction, sexual behavior, and romantic feelings. On the basis of their findings, they determined that there were five essential types of bisexuals: the *Pure Type*—people who prefer women and men equally; the *Mid Type*—people who prefer men and women equally in one dimension but favor one gender more in the other two dimensions; the *Heterosexual-Leaning Type* and the *Homosexual-Leaning Type*—people who ranked themselves high on one side of the scale in all three dimensions; and the *Varied Type*—people who ranked high on both ends of the scale. Markowitz (1995) comments on their findings:

> Overall, bisexual-identified men tended to turn to other men to meet their need for sex but to women for romance, and women seemed to experience love with another woman more than men did with another man. (p. 7)

Bisexuals obviously occupy a broad middle position on the sexual orientation continuum. Because they are neither only heterosexual nor only homosexual but are both, the ambiguity of their orientation tends to raise anxiety in both heterosexuals and homosexuals. As Garber (1999) notes:

> Bisexuality unsettles certainties: straight, gay, lesbian. It has affinities with all of these, and is delimited by none. It is, then, an identity that is also *not* an identity, a sign of the certainty of ambiguity, the stability of instability, a category that defines and defeats categorization. (p. 138)

It is important for counselors to understand these perspectives on bisexuality in order to assist their clients. Clients who identify as bisexual must struggle with the fact that their sexual orientation is often perceived as a threat by both heterosexuals and homosexuals. As

Klein (1993) comments, "Differences, freedom of choice, have been a threat to the group since before the beginning of recorded time" (p. 6). Bisexuals are seen as making choices, rather than adhering to the clearer-cut categories of gay-straight. In addition, as George (1993) points out, "The fact that bisexual people may not be so easily classifiable is often a cause for anxiety" (p. 102).

Klein (1993) explains another source of threat, of "biphobia":

> To most heterosexuals and homosexuals, the bisexual is an alien being whose dual sexuality opens up the possibility of their own sexual ambiguity. They cannot understand the bisexual's ability to share their own preferences but not their own aversions. (p. 11)

Markowitz (1995) adds that "The ambiguity shakes up straights' assumptions about how the world works, blurring the boundaries that either-or thinking requires" (p. 9). Either-or thinking and biphobia also exist in the lesbian and gay communities. Bisexuals are often viewed as being *really* lesbian or gay but not yet declared or as taking advantage of lesbian or gay pleasures but holding on to "heterosexual privilege."

Another powerful and destructive stereotype is that "bisexuals are promiscuous because of an inability to commit themselves to long-term monogamous relationships" (Rust, 1996, p. 127). Rust explains that

> The bisexual's ability to form relationships with members of both sexes is interpreted . . . as a need that cannot be fulfilled by any one relationship and that therefore dooms the bisexual to a life of promiscuity or, at best, serial monogamy in an effort to satisfy both sides of her [or his] conflicted self. (p. 128)

Rust (1996) describes another stereotype that is linked with the one about promiscuity—"that bisexuality is a phase or a temporary form of sexuality adopted by people who are either coming out as lesbian or gay or returning to heterosexuality" (p. 128).

Rust (1996) discusses the idea that bisexuals are considered to be immature because they are seen as promiscuous and engaged in a phase of sexual choice or development. Instead, bisexuals have taken a rather mature "approach that values a variety of relational forms . . ." (Rust, 1996, p. 132). Many bisexuals have adopted a newer form of relating called *polyamory,* "multiple sustaining relationships that can provide greater support [than monogamy] in a wider variety of circumstances" (Rust, 1996, p. 132). This relatively new term (and concept) seems to both describe and validate this way of being in the world. As Rust (1996) notes, "Both monogamous and nonmonogamous forms of relating can reflect emotional maturity, and neither one guarantees it" (p. 132). *Polyamory,* it should be noted, is not the sole possession of the bisexual community. It is a term and a concept and a way of being in the world embraced by many lesbians and gay men (Hutchins, 1996).

COUNSELING ISSUES

It is wonderfully freeing to realize that moderating and modulating oneself can enable one to be more fully and truly. One grows in appreciation of the zigzag, wiggle, and detour. The more one lets overtones and undertones of self and Other resonate, the more thrilling life becomes.

M. Eigen (1996, p. 166)

What is the meaning, the significance of all this for counselors? When working with clients who identify as bisexual, counselors need to keep in mind the specific issues facing such clients. For example, counselors should not assume that bisexual clients will be more comfortable at lesbian/gay AA/NA meetings than at heterosexual meetings or vice versa. They need to ask clients. It is also important for counselors to have a sense of the local meetings and to have contacts in local AA/NA so that understanding people can serve as temporary sponsors. It also is helpful for counselors to be supportive to bisexual clients who may have experienced or may be experiencing biphobia both in their lives and in the treatment program. Counselors need to challenge biphobia wherever it shows up, whether in staff, administration, or clients.

In addition to using this knowledge to help clients, counselors can use it to broaden their understanding of sexual orientation—its variety, its diversity, its complexity—and to challenge their own stereotypes and either-or thinking.

Labels

Human sexuality is a dynamic, changeable condition. A fairly large number of people shift their positions on the continuum of sexual/affectional orientation during the course of their lifetimes. It is extremely important, therefore, to understand that any of these labels—*homosexual, heterosexual, bisexual, asexual. pansexual*—can be inaccurate or misleading because they do not account for the subtleties and intricacies of human emotions and behavior or for changes in the human condition.

For example, what is the best way to describe a man who is primarily attracted to women but who has had a number of sexual/emotional experiences with men? What is this man's identity? Is he bisexual? Homosexual? Heterosexual? What is an accurate label for a woman whose primary emotional (and perhaps also sexual) interests are in women but who marries and has a family? What is her identity? What of the man who has had many same-sex attractions and experiences and has lived as a gay man for many years, then meets a woman and falls in love with her? What of the woman who has been married for many years, gets divorced, and later discovers that she is attracted to other women? What of the transgendered person who is biologically female but knows himself to be male and is attracted to men? These examples merely hint at the rich variety of human experiences, perspectives, and emotions, and point to the limiting and restrictive effects of labeling.

As Klein (1993) notes:

> We take comfort in the labels; they help define our relationships with one another and with the world at large. Yet with each label we acquire, we limit our infinite possibilities, our uniqueness. It is our insistence on labels that creates the "either-or" syndrome. (p. 8)

Although labeling can sometimes be helpful—"a tried and true method of eliminating the threats of uncertainty, ambiguity, fear" (Klein, 1993, p. 9)—it cannot possibly do justice to the complexities of human nature and experience (see Coleman, 1987). It is helpful to keep in mind the slogan that says—the *act* does not equal the orientation. Since people's sexual behavior alone is not necessarily an accurate indicator of their orientation, it is important for counselors *not* to label people. In addition, it is equally important not to label on the basis of gender identity because gender identity does *not* signify sexual orientation. Perhaps most important, the only person who has the right or the accuracy to attach a label is the person being labeled.

For example, a transgendered person who is biologically a male but whose gender identity is female may be heterosexual, bisexual, or homosexual, depending on who *she* is attracted to and how *she* identifies herself. No means other than the person's self-identification based on a number of factors is valid for determining that person's sexual orientation. Thus, labels need to be approached with great care and regarded with great caution. The approach needs to be that of *asking people* how they describe themselves and what (if anything) they wish to call themselves.

The Kinsey Scale

Alfred Kinsey and his colleagues (1948; 1953) made invaluable contributions to defining and understanding the enormous range and complexity of human sexual experience. To help describe the meaning of their findings based on over ten thousand interviews with men and women, they worked out the "Kinsey Scale" to reflect the continuum of human sexual experience (see Figure 2.1).

Kinsey and colleagues' research (1948) revealed that 50 percent of American males were "0's" (exclusively heterosexual) and that the remaining 50 percent were spread out along the continuum. These findings refuted the existing belief that the overwhelming majority of society (at least male society) is exclusively heterosexual. Klein (1978) provides a break-out of Kinsey's statistics which gives a clearer picture of the broad range of male sexual/affectional experience (Table 2.1).

Other factors revealed by Kinsey's data (1948; 1953) were equally illuminating. In regard to the period between adolescence and old age, over one in three men (37 percent) and over one in eight women (13 percent) disclosed that they had had at least one same-sex experience resulting in orgasm. In addition, other statistics indicate that over 30 million Americans have engaged in both heterosexual and

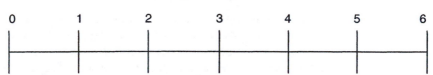

0 Exclusively heterosexual

1 Predominantly heterosexual, only incidentally homosexual

2 Predominantly heterosexual, but more than incidentally homosexual

3 Equally heterosexual and homosexual

4 Predominantly homosexual, but more than incidentally heterosexual

5 Predominantly homosexual, only incidentally heterosexual

6 Exclusively homosexual

FIGURE 2.1. The Kinsey Scale

TABLE 2.1. Kinsey's Statistics on Male Sexuality

Kinsey's Rating	Meaning of Rating	Percentage
0	Exclusively other-sex oriented in behavior and psychological response	50
1	Incidental same-sex behavior	15
2	More than incidental same-sex behavior	12
3	About equal amounts of same and other-sex behavior	9
4	More than incidental other-sex behavior	6
5	Incidental other-sex behavior	5
6	Exclusively same-sex oriented in behavior and psychological response	4

Note: Because percentages are rounded off, they add up to 101 percent.

homosexual experiences, a phenomenon that suggests that people can and do shift positions on the Kinsey Scale during their lifetimes (Bell and Weinberg, 1978; Klein, 1978, 1993).

Broadening the Perspectives

Counselors can be most helpful to all their clients if they broaden their perspectives on the dynamic nature of human sexuality and the potential for movement on the continuum of sexual experience. This discussion is not intended to imply that everyone changes positions on the continuum—such is certainly not the case—but rather to emphasize that not everyone's sexual orientation, attitudes, feelings, behavior, or experience are etched in stone. It can be reassuring to clients to hear that there is indeed a continuum of human sexual experience, feelings, and behaviors. The Kinsey Scale can be a helpful tool in assisting a client to begin talking about and looking at his or her sexual orientation. Asking clients to place themselves on the scale may be less threatening than asking them to answer a direct question about their sexual orientation or asking them to use the words lesbian, gay, bisexual, homosexual, or heterosexual. Often it is easier to say, "I guess I might be a '4'" than to say, "Yes—I am a lesbian" or "Yes—I am a gay male." Or to say, "Maybe I'm a '3'" rather than "Yes—I am a bisexual."

The Klein Sexual Orientation Grid

Using the Kinsey Scale as a starting point, Fritz Klein (1978, 1993) developed a way of viewing sexual orientation that is broader in scope, more specific, and more helpful. He looks at seven interrelated aspects of sexuality:

1. *Sexual attraction.* Who turns you on? Who do you find attractive as a real or potential sexual partner?
2. *Sexual behavior.* Who are your sexual contacts (partners)? Who do you actually have sex with?
3. *Sexual fantasies.* Who do you enjoy fantasizing about in erotic daydreams or while masturbating?
4. *Emotional preference.* With whom are you emotionally involved; with whom do you prefer to establish strong emotional bonds?
5. *Social preference.* Which sex do you prefer to spend your leisure time with, and with which sex do you feel most comfortable? With which sex do you prefer to socialize?
6. *Lifestyle.* How much does a person live in a hetero-, bi-, homosexual social world? Does this person have friends who are of other sexual orientations, socialize in other orientations' environments (e.g., LGB bars)?
7. *Self-identification.* How do you identify yourself, in terms of sexual orientation, on the Kinsey Scale?

The answers to these questions are not static; rather, they should be viewed as dynamic in nature, having a past, a present, and a future. Klein (1993, p. 19) presents a Sexual Orientation Grid (KSOG) (Figure 2.2) which can be used to help people gain a dynamic overview of their sexual orientation. (*Please Note:* Klein uses number 1 through 7 for his continuum rather than Kinsey's 0 through 6.)

People rate themselves on a 7-point scale from 1 to 7 as follows:

For variables A to E:

1. = Other sex only
2. = Other sex mostly
3. = Other sex somewhat more
4. = Both sexes equally
5. = Same sex somewhat more
6. = Same sex mostly
7. = Same sex only

For variables F and G:

1. = Hetero only
2. = Hetero mostly
3. = Hetero somewhat more
4. = Hetero/Gay-Lesbian equally
5. = Gay-Lesbian somewhat more
6. = Gay-Lesbian mostly
7. = Gay-Lesbian only

We have added the following: To provide for asexual behavior (no sexual behavior, feelings, experience, or fantasy), clients can place a dash (–) wherever appropriate. It is also important to advise them that the grid's categories are not really distinct and separate and need to be viewed as representing a continuum.

VARIABLE	PAST	PRESENT	IDEAL
A. Sexual Attraction			
B. Sexual Behavior			
C. Sexual Fantasies			
D. Emotional Preference			
E. Social Preference			
F. Hetero/Homo Lifestyle			
G. Self-Identification			

FIGURE 2.2. Klein's Sexual Orientation Grid

Filling out this grid can provide clients with a nonthreatening overview of their sexual orientation and can reassure clients by showing them that they belong—and where they belong—within the broad range of human sexual behavior. It can also assist them to begin to examine their sexual and affectional orientation and what that may mean for their lives and their recovery. The grid can also be used to teach clients about the wide range of human sexual, affectional, social, emotional, and intellectual experience. It can also be used to illuminate the truth that human sexuality and its expressions can change or remain the same over time.

It is important for counselors as well as clients to have the experience of filling out the grid. Doing so is a positive step towards greater openness and ease with the whole topic of sexuality. Such an experience can provide counselors with a vital awareness of their own sexual/affectional orientation and their sexuality. Carrying out such an exercise, evaluating their own sexuality, learning about such instruments as the Kinsey Scale and the Klein Grid, and gaining more information about sexual orientation will hopefully have the desired effect—counselors' broadening their view of healthy sexual/affectional orientation to include the whole continuum of human sexuality.

By doing so, counselors become better able to assist their clients in dealing with whatever pain or conflict they may be experiencing as a result of their fears and worries about sexual orientation. That assistance may take many different forms. It may mean getting clients to fill out the grid and then talk about its meaning; helping clients disclose their LGB identity in a group, if such disclosure is appropriate; or providing clients with a safe and accepting space in which they can feel free enough to look more closely at themselves.

SUMMARY

The following chart (Figure 2.3) presents continuums of the three major components of sexuality and their relationship to each other (Marcel, 1998). All of these components and the ways they interact with one another need to be considered when attempting to understand a person's overall sexual identity.

Every person falls somewhere on each of these continuums. In regard to the sexual anatomy continuum, a person may be of the male or

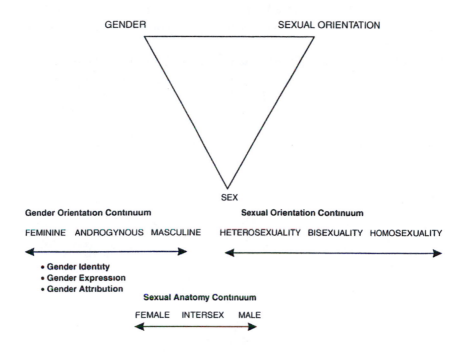

FIGURE 2.3. Continuums of Sexuality

female sex with male or female genitalia or the person may be intersex, with ambiguous or undifferentiated genitalia. It is important to note that people's sex does not necessarily determine their gender identity.

In regard to the gender orientation continuum, people can identify their gender as feminine, androgynous, masculine—or any combination thereof. Within those categories fall three aspects: gender identity, gender expression, and gender attribution.

- *Gender identity* is the way a person self-identifies and what that person feels his or her gender to be.
- *Gender expression* is how a person chooses to appear or present himself or herself to the world, e.g., through clothing, makeup, hairstyle, jewelry.

- *Gender attribution* is how others see the person, e.g., do they perceive the person as effeminate, masculine, gay, transgendered?

(*Note:* People's perceptions may or may not be accurate.)

In regard to the *sexual orientation continuum,* a person may identify as heterosexual, bisexual, or homosexual—or as pansexual. If a person identifies as asexual, the continuum does not apply. It is important to note that sexual orientation is *not* predicated on either gender identity or biological sex.

These three components—gender, sex, and sexual orientation—exist in every human being. Taken together, they are what enable us to understand the complex range of behavior, experience, thoughts, and feelings that comprise a person's sexual identity.

This complexity can be understood through some examples. Dennis Rodman is of the male sex. His gender expression is sometimes feminine, sometimes masculine, sometimes androgynous, but his gender attribution is masculine, and his gender identity seems to be primarily male. His sexual orientation seems to be heterosexual. RuPaul is of the male sex. His gender expression and his gender attribution are feminine, but his gender identity is masculine. His sexual orientation is gay male. Melissa Etheridge is of the female sex. Her gender identity, expression, and attribution are feminine. Her sexual orientation is lesbian.

Other less celebrated examples are drawn from client populations. "Nancy" is of the female sex. Her gender identity is feminine, but her gender expression is decidedly masculine—men's clothing, no makeup, no jewelry, engineer's boots; she "curses like a sailor," yells at her employees, and is fiercely competitive with friends and business acquaintances. Her gender attribution is masculine. Her sexual orientation is heterosexual.

"Alice" is an MTF transgendered person. She is of the male sex and still retains her male genitalia, though she takes hormones and has had extensive electrolysis. Her gender identity is feminine, as are her gender expression, and attribution. Her sexual orientation is heterosexual. "Stan" is an FTM transsexual who has had genital reassignment surgery. He is originally of the female sex but is now of the male sex. His gender identity is masculine, as are his gender expression, and attribution. His sexual orientation is bisexual.

These are just a few examples of the complex and rich diversity of human sexual identity. The combinations and variations are infinite. The point, of course, is that none of us can necessarily tell or say who someone is by the way they look or by the way they present themselves. It is not for us to label others when there is no sure way to know whether a label is accurate, fair, or true.

One other important matter should be noted—sex, gender, and sexual orientation are all shown on continuums. This is done to suggest the broad range of sexuality and that sexuality must be viewed as not necessarily fixed or static. A person's sexuality may stay the same his or her whole life, or it may shift over time. Most of all, these continuums are meant to indicate the tremendous range of differences that fall within the parameters of human sexual experience.

Chapter 3

Counselor Competence

When one is a stranger to oneself then one is estranged from others. If one is out of touch with oneself, then one cannot touch others.

> Anne Morrow Lindbergh
> *Gift from the Sea,* 1955

> Nobody, but nobody
> Can make it out here alone.

> Maya Angelou
> "Alone" in *Oh Pray My Wings*
> *Are Gonna Fit Me Well,* 1975

THE SCOPE OF THE PROBLEM

Two factors in particular contribute to an overall perspective on lesbian, gay, bisexual, and transgendered people who are substance abusers and on their treatment.

One factor is etiology, i.e., what is/are the cause(s) of homosexuality, bisexuality, and transgenderism. Many people ask this question with a hidden, often unconscious, notion that if the cause(s) were known, then the condition could (and should) be changed or "fixed." The second factor is the prevalence of substance abuse among LGBTs. What LGBT people face in terms of their substance use and abuse bears significantly on how they manage to cope with the oppressions they must confront on a daily basis.

Etiology of Homosexuality, Bisexuality, and Transgenderism

When the topics of homosexuality, bisexuality, and transgenderism arise, one of the most frequently asked questions is "What causes them?" Of course, the same question can be asked about heterosexuality. No one really knows the answer to either question.

A number of different "causes" of homosexuality and bisexuality have been posited: genetic factors, hormonal imbalances, arrested psychosexual development, and societal/familial conditioning are major ones (Bailey, 1995; Bohan, 1996; Fox, 1995, 1996; Klein, 1993). But the truth is that no one really knows. Bohan (1996) states a viable approach to questions about sexual orientation:

> It is reasonable to expect that the origin and the development of sexual orientation vary widely among people, with various components contributing differentially and at different times to the course of each person's evolution. For some, biology may play a major role; for others, choice predominates; for each, environmental forces likely contribute; for all, the meanings given by society shape how experiences will be understood and identities will be defined. (p. 88)

The "causes" of being transgendered are equally unclear and obscure (Schrang, 1997), but the development of gender identity is certainly heavily influenced by society's constructions of gender and gender identity (Bohan, 1996; Brown and Rounsley, 1996; Israel and Tarver, 1997; Lev, in press; Marcel, 1998). Transsexualism is thought by a number of scientists to be a medical condition created by hormone discrepancies, while others contend that at least some influences are exerted by early social learning (Brown and Rounsley, 1996; Marcel, 1998). However, according to Brown and Rounsley (1996), many gender identity experts now believe that transsexualism results from an interaction between nature and nurture. The "causes" of other forms of transgenderism are also obscure and probably influenced by the interaction between biology and environment.

The most helpful and healing perspective is that being homosexual, bisexual, or transgendered is a naturally occurring phenomenon. Certainly, life would be much better for LGBT people—as well as for heterosexuals—if everyone subscribed to this view.

Prevalence of LGBT Substance Abuse

Any discussion of substance abuse among LGBT people must, of necessity, be divided into groups. Much of the current research is focused on lesbians and gay men, sometimes strictly on lesbians or on gay men. Whatever research has been done on bisexuals is, for the most part, combined with or subsumed under the research about lesbians and gay men. There is at this time no study we know of that specifically focuses on bisexuals and substance abuse. In effect, bisexuals as substance abusers are almost completely invisible. The research on transgender substance abuse will be addressed as a discrete entity.

Problems for Researchers

Two major problems beset those who wish to study substance abuse problems among LGBT people. One is that people in each of the four groups are, to one degree or another, closeted and therefore hard to find. Although researchers can study those who are not closeted, they do not constitute a random sample. The second problem is that because these populations are at least partially invisible, researchers cannot really gain an accurate estimate of how large they are. Therefore, it is difficult to accurately calculate incidence or prevalence. Ultimately, there has to be some educated projecting.

Lesbian, Gay Male, and Bisexual Substance Abuse

It should be noted that only when bisexuals were specifically included in a study will that fact be indicated.

Alcohol and Other Drugs

The rest of the discussion in this section focuses on lesbians and gay men. Earlier research efforts suggested that substance abuse affects about one-third of American lesbians and gay men (Fifield, DeCresenzo, and Latham, 1975: Lohrenz et al., 1978; Saghir and Robins, 1973; Weinberg and Williams, 1974). Beatty (1983) reported on the findings of two gay counseling centers in Pennsylvania that 40 percent of their new admissions had MAST scores indicative of substance abuse. These studies were, however, affected by the problems mentioned above, problems of a closeted, non-random sample and based on self-report.

More recent research does not seem to fully bear out this high estimate. McKirnan and Peterson (1989a,b), found that the heavy use of alcohol was about the same among lesbians, gay men, and heterosexuals: 17 percent of the gay men, 9 percent of the lesbians, and 21 percent of the general population reported heavy use of alcohol and other drugs. Stall and Wiley (1988), McKirnan and Peterson (1992), and Ostrow and Kessler (1993) have all reported that there are less dramatic differences between lesbian/gay and heterosexual alcohol use/abuse than the 30 percent statistic would suggest.

Although there were no indications of significant differences in alcohol and other drugs (AOD) use, whatever people's sexual orientation was, other findings point to problems among lesbians and gay men. Lesbians and gay men use other drugs at higher rates than heterosexuals (e.g., their use of marijuana was three to four times higher) although their drug of choice was alcohol. Stall and Wiley (1988) found that gay men were three times more likely than heterosexual men to have used barbiturates in the past six months; five times more likely to have used MDMA (Ecstasy); and fifty eight times more likely to have used poppers (inhalants).

Skinner and Otis' (1992) findings support Stall and Wiley's study (1988): they report that gay men were more likely to use inhalants, sedatives, and stimulants than heterosexual men. Skinner and Otis (1996) later found that gay men had higher rates of inhalant and illicit drug use than heterosexual men. Frosch et al. (1996) studied gay, bisexual, and heterosexual men and found that while 33 percent of the overall sample reported injecting methamphetamine, over 50 percent of the gay and bisexual men reported doing so.

McKirnan and Peterson (1989a,b) also looked at whether people's use declined as they grew older. They found that both lesbians' and gay men's use did not decline with age, but that the heterosexuals' use did. Another, more recent study, the 1996 National Household Survey of Drug Abuse (NHSDA) report (SAMHSA, 1996), found that there are no significant age-related declines in drinking rates among lesbian and gay male populations (as there are among heterosexual men and women).

Other studies found that lesbians' use did not decline with age as did the use by heterosexual women (Bradford and Ryan, 1987; Bradford, Ryan, and Rothblum, 1994; Skinner, 1994). Lesbians tend to be at greater risk in that their use of marijuana and cocaine was higher than that of the general population (McKirnan and Peterson, 1989 a,b; Skinner and Otis, 1996). In addition, four studies showed they drank more heavily than heterosexuals (Bradford, Ryan, and Rothblum, 1994; Bux, 1996; Skinner, 1994; Skinner and Otis, 1996).

The research shows that lesbians in particular have more difficulties because of their AOD use. While McKirnan and Peterson (1989a,b) showed that both lesbians and gay men had twice the number of AOD-related problems as the general population, they also found that lesbians in their three older groups (twenty-six to thirty, thirty-one to forty, forty-one to sixty) reported three times as many alcohol-related problems as women in the general population with greater physiological vulnerability as a result (see also Cochran et al., 1996). Hughes et al. (2000) found that older lesbians (ages fifty-one to sixty) reported having more alcohol-related problems. Two other studies also found that lesbians had more problems because of their drinking than did heterosexual women (Bloomfield, 1993; Bux, 1996).

In addition, the 1996 NHSDA (SAMHSA, 1996) report found that lesbians were more likely than heterosexual women to be diagnosed as drug dependent. Cochran and Mays' (2000) examination of the 1996 NHSDA report found that women who were homosexually active would be more likely to have alcohol or drug dependency syndromes.

Several other studies of lesbian and bisexual women found between 2 percent and 6 percent were injection drug users (IDU) (San Francisco Department of Public Health, 1993a, 1993b; Stevens, 1993). One terrible finding of the 1993 San Francisco/Berkeley Women's Survey was that among IDUs, 7.69 percent were HIV positive (San Francisco Department of Public Health, 1993b). As Gomez (1995) notes, "studies of self-identified lesbian and bisexual women present data suggesting that these women may be more likely to inject drugs than are exclusively heterosexual women" (p. 24).

One other finding is that fewer lesbians and gay men (29 percent) than heterosexuals (14 percent) are likely to abstain (McKirnan and Peterson, 1989a,b). One possible reason for this difference is that AOD use has traditionally played such an important role in lesbian and gay male lifestyles.

Youth

Unfortunately, younger lesbians, gay men, and bisexuals are at high risk for substance abuse. Rosario, Hunter, and Gwadz (1997) found that young women (both lesbian and bisexual) were at higher risk for substance abuse than were young men (both gay and bisexual). Hughes et al. (2000) report that younger lesbians are at increased risk. Stall and Wiley (1988) and, eight years later, Skinner and Otis (1996) found high rates of drug use in young lesbians and gay men. Faulkner and Cranston (1998) state the results from their study of high school students:

> Students reporting same-sex contact were more likely to report fighting and victimization, frequent use of alcohol, other drug use, and recent suicidal behaviors . . . [and thus] may be at elevated risk of injury, disease, and death resulting from violence, substance abuse, and suicidal behaviors. (p. 262)

Savin-Williams (1994) echoes these findings. He notes that LGB youths use and abuse alcohol and other drugs to cope on a daily basis with stresses exerted by home, school, and society and to help them face their current lives and their futures as people who belong to stigmatized groups. These stresses are vividly captured by young people's comments following the Columbine (Littleton, Colorado) shootings. In an interview, they described how the two gunmen, Eric Harris and Dylan Klebold, had been taunted by other students because they did not "fit in."

MEG: They called them freaks, weirdos, faggots. . . . They couldn't handle it.
DEVON: They thought they were gay . . .
DUSTIN: When they called them fag. . . . I don't think they really meant that. They were like nerds. (*The New York Times*, 1999, p. A27)

Savin-Williams (1995) also points out that LGB youth who run away from intolerable conditions at home, school, hometown are "at extreme risk for substance abuse, prostitution, and suicide" (p. 176).

Tobacco

Recent studies on tobacco use among lesbians and gay men have produced some appalling information. Du Rant, Krowchuck, and

Sinal (1998) report that adolescent males with same-sex behavior have increased rates of tobacco use relative to their peers. Stall, Greenwood, et al. (1999) found that 41.5 percent of gay male adults smoke, a rate far above the national rate of 28.6 percent of the general male population (CDC, 1994). Skinner and Otis (1996) report that lesbians smoke more than their gay male counterparts. Bradford, Ryan, and Rothblum (1994) found that 30 percent of the lesbians they surveyed smoked cigarettes on a daily basis, an additional 11 percent smoked occasionally, and that 49 percent of African-American lesbians surveyed regularly used tobacco. Three other studies found that lesbians smoke more and have a higher body mass index than heterosexual women. These factors tend to put lesbians at higher risk for cancer and cardiovascular diseases (Bradford et al., 1994; Moran, 1996; White and Dull, 1997).

Obviously, smoking—this long-ignored form of substance abuse—has a powerful impact on the lesbian and gay male communities, and, very likely, on the bisexual and transgender communities as well.

Transgender Substance Abuse

When considering issues affecting transgendered people, it is important to remember that TGs' sexual orientation ranges over the whole sexual orientation continuum—from heterosexual to bisexual to homosexual. Thus, when discussing substance abuse in the transgender community, it is important to note that bisexuals are included in the studies but often are not separately acknowledged.

Substance abuse problems are rampant in the transgender population. Valentine's study (1998) of intake records at the Gender Identity Project in New York City showed high rates of substance abuse in the transgender population: 27.1 percent reported alcohol abuse; 23.6 percent reported drug abuse. Three hundred ninety-two MTF transgenders participated in Clements' study (1999). Eighty-two (21 percent) identified as bisexual. Sixteen percent of the total number revealed they had received treatment for alcohol problems, and 23 percent for drug problems. The reports of lifetime non-injection drug use were staggering: for example, marijuana—90 percent; cocaine—66 percent; crack—48 percent; heroin—24 percent. Of the injection drug users, 84 percent used speed; 58 percent heroin; 54 percent cocaine.

Of the 252 participants in Xavier's Washington, DC, study (2000), thirty-three people (13.1 percent) self-identified as bisexual. Thirty-four percent of all the participants stated that alcohol was a problem for them; 36 percent reported drugs to be a problem. Furthermore, 46 percent reported having sex while drunk or high; 22 percent cited drug use as their reason for engaging in unsafe sex. Marcel (1998) also states that the rate of substance abuse in Boston is very high; he notes, for instance, that 80 percent of the transgendered people surveyed reported using crack. A 1995 study showed that 80 percent of the transgendered people surveyed reported using crack.

One of the more terrible results of acknowledging one's gender identity can be loss of jobs, families, friends, and/or partners that make up one's social structure (see Israel and Tarver, 1997). As the Transgender Health and Education Network (Marcel, 1998) study notes, "Without a social structure many TS/TG people, especially those from minority communities and low-income families, turn to the sex industry for financial survival and sexual relationships . . ." (p. 9).

Being sex workers puts people at high risk. Nemoto et al. (1998) note that "Sex work offers a means to support drug use, and sex becomes riskier when using drugs" (p. 2). Marcel (1998) points out that "those who work in the sex industry are at high risk for substance abuse because of the prevalence of drugs and alcohol in this environment" (p. 9). Reback and Lombardi's study (1999) of Los Angeles TGs reveals that those engaged in sex work showed much higher percentages of alcohol/drug use than non-sex workers. For example, 51 percent of sex workers versus 29 percent of non-sex workers reported alcohol use; 25 percent versus 3 percent reported crack use. Reback and Lombardi (1999) also found that sex workers were more likely to inject drugs (8 percent versus 2 percent) and their use of crystal methamphetamine was high (11 percent).

Treatment Outlook for Lesbians, Gay Men, Bisexuals, and Transgendered People

Lesbians, Gays, Bisexuals

Although the outlook for LGBs is not as bleak as it was in 1987 when this book was first written, the prospects of finding and receiving LGB-affirmative substance abuse treatment are not terribly promising. For one thing, there seem to be no treatment opportunities specifically for bisexuals. They are, per usual, put together with lesbians and gay men and are not considered a discrete population.

There are a few in-patient treatment facilities specifically for LGB substance abusers and psychiatric patients—Pride Institute in Minneapolis and Alternatives, which has facilities in several cities. Some other in- and outpatient facilities either have a "gay track" (which may offer groups and lectures specifically for LGB clients) or have a policy of being LGB-affirmative. Since 1987, many more lesbian and gay AA and NA meetings have come into existence, and the lesbian and gay community centers in many cities provide programs and AA/NA meetings specifically for lesbian, gay male, and bisexual substance abusers.

Transgendered People

> Because it is legally mandated that our lives must fit into one of those tiny boxes [male or female], many of us actually face imprisonment or institutionalization merely because we don't. We live under the constant threat of horrifying violence. We have to worry about what bathroom to use when our bladders are aching. We are forced to consider whether we'll be dragged out of a bathroom and arrested or face a fistfight while our bladders are still aching. It's an everyday reality for us. Human beings must use toilets.
>
> L. Feinberg (1998, p. 68)

The outlook for transgendered substance abusers is very bleak indeed. Clements' study (1999) in San Francisco of 392 MTF transgenders revealed that all of them "reported some type of abuse and discrimination because of their gender identity or gender presentation" (p. 8). Eighty-three percent reported verbal abuse; 46 percent employment discrimination; 37 percent physical abuse; 27 percent housing discrimination; and 13 percent reported problems getting health care. As Lombardi and van Servellen (2000) note, "transgendered individuals must navigate through a health-care system that is unable to comprehend let alone support transgendered individuals" (p. 293).

The same kinds of problems face transgenders who seek substance abuse treatment. Focus groups in Minneapolis and San Francisco discovered that HIV/substance abuse programs discriminated against transgendered people. It was also found that a number of substance abuse programs do not provide transgender-specific or sensitive treatment (Bockting, Robinson, and Rosser, 1998; San Francisco Department of Public Health, AIDS Office, 1997).

Transgendered people in substance abuse treatment programs have also been exposed to abusive and inappropriate experiences, including physical/verbal abuse by other patients and by staff members; being forced to wear only clothing deemed appropriate to their birth gender; and having to use showers and sleep in areas deemed appropriate to their birth gender (The Transgender Substance Abuse Treatment Policy Group of the San Francisco Lesbian, Gay, Bisexual, and Transgender Substance Abuse Task Force, 1995).

The Transgender Education Network: JRI Health study (Marcel, 1998) reported that TG/TS clients in inpatient substance abuse programs received mixed treatment regarding their gender identity as a determining factor for sleeping arrangements. Some programs placed their MTF clients in housing matched to their gender identity. But others placed clients in housing matched to their birth gender. All of the male inpatient programs required these MTF to dress as men.

This study examined the services provided by twenty-one programs—inpatient and outpatient. In nineteen of the twenty-one sites, gender issues were never addressed in groups. In twenty of the twenty-one sites, the focus was always on substance abuse and gender issues were viewed as secondary to substance abuse issues.

The Transgender Education Network: JRI Health study (Marcel, 1998) clearly states that

> The largest issue reported by staff for TS/TG clients in recovery was the lack of services available in after-care programs (residential, sober housing, substance abuse support groups which integrate TS/TG issues) that accept and support the clients' gender identity. Especially in after-care, it is necessary to focus on substance abuse problems as well as life issues of being TS/TG. Without this kind of support clients reported having to resort to finding community from their previous social network in the bars. (p. 31)

Kammerer, Mason, and Connors (1999) also reported that in Boston there were no alcohol or drug treatment groups or facilities specifically for transgendered people. In addition, when transgenders went to lesbian and/or gay twelve step meetings, there was often friction about their presence.

The bleakness of this picture is considerable. It is tempered somewhat by the growth of community centers around the country which are to some degree filling the enormous gap in treatment and support. For example, the New York City Gay and Lesbian Community Center has a program, Project Connect, that provides services to LGBT substance abusers. In addition, they have a Gender Identity Project that addresses transgendered people's issues and problems, including substance abuse. The Center houses all kinds of support groups and twelve step meetings that address many different people's specific issues.

Summary

The research paints a grim picture. Substance abuse problems intertwined with oppression often make LGBTs' struggles to cope with life extremely difficult. Clearly, the importance of compassionate and supportive counselors cannot be overstressed. Oftentimes, counselors can serve as lifelines and as beacons of hope.

ADDRESSING THE PROBLEM

To heal is to touch with love that which we previously touched with fear.

S. Levine
Healing into Life and Death, 1987

If counselors are to help and support their lesbian, gay, bisexual, and transgendered clients who are substance abusers, it is essential that they address certain matters.

The Counseling Relationship

The relationship between counselor and client is at the heart of all substance abuse counseling and indeed of all counseling. As Herman

(1992) notes, "Recovery [from trauma] . . . is based upon the empowerment of the survivor and the creation of new connections. *Recovery can take place only within the context of relationships; it cannot occur in isolation* [our italics] (p.133).

The reason that counseling relationships are paramount is that substance abusers are people who have been traumatized, as are lesbians, gay men, bisexuals, and transgendered people. As Herman (1992) points out, trauma shatters images of the self and ruptures connections with others. "The core experiences of psychological trauma are disempowerment and disconnection from others" (Herman, 1992, p. 133). Active addiction also traumatizes people (Bean, 1981; Brown, 1998; Levin, 1998). Bean (1981) describes the trauma of alcoholism as a "Catastrophic experience—terrible losses, deprivations, the sense of being at hazard, shame and the uncertainty one can never atone, the ruin of self-esteem, the utter loss of hope" (p. 90).

Homo/bi/transphobia and heterosexism traumatize people affected by those oppressions (Alvarez, 1994; Dillon, 1993; Finnegan and McNally, 1996). Alvarez (1994) states that lesbians and gay men are very often victims of emotional, and often physical, abuse and likens them to sexual abuse survivors. Certainly LGBT people are the casualties of a vast range of abuses—from vicious name-calling to gay-bashing to rejection by family and friends. They are often subjected to physical violence, rape, and emotional abuse if they do not conform, keep quiet, stay in the closet and thereby deny their identity, negate their truths, and invalidate their Selves. All of this is traumatizing. And added to these traumas may be others—growing up in an alcoholic and/or drug abusing home and/or sexual abuse.

As Surrey (1992) states, addiction is a contraction of connection (with self and others) and recovery is an expansion of connection (with self and others). The connection that occurs between counselors and clients can contribute greatly to the recovery process.

Countertransference

We learn we are not only entitled but also obligated not to reduce ourselves to one version of ourselves. We turn ourselves over this way and that. The turning never stops. We put it aside to rest, to do something else, to recover from the movement. But when we are ready, we dip in and ride the rapids as best we can. We do not know ahead of time what current will take us where.

M. Eigen (1996, p. 167)

Whatever affects the counseling relationship is of crucial importance to the well-being of the client. The factor having the most powerful effect on the relationship is counselors' *countertransference*— all their responses to clients. Some of these responses are conscious ones in reaction to what clients do. These responses are considered forms of *objective* countertransference because there is an objective reality involved—for example, suppose a client yells an obscenity at the counselor when the counselor asks a personal question. The counselor might feel shock or anger and might reply angrily. That would be a response to an objective reality. However, if this same counselor's response were to storm out of the room or to insult the client, that response would be one of *subjective* countertransference—i.e., pre-conscious or unconscious responses to clients which are based on unresolved issues from the counselor's past and which, therefore, are to some degree not appropriate to the current reality of the counseling relationship (Flores, 1988; Imhof, Hirsch, and Terenzi, 1984; Loris, 1994; Vannicelli, 1989; Watkins, 1985).

For example, suppose a male counselor's father frequently told him not to cry because "only girls and sissies cry" and constantly told him to "be a man." In addition, suppose his father also told him repeatedly that if he didn't act like a man, he was "a faggot." If this counselor has not resolved the conflicts caused by his father's treatment of him, he may react hostilely to a gay male client who has effeminate gestures. The counselor's hostility is his unconscious way of distancing himself from this client so that the counselor can feel very different and distinct from his "sissy" client and from his own feminine side.

Counselors working with substance abusers who are lesbian, gay, bisexual, or transgendered are dealing with The Other—i.e., people who are different from them or who may represent a part of themselves they may be afraid to own. The more different from us a person is, the more likely we are to react in primitive and powerful—often unconscious—ways. Certainly lesbians, gay men, bisexuals, and transgendered people constitute The Other; their difference represents the "forbidden" or, according to the distorted teachings of homo/bi/transphobia and hatred, represents the "abnormal," the dark side. This Otherness is a threat that stirs deep, primitive fears and aggressiveness in people. It becomes critically important, therefore, that counselors monitor their feelings, attitudes, and behaviors and receive good training, supervision, and support.

Watkins (1985) discusses four destructive forms that countertransference can take, a list that can be helpful in monitoring self.

1. *Overprotectiveness:* being overprotective toward the seemingly fragile client, counselors prevent clients from coming to grips with their issues and therefore not achieving self-mastery.
2. *Focusing on the positive:* fearing clients' anger or needing to be liked, counselors focus on the positive and ignore the negative, thereby colluding in denial.
3. *Rejection:* viewing the client as needy or overly dependent, counselors act aloof and distant, thus pushing the client away and enlarging the separation between counselor and client.
4. *Hostility:* fearing they are like the client, counselors distance themselves via hostile remarks and behavior.

As presented, these four types are clear-cut and obvious. In actual, everyday counseling, they are often not so obvious. Thus it becomes necessary to know what other markers to watch for. Vannicelli (1989) provides "Signals of Countertransference," both covert and overt, which are helpful in the monitoring process.

> *Covert* signs . . . (1) unexpected shifts in attitude toward the patient . . . ; (2) preoccupation with a given patient . . . as expressed through dreams, recurring thoughts. or rehashes in one's head about a session . . . ; and (3) feeling mired down, exhausted, or stuck, or having fantasies about missing a session. *Overt* signs . . . (1) stereotyped or fixed responses to the patient . . . ; (2) inappropriate affective responses to the patient (i.e., responses that differ from the therapist's usual behavior); and (3) changes in the therapeutic contract—therapist's lateness, sleepiness during the hour, changing the time of appointments or cutting them short, neglecting to return phone calls, and laxness about the patient's failure to respect the therapeutic contract [our italics]. (p. 78)

Because almost everyone who grows up in this culture acquires some homo/bi/transphobia, some heterosexism, counselors need to be especially alert to those signs in themselves when they counsel LGBT clients. Only such alertness can help counselors provide safety and competent counseling.

Traumatic Countertransference

One other matter needs to considered here. In addition to providing safety to their clients, counselors need to attend to their own well-being. Herman (1992) speaks powerfully to this issue:

> Trauma is contagious. In the role of witness to disaster or atrocity, the therapist at times is emotionally overwhelmed. She [or he] experiences, to a lesser degree, the same terror, rage, and despair as the patient. This phenomenon is known as "traumatic countertransference" or "vicarious traumatization." (p. 140)

Herman (1992) discusses the problems created by this condition. These may include reactions such as overidentifying with the client's helplessness and "violating the bounds of therapy and assuming the role of rescuer" (p. 143); identifying with the client's rage; experiencing tremendous grief; experiencing "survivor guilt"; identifying with the client's tormentors (see Herman, 1992, pp. 140-154, for a full and extremely helpful discussion of this phenomenon; see also McCann and Pearlman, 1990b).

In order to protect their clients and themselves, counselors need to use the tools that Watkins (1985), Vannicelli (1989), and Herman (1992) present (see preceding). In addition, counselors need to find and avail themselves of good supervision, and they need to seek out and find peer support. As Herman so aptly notes, "Just as no survivor can recover alone, no therapist can work with trauma alone" (p. 141).

Values/Attitudes

> Editing is a part of the pleasure of life. One edits oneself as one goes along. Life edits one.

> M. Eigen (1996, p. 166)

As a specific part of their monitoring process, counselors need to recognize, clarify, and, if necessary, challenge and perhaps alter their own values and attitudes about gender and sexuality—homosexuality, bisexuality, and transgenderism in particular. Certainly they need to address their own heterosexism, homo/bi/transphobia, and homo/bi/transhatred. It is critically important for counselors to pay close attention to their "gut reactions" when they interact with people whose experiences are very different from their own; e.g., the man who is effeminate; the woman who is "overly" masculine; the man who cross-dresses; the woman who knows he is really a man even though his body is that of a female.

Counselors need to think about and determine what they consider to be the parameters of health. Is there room in their definition of health for alternative lifestyles? Do they believe that being transgendered is a natural expression of gender? That homosexuality, like being left-handed, is a naturally occurring phenomenon? That bisexuality is a viable orientation? In addition, counselors need to identify areas where they lack education and information and fill these gaps. They will then be more comfortable with and knowledgeable about gender and sexuality, including homosexuality, bisexuality, and transgenderism, and they will be less likely to visit their countertransference on clients who are Other.

Knowledge

> Every human being is actually many males, many females. If we took this as an axiom of daily life, we might get along better. We might make room for ourselves and each other. We ought not assume we know too much about the capacities that constitute us, who we are, and what we are made of. We are and remain mysteries all our lives. If we are lucky, we learn a little about being partners with ourselves.

M. Eigen (1996, p. 168)

It is imperative that counselors be as clear as possible about issues regarding gender, sexuality, and sexual orientation because clients, whether LGBT or not, are often confused and frightened about these matters. Many of these clients were confused about gender and sexual identity before they started using alcohol and drugs, partly because many of them began using and abusing substances at very early ages. During their active substance abuse, many of them engaged in sexual behaviors with and/or experienced emotional attractions to people of the same sex which further confused and frightened them. When they begin getting clean and sober and start struggling with issues related to their gender identity and sexuality, they may experience a great deal of turmoil.

For example, Sarah insisted to herself and others that she was not a lesbian and she slept with many men to prove it. But when she got really drunk and blacked out, she was always amazed to wake up in bed with a woman whose name she often did not even know. She explained away these alcohol-induced episodes by claiming the women "took advantage of her." But, in her recovery, when she began feeling attracted to women she met in Alcoholics Anonymous (AA), she felt confused and frightened. Another example is Jeff, a seventeen-year-old who hustled men to get money for his drugs. When he started to get clean and sober, Jeff was faced with the terrifying questions of "Who am I?" and "What is my sexual identity?" Knowledgeable counselors with nonjudgmental attitudes can help to ease their clients' turmoil somewhat and reassure them that it is possible to get and stay clean and sober and come to terms with themselves and their lives in recovery, without the anesthesia of alcohol or other drugs.

Counselors often see clients whose lives are seriously threatened by the turmoil they are experiencing. Ted, a thirty-six-year-old man, signed himself into an substance abuse unit because he could not stop drinking and was depressed and suicidal. He had taken an overdose of aspirin three weeks prior and had attempted to slash his wrists a few days before. Although he attended AA regularly, he kept relapsing and wanted to die. When questioned by a counselor whose manner was both accepting and matter-of-fact, he haltingly and painfully shared his past for the first time with anyone. He revealed that as an adolescent he dressed up in women's clothing and that even though he stopped doing so after a few years, he continued to feel very confused and guilty about his behavior.

During the past fifteen years, he reported having both heterosexual and homosexual experiences, including a four-year relationship with a woman. In the past few years he has struggled to get and stay clean and sober, but has not been successful. Although he often goes to AA meetings, he says he feels alienated and unable to trust others and does not feel free to talk to anyone about his feelings or experiences. He does not know where he belongs, who he is, or what he should do. He does not know whether he is gay or straight or bisexual. He does not know what his experiences with cross-dressing mean. He is terrified of finding out who he is, and his despair is profound.

To begin to understand this man and to help him understand and accept himself is a difficult and delicate task. But along with helping him address his substance abuse, the attempt must be made because his gender and sexual identity confusion seem to be affecting his ability to remain clean and sober. An accurate assessment requires the counselor to know a certain amount about transgenderism including cross-dressing, and about homosexuality, heterosexuality, and bisexuality. If, for example, a counselor does not know that the majority of cross-dressers are heterosexual, he or she might assume that this man is gay because of his cross-dressing and because of a few same-sex experiences. Conversely, the counselor must be careful not to jump to the conclusion that this man is heterosexual because he had a four-year relationship with a woman. The results of a counselor's conclusions are very important. For example, if the man is assumed to be gay, the counselor might urge him to go to a gay AA meeting. If the man is assumed not to be gay, the counselor might fail to consider gay AA meetings as a resource and not mention them. Such counseling decisions must be made on the basis of a thorough and informed assessment. Otherwise, the decisions could well be inaccurate, premature, and probably very distressing, if not destructive.

If, however, the counselor is relatively well-informed about matters of gender and sexuality and is comfortable discussing them, he or she can help this client explore the meanings of his behaviors and feelings and not jump to conclusions or urge actions upon him that may not be appropriate. In effect, the counselor must be able to occupy a position of ambiguity rather than take a definite position before enough is known. The counselor must not give in to his or her own need or the client's need for certainty.

Probably the first step is to tell the client there can be no answers to his questions until he has gotten and stayed clean and sober for a period of time. Explaining that determining identity is a long-term process may reassure him and give him hope, helping him to relax and give himself time. Also, if a knowledgeable therapist is available, telling the client he can be referred to that person may be reassuring.

Another helpful action is to have this client read books and magazines that will clarify some of these issues.

It is not the counselor's job to treat a client's sexual or gender identity confusion. What is most important is that the counselor attend to the client's statements and feelings; that the counselor be empathic and supportive; that the counselor help the client to begin recovery; and, most of all, that the counselor offer some hope to the client—that resolutions of his confusion and pain are possible in recovery.

Cultural Competence

Another extremely important aspect of counselor competence is that of *cultural* competence (SAMHSA:CSAT, 1999). What is cultural competence? It is the ability to provide effective and helpful services to people from varied cultures and communities in a respectful and informed manner. Such competence requires that counselors honor the diversity in people's attitudes, beliefs, values, mores, and actions and that they promote inclusion rather than simply tolerate difference (Wright et al., 2001). In these ways, counselors can make prevention and treatment environments safe so that clients are protected while they strive to recover from the ravages of their substance abuse.

Some definitions are in order here. *Race* is ordinarily defined as similar physical characteristics that distinguish groups of people. *Ethnicity* refers to groups' common national, geographical, and/or cultural heritage marked by shared customs, language, beliefs, and history. Thus, for example, someone's *race* might be Asian, African, Caucasian, Hispanic; someone's *ethnicity* might be African American, Irish, Cherokee, Vietnamese.

Eurocentrism, as Woll (1996) notes, means adherence "to a set of white European-male-based cultural values which are often used by society to define what's perceived as 'normal'" (p. 71). Eurocentrism is one form (and the predominant form in American society) of ethnocentrism, defined by Smith (1997) as "the belief that one's own cultural approach is the normative lens through which to view a situation or experience" (p. 287).

Identity Issues of LGBTs from Racial/Ethnic Minorities

Racial and ethnic groups have powerful and far-reaching values, customs, beliefs, and mores which tend to influence, and often govern, the lives of their members. Many of the existing racial and ethnic groups tend to be rather homo/bi/transphobic. What happens, then, when a member of a racial and/or ethnic minority is also lesbian, gay, bisexual, or transgendered?

Counselors need to know the answers to this question in order to effectively (and compassionately) evaluate and help their minority LGBT clients. Counselors need to know what issues and pressures racial and ethnic minority people face when they are trying to form or come to terms with *both* their sexual and/or gender identity and their racial/ethnic identity. In this way, counselors can appreciate their clients' struggles, feelings, attitudes, and behaviors and the obstacles and difficulties they may face.

Multiple Oppressions

> You cannot make yourself feel something you do not feel, but you can make yourself do right in spite of your feelings.

> Pearl Buck
> *To My Daughters, with Love,* 1967

In this heterosexist, homo/bi/transphobic society, LGBT people are subjected to much bad treatment, ranging from verbal to physical harassment and abuse. In this racist, Eurocentric society, people who belong to a racial or ethnic minority are subject to oppressions ranging from subtle attitudes to blatant insults, from verbal to physical assaults. If a person belongs to both a racial/ethnic and a sexual/gender identity minority, he or she is the target of double, triple, or multiple oppressions.

For example, an African-American lesbian will be oppressed for her race, her gender, and her sexual orientation. If, in addition, she is transgendered, she will be oppressed for her gender identity as well. If she comes out to her family, she runs the risk of their homo/transphobia and possible rejection. If she is an active substance abuser, she may be rejected or stigmatized by her racial/ethnic group for her addiction. If she is a recovering substance abuser, she may be stigmatized by at least some segments of the lesbian community who are "alco/drugphobic"—i.e., they do not want to know about or deal with substance abuse, and some of them may reject her because of transphobia.

It is important for counselors to recognize what their racial/ethnic minority LGBT clients may face when they try to answer the great human questions of Who am I? and Where do I belong? Bohan (1996) points out the terrible irony that "For minority LGBs, there is the additional marginalization that results from the erasure of one's minority identity in the LGB community and of one's LGB identity in the minority community" (p. 126). The same dynamics hold true for minority transgendered people, but with an added twist. The LGB community tends to be not just racist but also transphobic which further marginalizes the transgenders. Unfortunately, many transgendered people are racist, homo/biphobic, *and* transphobic.

This intersection of identities and oppressions makes people's life choices difficult and complex.

Racism in the Lesbian, Gay Male, Bisexual, and Transgender Communities

As Bohan (1996) notes, the LGB communities are smaller versions of the larger society and often manifest its racism, Eurocentrism, classism, sexism, ageism, and other prejudices. Choi et al. (1995) agree, pointing out the example of racist attitudes directed toward gays who are Asian-Pacific Islanders (API). Basically, the same prejudices exist in transgendered communities (Gainor, 2000). Israel and Tarver (1997) comment on the effects of racism/ethnocentrism *within* the transgender community: "many transgender people of color either remain isolated within their ethnic minority communities or exiled from the *white dominant culture* of the transgender community and community services" [our italics] (p. 129). They go on to note the "racism, elitism, and sexism that many transgendered people of color regularly face" (p. 130). Thus LGBT people of color who seek support from the LGBT communities for their struggle to develop and maintain their sexual/gender identities frequently have to contend with a lack of affirmation and often with overt prejudice.

Homo/Bi/Transphobia in Racial/Ethnic Communities

Bohan (1996) notes that "Some have argued that homonegativity is greater in minority communities than in the culture as a whole" (p. 127). Although there is little research about this matter, there are obvious factors at work in these communities that create strong homo/bi/transphobic feelings. attitudes, and behaviors which discourage or work against LGBT people coming to terms with and claiming their sexual/gender identities.

Although there are obvious and significant differences among various races and ethnic groups, some similarities run through most of them that negatively affect their attitudes and beliefs about being LGBT.

1. As Smith (1997) points out, "The coming out process is . . . [seen] as a White, Western, middle-class phenomenon . . ." (p. 287) (see also Bohan, 1996; Chan, 1997; Choi et al., 1995). Thus taking on a LGBT identity may be perceived as giving in to or embracing white values and denying one's racial/ethnic roots (Chan, 1995).
2. Smith (1997) notes that white LGB communities emphasize independence and distinguishing oneself from family of origin as the way to come out and form an LGB identity. These values run strongly counter to the primary value most minority groups place on the heterosexual family as the key means to survival and to the well-being of members (Bohan, 1996; Chan, 1995; Choi et al., 1995).
3. As Bohan (1996) points out, gender roles and expectations underpin the well-being of the family and therefore the culture. But LGBT identities challenge and transgress traditional gender roles/expectations and thereby threaten the very structure of the family/culture.
4. Religion plays a central role in the life and beliefs of many minority cultures and teaches and reinforces homo/bi/transphobic values.

These and other rationales have a constricting effect on LGBTs' opportunities to own their sexual and/or gender identity (Chan, 1995; Choi et al., 1995; Gainor, 2000; Israel and Tarver. 1997; Smith, 1997). As Bohan (1996) comments, "To the extent that their cultures embrace these rationales, identifying as gay, lesbian, or bisexual is tantamount to challenging values that define the very essence of one's culture and therefore of oneself" (p. 128). The same, of course, applies to transgendered people because their self-identification or coming out are the clearest and most overt transgressions of cultural values.

Minority LGBTs are often caught between two worlds, discriminated against by both, often not receiving important support from either. Although this situation may afford possible opportunities for growth (Bohan, 1996), it also provides a breeding ground for the use and abuse of alcohol and other drugs. The stresses inherent in straddling but not fully belonging to the two most important worlds in people's lives may lead them to seek the oblivion offered by mood-altering substances.

Counselor Awareness

Counselors need to be aware of the stresses, the possible self-medicating remedies people seek, and the coping strategies they may need to employ. Because they often look the same, it is important to distinguish between what are adaptive strategies and what are expressions of self-hatred and internalized homo/bi/transphobia. For example, passing may be highly adaptive in a job market that would never accept an LGBT person. Another empowering strategy may be that of withholding information about self because that is what one has control over. Another strategy may be to not come out as a way of maintaining one's own privacy and simultaneously respecting others' boundaries (Smith, 1997).

Counselors also need to be aware that there are sometimes major differences in the ways some cultures view same-sex behavior. For example, in Hispanic cultures, men have insertive anal sex with other men but do not necessarily see themselves and are not seen as homosexual. Hispanic women may physically express affection to other women without seeing themselves or being seen as lesbian partly because women are thought to be ignorant about sexuality or primarily non-sexual (Bohan, 1996). Many African-American men see themselves as heterosexual even though they also have sex with men. These differing cultural perspectives argue for sensitive intake procedures and skilled questioning to elicit accurate information.

In light of cultural differences, it is extremely important that counselors monitor their own attitudes, beliefs, and values. Counselors need to explore whether they are Euro- or ethnocentric and the effects of those characteristics. They need to consider whether they are experi-

encing negative countertransferential reactions to clients of ra-
cial/ethnic minorities or are delivering racially and/or ethnically inappropriate treatment based on ignorance. If any of these conditions
apply, then counselors need to challenge and work on altering their
ethnocentric views, attitudes, and behaviors.

In addition, they need to understand, honor, and respect the diversity of their lesbian, gay, bisexual, and transgendered clients. This requires both knowledge and an understanding of the interrelationships
among all these factors. Competence also includes an understanding
of how substance abuse interfaces with the stresses inherent in these
conflicts.

Chapter 4

Societal Prejudice and Oppression

Bigotry exacts its toll in flesh and blood. And left unchecked and unchallenged, prejudices create a poisonous climate for us all. Each of us has a stake in the demand that every human being has a right to a job, shelter, to health care, dignity, and respect.

L. Feinberg (1998, p. 3)

Afraid is a country where they issue us passports at birth and hope we never seek citizenship in any other country.

Audre Lorde
"Stations," in *Our Dead Behind Us,* 1986

There are many issues and problems specific to lesbian, gay, bisexual, and transgender substance abusers' experience that can make their recovery from substance abuse difficult. But there is one central issue, from which all the others seem to arise—*homophobia.* Since Weinberg coined the word in 1972, its meanings and connotations have expanded to refer to *all* prejudicial attitudes and feelings toward homosexuals and homosexuality. Homophobia now means both irrational fear of and hatred and contempt for homosexuals and homosexuality and indeed any sexual orientation that varies from heterosexuality. In addition, biphobia and transphobia go hand in hand with homophobia.

Bolstering and feeding homo/bi/transphobia is *heterosexism,* what Herek (1995) defines as "the ideological system that denies, denigrates, and stigmatizes any nonheterosexual form of behavior, identity, relationship, or community" (p. 321). It is the prevailing cultural belief that heterosexuality is the *only* normal mode of sexuality and sexual expression and experience. Thus, according to these beliefs, anyone who is heterosexual is normal; anyone whose sexuality, sexual expression, feelings, attractions, and experience are not heterosexual is abnormal and is to be despised. By definition, then, bisexuals are abnormal and transgendered people whose orientation is not heterosexual are abnormal. Thus bisexual and transgendered people, as well as lesbians and gay men, are targets of homo/bi/transphobia.

Furthermore, even if transgendered people are heterosexual, they are subjected to homophobia because this culture views deviations from gender roles as clear evidence of homosexuality. As Bohan (1996) points out:

> the anchor of heterosexuality is gender-role compliance. It may be that the greatest risk posed by LGB identity is precisely the profound transgression of gender norms by such identities. Indeed, the very existence of same-sex relationships is an affront to gender roles. (p. 35)

Transgendered people—by definition—"transgress" gender norms and thereby become targets not only of homophobia but also *transphobia*. This is the specific fear, revulsion, and hatred directed at those who "violate" the culture's gender rules.

Bisexual people are subjected to *biphobia*—fear, anger, contempt, hatred, mistrust—from both heterosexual *and* homosexual people. The negative attitudes of heterosexual people spring from their homophobia—bisexual people are seen as deviating from heterosexual norms. Lesbian and gay men's negative attitudes often derive from beliefs that bisexuals want to have heterosexual privilege or cannot deal with their "real" identity of being homosexual (Bohan, 1996; D'Augelli and Garnets, 1995; Savin-Williams, 1995).

Another source of lesbians' and gays' biphobia is their mistrust of bisexuals. This mistrust is based in part on lesbians and gay men defining their identities by rejecting intimate relationships with heterosexuals whereas many bisexuals embrace such intimate relationships (Bohan, 1996). It is important, therefore, to keep in mind that bisexuals may hide their identity because they are often caught between two unwelcoming groups and may be subjected to biphobia if they self-disclose.

Homo/bi/transphobia and heterosexism permeate American culture and constitute the one prejudice that is still socially condoned (Bohan, 1996). It is virtually impossible for anyone to grow up without acquiring negative views and attitudes. From the moment people are born into this culture, they are subjected to teachings about what is and what is not normal and to the view that there are only two possible genders in life which have narrow, rigid scripts specifying what is acceptable behavior for girls and for boys. People grow up and live their adult lives hearing about "faggots," "dykes," "AC-DCs," "he-shes," and "queers." Everyone hears that "these people" are perverts to be feared, hated, shunned, and isolated. It is impossible to live in this culture and not be exposed to these virulent teachings. Since they are as common as the air everyone breathes, it is almost impossible for people not to incorporate them into their belief systems. Thus, almost everyone—whatever their sexual orientation or gender identity—is homo/bi/transphobic and heterosexist to some degree.

Homo/bi/transphobia (hereafter used as a cover term which includes heterosexism) is comprised of all the negative, unfounded, and prejudicial teachings and beliefs about sexual orientation and gender identity that the culture perpetuates through its various institutions. These negative attitudes affect both LGBT and non-LGBT people. For example, heterosexual women who walk down the street hand in hand or arm in arm run the risk of being branded as lesbians; and if heterosexual men were to do so, they would most likely be ridiculed as "faggots" or "fairies" or be attacked, verbally and/or physically. If a man were to dress in women's clothing, he would probably be attacked either verbally or physically, or both. Thus homo/bi/transphobia seriously restricts the freedom and spontaneity of everyone.

Weinberg (1972) contends that homophobia affects everyone's mental health. In like manner, so do biphobia and transphobia. If people are homo/bi/transphobic, their choices of responding to others and to life are severely restricted and compromised by the culture's demands for conformity and its punishment of non-conformity. However, while everyone is affected by homo/bi/transphobia, society's negative attitudes are incalculably more powerful and destructive for LGBT people.

Recognizing and appreciating these effects can help counselors begin to understand why their LGBT clients might be frightened to reveal their sexual orientation and/or gender identity, be extremely mistrustful, and have special issues that significantly affect their recovery from substance abuse.

INSTITUTIONALIZED HOMO/BI/TRANSPHOBIA

Our identity includes many subidentities. As a species, we tend to try what we imagine. If we can imagine it, someone is trying to do it. And, probably, there is also someone speaking out against it.

M. Eigen (1996, p. 170)

This culture perpetuates and enforces its homophobic teachings through a number of different institutions—religion, the medical/psychiatric establishment, the legal system, and the media.

RELIGION

Religious homophobia attacks everyone who "deviates" from (i.e., differs from) mainstream heterosexist injunctions. Thus lesbians, gay men, and bisexuals come under fire because of their "deviant" sexual orientation, and transgendered people come under attack because they are *presumed* to be homosexual as a result of their transgressing gender role restrictions. Citing from Scripture and dogma, many religious institutions attack homosexuality, branding it as sinful, immoral, and against the laws of God and Nature. Although in recent years some churches have taken a more liberal view, many continue to condemn homosexuality and gender nonconformity as an affront to God and a threat to Judaeo-Christian values such as marriage and family.

LGBT people are well aware of religious homophobia. It appears in newspaper columns written by fundamentalists who see homosexuality as a threat to the moral fiber of America. A few of these fanatics call for the extermination of homosexuals. It appears in the Catholic Church's view that acting upon one's homosexual feelings is a sin. It appears in the religious right's attacks claiming that lesbians and gay men are pushing their "homosexual agenda" in schools and in society at large. It appears in some people's attitudes that gay men brought the plague of AIDS on themselves by their wicked behavior and that AIDS is God's punishment for the sin of homosexuality (Paul, Hays, and

Coates, 1995). It appears in the loud silence of some church leaders in the face of vicious attacks on LGBT people, such as the murders of Brandon Teena and Matthew Shepard. It even appears on placards displayed in the street outside Matthew Shepard's funeral service, placards that read, "He's gone to hell where all faggots belong."

Religious homophobia does not confine its destructive effects to homosexuality. A number of fundamentalists equate homosexuality with substance abuse and view both states as self-induced, self-inflicted moral sicknesses. These homophobic people contend that all homosexuals and substance abusers have to do is repent, pray, and give up their sinful condition; that perhaps they cannot help becoming substance abusers or homosexuals, but they can (and must) become abstinent. "Just say no," as it were. Such attitudes and preachings tend to evoke rage—and often despair as well—in people who are targets of such homophobia.

The clients who sit across from the counselor may well have stopped going to church long before because of the tremendous guilt instilled by their religion or because of the hostile treatment they have received in their churches. A number of LGBT people report the traumatic results of confessing their homosexual or nonconforming behavior or perhaps just their feelings to priests, rabbis, or ministers and having those clergy castigate them, refuse absolution, or ask them to leave the church (Denny, 1994).

Kroll (1997), who is a transsexual, describes the power of censorious religious attitudes which she terms "fundamental legalism." This school of belief

> stresses a strict or literal adherence to a set of moral principles within a structured code of conduct. . . . Adherents of this school of thought take their "black and white" concepts and equate them with the divine. . . . [In effect,] they are saying that anyone who cannot accept these concepts cannot be saved by God. Everything must be judged as either right or wrong, and the institution drawing up these concepts becomes equivalent to God. (p. 491)

According to these strictures, anyone who "chooses" to go against the "teachings of God" (as interpreted by the fundamental legalists) is

wrong and cannot be saved. Since many religions and religious ad-
herents believe that homosexuals, bisexuals, and transgendered people *choose* to "deviate" from God's teachings, they believe these
people are damned—unless they "choose" to change.

Many who hold these religious views argue that "God made you a
woman/man so it is a sin to change God's work." But as Kroll (1997)
and Harris (1997)—among others—contend, this argument withers
in the face of questions about operations to separate viable Siamese
twins or to correct birth defects. The distorting heart of this false argument is, of course, that transsexuals (and other transgendered people) can choose not to be transsexual or transgendered, whereas babies with birth defects cannot. The truth is that the choice lies in how
one will live one's life.

In recent years, there has been a rise in claims made by some fun-
damentalist Christian groups regarding "conversions" of homosexuals. These groups contend that through prayer and accepting Christ as
their savior homosexuals can change their sexual orientation and become heterosexual. The driving force behind these homophobic con-
tentions is that homosexuality is wrong and therefore people should
change to heterosexuality and, most important, that *such a change is
possible*—and desirable.

There is absolutely no scientific evidence that people can change
their sexual orientation at will. What confuses the issue is that people
can alter their sexual *behavior* and thereby appear to be and live as
heterosexuals. Indeed, some people do just that. *Why* someone would
do so is another matter. But duress is a strong motivator. The pressures to please parents and family, to belong to the mainstream and
not be different, to not be stigmatized, and, most strongly, to be saved
(according to the narrow "fundamental legalism" of some Christian
groups)—those are powerful inducements for some people.

Claims of "conversions" to heterosexuality, based as they are on
behavioral changes, seem rather fraudulent because true conversions
of the spirit entail not behavior changes but rather soul changes.

Many LGBT people describe the despair they experienced when at
some point they measured their feelings and behavior against their
churches' teachings and realized that by those standards they were
sinners. Because of these kinds of conflicts and emotional scars,
many LGBT people may have extra trouble in recovery with spiritual
concepts involving "moral" inventories and a belief in God or a

Higher Power. Fortunately, understanding priests, ministers, or rabbis can often help heal some of the scars simply by being accepting.

THE MEDICAL/PSYCHIATRIC/PSYCHOLOGICAL PROFESSION

Late in the nineteenth century, the medical/psychiatric/psychological profession somewhat tempered the prevailing religious view of homosexuality by defining it as a mental aberration, a form of illness, and claiming that it should be treated, not condemned as sinful. Since that time, much homophobia has simply taken on a pseudo-scientific aura, and many lesbians, gay men, and bisexuals have been subjected to all kinds of indignities, insults, and poor treatment by health professionals under the guise of therapy or treatment.

Lesbians, Gay Men, and Bisexuals

Unfortunately, the medical and health care professions are often as homophobic and biphobic as the general population. As Dean et al. (2000) point out, "Bias from healthcare professionals and perceptions of such bias have been identified as personal and cultural barriers to care, leading to reduction in help-seeking and quality of care . . . (p. 103). They also note that homo/biphobia and ignorance may lead to health care professionals' not providing preventive care or treatment suited to the needs of LGB people (e.g., not providing Pap smears to lesbians; not checking gay or bisexual men for infections of the anal canal).

A number of lesbians have reported that their gynecologists have told them to have intercourse to help them "get over" or "outgrow" their lesbianism (McNally, 1989). Gay men have been subjected to electric shocks in aversive therapy to condition them not to respond erotically to other men. There are reports of lobotomies and other brain surgeries having been performed on lesbians and gay men in attempts to "cure" them of their homosexuality (Katz, 1976).

Until 1973, the American Psychiatric Association (APA) viewed homosexuality as an illness, and it was so listed in the *Diagnostic and Statistical Manual of Mental Disorders* (Second Edition) (DSM-II) (1968). After careful consideration as well as an intense political battle, the APA declared that homosexuality "by itself does not necessarily constitute a psychiatric disorder." It went on to say that only if a person is unable to accept and adjust to being homosexual can he or she be considered as sick, a state labeled "Ego-Dystonic Homosexuality" (DSM-III, 1980). Apparently the APA did not recognize the irony inherent in labeling the inability to accept one's homosexuality as pathological when high levels of homophobia in the culture made such acceptance extraordinarily difficult to achieve. In a later edition of the DSM (DSM-IV, 1994), the APA deleted this diagnostic category.

Getting rid of labels by official decree does not automatically get rid of homophobic attitudes and practices. Many psychologists and psychiatrists continue to view homosexuality as mental illness. It is not unusual to hear of lesbians, gay men, and bisexuals being treated as though the essential cause of any emotional problems they may have is their "abnormal" lifestyles. Despite strong positive statements by both the American Psychiatric and the American Psychological Associations, many lesbians, gay men, and bisexuals still report having psychiatrists, psychologists, and other professionals suggest that they get "reparative therapy" which is intended to change their sexual orientation or to "cure" them (Berger, 1994; Ryan, Bradford, and Honnold, 1999).

Countless lesbians, gay men, and bisexuals have been subjected to hostile and destructive treatment based on the psychological views that they are the way they are because of "arrested psychosexual development" or because of neuroses (Garnets et al., 1991). This latter, unfortunately common situation, is analogous to the view that substance abuse is a symptom of an underlying personality disorder. Urging lesbians, gay men, or bisexuals to gain insight, change their behavior, and thereby be "cured of homosexuality" is much like exhorting substance abusers to just say no to their addiction, to just stop being substance abusers. Calls for this kind of change are rooted in ignorance, prejudice, and hostility.

Transgendered People

> Trans-identity is not a natural fact. Rather, it is the political category we are forced to occupy when we do certain things with our bodies. That so many of us try to take our own lives, mutilate ourselves, or just succeed in dying quietly of shame, depression,

or loneliness is not an accident. We are supposed to feel isolated and desperate. Outcast. That is the whole point of the system. Our feelings are not causes but effects.

R. A. Wilchins (1997, p. 25)

Transphobia is, unfortunately, all too common among medical, psychiatric, and psychological professionals. Although intermingled with prejudice against homosexuals and bisexuals, transphobia carries with it negative charges and effects that go far beyond homo/biphobia.

Gender dysphoria—the emotional anguish and painful confusion resulting from a person's experiences of an incongruity between anatomical sex and gender identity—is often seen as confirmation of mental health problems (Brown and Rounsley, 1996), as a "highly pathologized condition . . ." (Denny, 1997, p. 40). At the very least, transgendered behavior is seen as "acting out behavior."

Israel and Tarver (1997) note:

> Until recently, the field of mental health remained rooted in treating transsexualism or any uncertainty about gender identity as a sexual perversion, immature developmental stage, psychotic state, or delusional distortion of self-image. This historical diagnostic labeling of all forms of transgender identification is gradually giving way to a depathologized view of transgender individuals. (p. 24)

As Israel and Tarver (1997) point out, the *Diagnostic and Statistical Manual* (DSM-IV) (1994) narrows the transgendered population who may be diagnosed as "exhibiting a bona fide mental disorder" (p. 24) to a subgroup of emotionally distressed transgendered people suffering from Gender Identity Disorder (GID). Ultimately, they believe, the DSM will drop this diagnostic category altogether—just as they dropped Ego-Dystonic Homosexuality.

However, as Israel and Tarver (1997) state,

> Numerous medical and psychotherapy texts, diagnostic tools, and medical or psychotherapy research and treatment protocols are still likely to refer to transsexualism and associated gender issues as pathologic conditions or sexual perversions. (p. 25)

Not only the formal medical/psychiatric institutions pathologize transgendered people. Unfortunately, it happens all the time in the "trenches" of everyday medical and psychiatric care. A recent study, *Access to Health Care for Transgendered Persons in Greater Boston*, conducted by JSI Research and Training Institute, Inc. (JSI) (July 2000) states:

> In all four focus groups, a constant theme was a perception of vast provider ignorance of trans people and concerns. From the level of health care systems down to individual providers and front-line staff, TG/TS people reported provider unawareness of, disrespect toward, and outright refusal of treatment for their health needs, both basic and trans-related. (p. 35)

Some of the health care needs the participants identified were endocrinology, mental health, substance abuse treatment, HIV/AIDS care, and primary/general medical care. Some of the health care problems and concerns they discussed were obtaining hormones and being properly treated in regard to them; receiving adequate gynecological care; therapists' ignorance about gender issues; and substance abuse counselors' insistence on dealing only with substance abuse and ignoring gender issues (JSI, 2000).

This rather abstract list of needs and problems pales before the personal accounts of individual participants. One MTF youth described obstacles to getting hormone therapy while in treatment at a state-run agency which she characterized as "'so vicious towards transsexuals'" (JSI, 2000, p. 17). An adult FTM participant stated that "a therapist asked him, 'Why didn't you just stay a woman?'" Another FTM participant reported that "a mental health provider said to him, 'You're just a different kind of woman'" (p. 19). One FTM adult recounted that some substance abuse therapists "refused to help him deal simultaneously with his substance abuse and gender issues . . . [saying], 'Deal with your substance abuse, and then come back'" (pp. 19-20). FTM youth reported that they often met with verbal abuse and humiliation from frontline health care staff. One stated that "'I can't even make it through the front door without staff staring at me, laughing at me or whispering about my gender presentation.'" All the participants in the FTM youth group "agreed that they did not feel safe receiving health care; one described his health care experience as 'traumatizing'" (p. 20).

Two other accounts strongly underscore the pain, humiliation, and extreme difficulty involved in interacting with the health care system. One FTM youth reported that "'I was actually turned away [from an emergency room] because the doctor said he did not treat people like me'" (p. 23). Another participant, an "MTF adult said that when a provider discovered her transsexuality, the provider refused to treat her and commented that she should 'see a veterinarian,' as a medical doctor was 'a doctor for people'" (pp. 25-26).

The unbelievably cruel and destructive consequences of transphobia reach beyond even these examples of brutal prejudice. Transgendered people are routinely shamed and humiliated by such treatment. In addition to the emotional scarring visited upon them, however, there are immediate and far-reaching practical effects. As one MTF person who has retained her penis said, "I'd rather die of cancer than get a prostate exam." An FTM person vehemently stated, "I'd rather die of ovarian cancer than have a gynecological exam" (Marcel, 2000). Many transgendered people do not go for treatment ("unless," as one said, "I'm dying"); many will not disclose their TG status or their medical background unless forced to; and they do not get the kind of care they need.

Summary

In addition to the devastation wrought by overt forms of homo/bi/transphobia is the damage inflicted by the more subtle instances in which counselors ignore the issue of gender identity and sexual orientation. Because of their ignorance and their homo/bi/transphobia, they may be in denial and not attend to the realities of the person in front of them by asking and actively seeking to know about the person's background, experiences, and feelings about gender, sexuality, and sexual orientation. This is similar to the way many psychiatrists, psychologists, and medical doctors fail to ask clients about their alcohol and other drug use and abuse—because of prejudices and resultant denial. Obviously, it is difficult if not impossible to give proper care and service when blinded and limited by prejudice.

THE LEGAL SYSTEM

This is another area in which homo/bi/transphobia exerts powerful negative influences. It is possible that LGBT clients may be filled with terror at being discovered, either because they have already been caught in the legal system or because they are frightened by the threat of legal action against them. Many LGBT people have been in a lesbian, gay, or transgender bar when a police raid swept through. Other LGBTs have been roughed up or arrested by the police on flimsy charges. And most LGBTs live on a daily basis with the knowledge and fear that, if discovered, they could lose their jobs, their homes, or their children via custody battles because in most cases the law does not afford them the same protection it affords heterosexual people.

"No federal law protects lesbian, gay, bisexual or transgendered workers from discrimination on the basis of their sexual orientation or gender identity" (Human Rights Campaign Foundation, 2000, p. 15). Nor does federal law protect LGBTs from overt discrimination in housing and access to public accommodations (D'Augelli and Garnets, 1995). Only eleven states, 116 cities and counties, and the District of Columbia have legislation barring employment discrimination based on sexual orientation. Only "Two states (Minnesota and Iowa), the District of Columbia, and 28 municipalities protect transgendered or gender-different people either through legislation or executive order" (Human Rights Campaign Foundation, 2000, p. 21).

In fifteen states, it is still a crime punishable by imprisonment for consenting adults of either the same or the opposite sex to have anal sex with one another. In an additional seven states, sodomy is a crime specifically for same-sex partners. Since the Supreme Court upheld the Georgia "Sodomy Law" in 1986, states have the right to arrest people engaged in acts of sodomy *even in the privacy of their own homes* (Swan, 1997). Furthermore, at this time only twenty states have hate crime laws that specifically protect lesbians and gay men. Currently, although there is a federal law requiring national reporting of hate crimes, there is no federal law *barring* hate crimes against LGBTs (Swan, 1997). Efforts to pass such a law have met with virulent homo/bi/transphobia and claims that LGBT people want "special" civil rights.

As D'Augelli and Garnets (1995) point out, there are strong heterosexist assumptions built in to family law that can be effectively used in many states to take away custody from LGBT parents (see also Swan, 1997). And most "institutional policies (e.g., insurance regulations, inheritance laws, hospital visitation rules)" ignore or deny the validity of LGBT claims (D'Augelli and Garnets, 1995, p. 304). Counselors need to help their LGBT clients navigate the legal minefields, at least by suggesting that clients get legal advice and assistance if any of these issues are relevant.

One other specialized area of concern needs to be considered here. Transsexuals who are living full time in their new gender role must change many legal documents (e.g., legal name, birth certificate, driver's license, marriage license, passport) in order to verify and legitimize their new identity so they can fit in to society. This is a detailed and complex set of tasks which can be beset by problems, delays, and frustrations. Counselors may need to help transsexual clients assess where they are in the process, help them find information (see Denny, 1994), and refer them to an appropriate professional.

There are great injustices built in to the legal system. Thus, although LGBT clients may need help from a counselor, they may be determined not to open up, not to reveal who they really are, for fear their revelation may somehow be used against them. Fear of the law and how people may use it is extremely powerful. It is important, therefore, that counselors develop good relationships with clients so that they can trust their counselors and turn to them for help, such as referral to an LGBT-affirming lawyer or legal service and guidance about resources.

THE MEDIA

In the fifteen years since this book was first written, many changes have taken place in society, especially in the media and the entertainment world. In the 1980s, when the news got out that Rock Hudson was gay (and had AIDS), the media had a field day, squeezing every drop of sensationalism out his life and death. Other, more subtle forms of homophobia were commonplace: portrayals of ordinary lesbian/gay people on TV or in movies were almost non-existent, making gay people invisible. When gay or lesbian characters did appear in TV shows or movies or in novels, they usually were portrayed as disturbed or unlikable. Often the stories ended with these characters committing suicide.

Presently, attitudes are more relaxed and the atmosphere is more open. Now, there are openly lesbian, gay, bisexual, and transgendered performers on TV, on Broadway, in rock bands, as rappers. The relationship breakups of television and movie stars such as Ellen DeGeneres and Anne Heche have been treated in rather matter-of-fact ways by the media; an out and vocal lesbian, Lea DeLaria, has starred on Broadway and in movies; all three shows of the television program *Survivor* have had a gay man; Showtime's *Queer As Folk,* about gay life, has gained popularity; and negotiations are under way to start a gay TV channel.

The Crying Game, which featured a transgendered person in a serious drama about politics, love, and life, was well-received; the movie *Boys Don't Cry,* the story of Brandon Teena, a female-to-male transgendered person who was beaten and ultimately murdered, captured moviegoers' attention with its honesty and realism. *Southern Comfort,* about a female-to-male (Robert Eads) and a male-to-female transsexual (Lola Cola), won the 2001 Sundance Grand Jury Prize for Best Documentary. The film chronicles their committed relationship and focuses on Robert's last year of life before he died of ovarian cancer.

There are openly lesbian and gay people on the radio; LGBT people are writing (and publishing) short stories, memoirs, articles, novels, plays, screenplays; taking active and important roles in the movie and TV industry. From time to time, the print media—newspapers, magazines (e.g., *Newsweek* and *Time)*—feature positive articles and columns about gays and lesbians.

Positive as all this progress is, however, American culture seems to have a split personality with regard to lesbians, gay men, bisexuals, and transgendered people. Bisexuals, for the most part, remain an invisible population. It is no mistake that there is only *one* example given of a bisexual performer (Sandra Bernhard). That may be because of biphobia which is directed at bisexuals from both the heterosexual and the lesbian and gay communities. It may also result from there being almost no unified bisexual community that could support and encourage bisexual performers.

Martina Navratilova, one of the world's greatest tennis players, could not get many corporate sponsors because she is a lesbian. Talk show hosts such as "Dr. Laura" Schlessinger flourish and convey messages of hate against gays to over 18 million listeners. She has called homosexuality "a biological error"; perpetuated the myth that " 'a huge portion of the male homosexual populace is predatory on young boys' "; and promoted the destructive "notion that homosexuality should (and can) be 'cured' " (France, 2000, p. 80).

Hip-hop artists and rappers spew virulently homophobic "lyrics" urging violence against LGBT people with no fear of any controls— e.g., Eminem's (2000) lines: "You faggots can vanish to volcano ash/And reappear in hell with a can of gas, AND a match. . . ."

The religious right uses its radio and TV stations and its newspaper columns to preach about the sinfulness of homosexuality (and by extension, bisexuality) and transgender behavior. Often it attempts to promote its belief that homosexuality can (and should) be cured through Christ. It has also made videos purporting to show the spread of "the homosexual agenda" in schools. The religious right still has the clout to threaten or smear political candidates for "being soft" about the "menace" of homosexuality by implying that they are anti-family, anti-American, anti-God.

Another form of homo/bi/transphobia that LGBT people are subjected to is loud and frequent public debates about their character, their rights, their very existence. Newspapers and TV stations regularly report on school boards that argue about and vote down the inclusion of sexual orientation in antidiscrimination policies designed to protect both teachers and students. State legislatures debate about and pass laws prohibiting same-sex marriages. Many states have tried to pass laws which do not protect people from discrimination based on their sexual orientation and gender orientation. Other states have launched referendums to take away antidiscrimination laws. The Supreme Court has ruled that the Boy Scouts of America may discriminate against boys and men who are gay. The destructive force of having one's lifestyle, one's sexual/affectional orientation, one's gender identity, one's very life debated in public with no regard for feelings or privacy is incalculable (Herek, 1995; Human Rights Campaign Foundation, 2000).

Even so, this is a time of some hope. The struggle for visibility and tolerance seems to have gained considerable ground. Changes reflected in the media are extremely important because they provide positive role models for LGBT people and make being visible a strong possibility. Seeing other lesbians, gay men, bisexuals, and transgendered people who are "out" can help LGBTs feel less isolated, less alienated, less alone. They see others like them who reflect something of their own lives. These experiences help to normalize what has been branded by society as deviant.

THE STRESS OF HOMO/BI/TRANSPHOBIA AND HETEROSEXISM

The secondary reactions to psychological trauma—such as emotional constriction, sensation seeking and reenactment, and drug and alcohol abuse—all create new and usually overwhelming problems.

B. A. van der Kolk
Psychological Trauma, 1987

In addition to hearing negative messages via the media, most LGBT people are subjected to insulting, demeaning remarks every day because most of them are forced to pass in their everyday lives. These ordinary, invisible LGBT people must hear all the slurs and jokes that other people feel free to utter because they are operating on the unconscious assumption that everybody around them is heterosexual and is living as their anatomical gender. These LGBT people hear the derogatory language casually used to describe them—"faggots, fairies, dykes, lezbos, AC-DCs, swingers, she-males, he-shes, freaks, queers, pansies, sissies, girls" and on and on, ad nauseam. The contempt, fear, and hatred conveyed by these words are a part of the pulsebeat of American life.

Living in the midst of homo/bi/transphobia is one of the more stressful experiences to which a person can be subjected. It requires an almost constant struggle to answer such questions as, "Where do I belong?" "Who am I?" "Who will accept me?" "What value do I have?" It frequently involves recognizing that the price of openness about self may well be as high as rejection by family and friends and/or loss of jobs, the two institutions most directly involved with developing and maintaining identity, self-esteem, and a sense of belonging. Obviously, the stress created by the pressures of homo/bi/transphobia and heterosexism is extremely strong and demoralizing.

When counselors can get in touch with the power of this constant assault on LGBT sensibilities and lives, they can become a positive, counteractive force in clients' recovery. An awareness of the impact of homo/bi/transphobia makes it possible for counselors to understand empathetically why their LGBT clients may have tried to be or are honestly claiming to be heterosexual; why their bisexual clients may claim to be lesbian or gay; why their transgendered clients are not forthcoming about their gender. They can understand why clients may feel almost unbearable guilt and scalding shame, why they may be filled with rage or denial or self-pity, why they may have turned to substance abuse as a way of coping.

By understanding the implications of life in a society driven by homo/bi/transphobia, counselors are enabled to have a powerful, positive impact on clients' lives. As people who really do understand and care, as people who are accepting and consciously LGBT affirmative, counselors can help provide a safe environment for LGBT clients, an experience which offers them that most powerful of all emotions—hope.

Chapter 5

Internalized Homo/Bi/Transphobia

You gain strength, courage, and confidence by every experience in which you really stop to look fear in the face.

Eleanor Roosevelt
You Learn by Living, 1960

When we speak up, we heal . . . we stand up for ourselves . . . confronting the oppression we face. We move from victim to survivor, from silence to action.

J. Neisen
Reclaiming Pride, 1994b

Having to contend with the ever-present pressures of external homo/bi/transphobia on a day-to-day basis can be extremely demanding, demoralizing, and stressful. Perhaps even worse is the task of dealing with the *internalized* prejudices of fear, hate, revulsion, loathing. As they grow up, LGBT people (along with everyone else) are exposed to and taught the homophobic, biphobic, and transphobic values held by the culture. Gradually, they internalize these values—learn them, accept them as "truth," and incorporate them into their belief system. They take the enemy of homo/bi/transphobia into themselves—as Pogo says, "We have met the enemy and it is us!"

Homophobia most certainly affects lesbians and gay men. It is the hatred directed at homosexual orientation. But bisexuals and transgendered people whose sexual orientation is either homosexual or bisexual are also affected by homophobia. Ironically, probably most, if not all, transgendered people—*whatever* their sexual orientation—are likely to be subjected to homophobia because of this culture's powerful stereotype that homosexuality is indicated by gender nonconformity.

Bisexuals are also subject to *biphobia* (Bohan, 1996; D'Augelli and Garnets, 1995; Klein, 1993)—because they "break both codes." Their homosexuality makes them a target for mainstream homophobic values and their heterosexuality offends lesbian and gay sensitivities by seeming to cozy up to "the enemy" (homophobic heterosexuals). The internalized biphobia results not just in self-hatred but also in the self-doubt of "Who (and what) am I? I don't belong anywhere."

In addition to dealing with homophobia, transgendered people must cope with the ravages of *transphobia*—society's fear of and hatred toward anyone who does not conform to the culture's gender roles, expectations, and requirements. The range of gender nonconformity is very great, ranging from dressing in drag to transsexuality. But those transgendered people who have grown up with all the feelings of being different, of not fitting in, and, for transsexuals, of knowing their anatomical sex does not match their gender identity—these people are often beset by powerful internalized transphobia. They internalize society's belief (supported by the medical/psychiatric establishment) that transgendered people are suffering from mental illness. They must struggle with gender dysphoria—the often intense discomfort with their ascribed gender. They are not comfortable with the gender assigned to them by society according to their biological sex, but to live or be otherwise is to face the entire weight of societal disapproval. They internalize feelings of shame, guilt, self-doubt, unworthiness, self-hatred, and despair. Many transsexuals come to hate their bodies, their biological sex (Brown and Rounsley, 1996; Marcel, 1998).

Many LGBT people report that as they were growing up and internalizing all these negative teachings about these unacceptable "Others," they experienced many feelings of unease about themselves. They felt different, that "something" was the matter with them, but often they did not know what. As they began to sense or discover how they were different—that *they* were the Other—they were horrified to learn they belonged to a group reviled and despised by this culture.

When turned against the self, the feelings generated by internalized homo/bi/transphobia are extremely painful. They are the feelings of a self divided, of a self against itself. Many lesbians, gay men, bisexuals, and transgendered people feel that the very center of their being is tainted, unacceptable. That which defines who they are becomes the enemy. Now they are beset by two hostile forces—from without and from within.

These hostile forces have an especially harsh effect on young people as they become aware that they are different. As they move through their adolescent years, they are frequently subjected to hostility from parents, other young people, school personnel, religious leaders, the media, and others. All this hostility and cruelty come together to oppress and sometimes crush their developing sense of self and identity as a lesbian, a gay male, a bisexual, or a transgendered person. The wonder is that anyone survives this harshness. Some do not.

BASIC REACTIONS AND EFFECTS

The difficulties of growing up gay are enormous and separate us from other children. Early feelings of isolation, rejection and loneliness had a great effect on us. We sensed that we were on the outside looking in.

A. Milton
Lavender Light (1995)

The consequences of homo/bi/transphobia are often harsh and far-reaching. Some LGBT people react with rage, some with rebellion, some with resignation and conformity. Some of them react in ways dangerous to themselves. Some try to, some actually do, commit suicide. Forty-two percent of lesbian/gay/bisexual teenagers surveyed report attempting suicide at least once (D'Augelli and Hershberger, 1993). Israel and Tarver (1997) state that over 50 percent of transgendered youth "have seriously considered or attempted suicide" (p. 133). Brown and Rounsley (1996) note that "Estimates of attempted suicide by transsexuals range from 17 percent to 20 percent" (p. 11).

Many react by living and measuring their lives according to society's homo/bi/transphobic and heterosexist values. Thus it is not unusual for lesbians, gay men, bisexuals, and transgendered people to believe that heterosexuals are superior, homosexuals inferior. It is not unusual for transgendered people to believe that heterosexist role expectations are normal and that anyone who doesn't conform to them is abnormal. One destructive result of these beliefs is that LGBT clients may not want counselors who are LGBT, considering them to be "second-class citizens" also.

People deal with these beliefs in various ways. Some lesbians, gay men, bisexuals, and transgendered people make an "accommodation" with what they see as this "unnatural" homosexual part of themselves by grimly living as heterosexuals—because to live as a lesbian or gay man would mean to them that they are lesser beings, immoral, stigmatized, unwanted. As a result of their internalized homophobia, some LGBTs split their lives and have same-sex experiences and relationships while in heterosexual relationships but do not see themselves as homosexual or bisexual. Although they may engage in homosexual behavior, in their minds they are heterosexual.

Such is the power of denial in the face of life—or sanity—threatening circumstances. Some bisexuals may choose to live exclusively as lesbians or gays: they feel they cannot live completely as heterosexual but can't accept being bisexual because of their internalized biphobia. Some transgendered people will live as the "wrong" gender, the one they know is not truly who they are, because they cannot face the pressures and oppression of being transgendered.

Some lesbians, gay men, bisexuals, and transgendered people seek what they perceive to be the safety of a celibate life in a religious order. Others may unconsciously seek very homophobic settings such as the armed forces. Lesbians, gay men, and bisexuals may see the service as a way of "solving" their sexual/affectional conflicts because the powerful dictates against same-sex behavior will, they hope, help them curb their forbidden sexual impulses. Male-to-female transsexuals may join the armed forces or seek jobs in male-dominated occupations in order to deny their true gender identity of female by behavior designed to confirm their masculinity (Brown and Rounsley, 1996). [It should be noted, however, that some LGBT people simply want the opportunity to serve their country or their religion and to belong to something bigger than themselves].

Some transgendered people marry in order to live as their original birth sex and thus deny their true sense of self. Some lesbians, gay men, and bisexuals marry in order to deny their sexual orientation or to reassure themselves they are heterosexual.

Unfortunately, the measures people take to cope with homo/bi/transphobia often tend to increase their feelings of shame, self-loathing, and self-blame. All too frequently, people turn to alcohol and/or drugs as a culturally acceptable way to decrease and soothe their psychic pain. All too often, that way leads to substance abuse.

Depression

One major effect of external and internalized homo/bi/transphobia is depression, a condition fed by self-hatred, self-loathing, self-contempt (Brown and Rounsley, 1996; Herek, 1995; Israel and Tarver, 1997). These feelings can, in turn, contribute to people's substance abuse and suicidal thoughts or actions. LGBT people may drink and/or use other drugs to alleviate their depression, to fill the void, to kill the pain, or to create the illusion of not being different. But all the while their use of mood-altering chemicals is depressing them further. There is a synergistic interaction, a synergistic vicious circle, in which the depression created by homo/bi/transphobia is heightened and intensified by depression resulting from the physiological and psychological effects of substance abuse, and vice versa.

This phenomenon also creates potential dangers for LGBT substance abusers trying to recover. The depression resulting from internalized homo/bi/transphobia will not necessarily or even usually be removed with the removal of alcohol and other drugs. In fact, the depression may deepen and place these clients at great risk of relapse.

It is important, therefore, that counselors help their LGBT clients begin to find constructive and practical ways to deal with their depression (and thus their homo/bi/transphobia). It also helps to point out to clients that their depression is an appropriate and common response both to the loss of alcohol/other drugs which shielded them from the assaults of external and internalized homo/bi/transphobia and to the assaults themselves.

Anxiety

In addition to self-hatred and depression, many LGBTs experience powerful, sometimes crippling anxiety (Brown and Rounsley, 1996; Herek, 1995; Israel and Tarver, 1997). *Anxiety* may be defined as the physiological and emotional response to what is perceived as dangerous and threatening. Since this society visits humiliation, punishment, physical violence, and/or isolation on LGBT people because they are seen as threats to its values, it is little wonder that many LGBTs view discovery of their sexual orientation and/or gender identity as very dangerous and therefore experience great anxiety.

Because of their internalized homo/bi/transphobia which says that the very center of their being is sick and disgusting, many LGBT people feel their sexual/affectional orientation and/or their gender identity must be hidden at all costs. The overriding fear generated by these feelings is of discovery by others and/or by self. "I couldn't bear it if I were gay." "I'd hate myself if I were a lesbian." "I couldn't live with myself if I found out I was a transsexual." "What would they think of me if they found out I'm bisexual (transsexual, homosexual)?" "If they only knew, they wouldn't like me—or I'd lose my job—or I'd lose my family."

It is not uncommon for people who are LGBT to go to some lengths to hide their sexual orientation and/or gender identity from others. Some may even fabricate detailed cover stories. For example, some gay men will get women friends to go with them to family functions (e.g., weddings, parties) posing as girlfriends or fiancées so that people will not know or suspect their sexual orientation. Lesbians who work in traditionally all-male occupations (e.g., construction) may create a fictional boyfriend with a name, pictures, and a history to fend off the vicious homophobia and sexism they are exposed to. Some bisexuals will suppress information about experiences or relationships with same-sex partners. Transgendered people may choose at times to dress in the clothing ascribed to their birth gender.

Coming to terms with and learning how to cope with both external and internalized homo/bi/transphobia is a long, complex, painful, and arduous process. The effects of having a stigmatized identity can be devastating and certainly can make living a reasonably stable and satisfying life rather difficult. The struggle is made even greater by many LGBT people's deep, underlying fear that at their very core they are irreparably defective and forever unacceptable to society, to their families, to themselves. With this can come the belief that no matter how well they may do in other aspects of their lives, no matter how brilliant or famous or accomplished they may become—underneath they are no good. Thus, many of them live their lives riddled with anxiety—that somehow, some way, some day, someone will discover their secret.

Living with such intense anxiety, whether conscious or not, tends to make some LGBTs feel very paranoid and they may become hypervigilant, always on the lookout for possible danger. The anxiety produced by living with such fears takes its toll. One major toll is that under such stress it becomes difficult to sort out real from perceived dangers and difficult not to distort reality in some way. The anxiety generated by homo/bi/transphobia can turn people's lives into funhouse mirrors.

For example, a lesbian might come to believe that she cannot trust *anybody* with the knowledge of who she is. Thus she might not share her orientation with her best friend because she perceives that friend as not accepting her—which may or may not be true. One way that many LGBT people learn to deal with the stress of such anxiety is to medicate themselves with alcohol and/or other drugs, a strategy which can all too easily boomerang into addiction. Then they are likely to be afflicted with the agitation, unknown fears, and "paranoia" common to substance abuse—feelings which heighten and intensify already existing anxiety.

As is true with depression, abstinence usually does not remove the anxiety that external and internalized homo/bi/transphobia produces. In fact, it may make matters worse. Without anesthesia, LGBT substance abusers' awareness of their anxiety may be much sharper and far less tolerable. Thus they are likely to be at greater risk of relapse.

It is important, therefore, that counselors help LGBT clients learn constructive ways to reduce anxiety, to self-soothe. It is also helpful for counselors to acknowledge the powerful, anxiety-producing effects of homo/bi/transphobia, both external and internalized, because such acknowledgment validates their clients' feelings and aids their reality testing. In addition, such counselor responses are very supportive to frightened clients. The importance of addressing and helping with LGBT clients' anxiety cannot be overstressed. At best, unresolved anxiety is likely to make these clients' recovery less fulfilling or comfortable than it otherwise might be. At worst, it can lead to relapse.

DEFENSES

Depression and anxiety, the two major psychological consequences of homo/bi/transphobia, are very destructive and extremely painful; and to the best of their ability, people naturally defend themselves against pain. Counselors need to understand the ways LGBT people defend against the pernicious effects of homo/bi/transphobia in order to know how to react to and deal with their clients' protective stances.

Everyone has defenses. They help people survive. Defenses are the ways people's minds have of shielding them from what they perceive as threats and danger; defenses protect the ways people see and feel about themselves and help prevent their concepts of self from being devalued. Breakwell (1986) describes how coping strategies—or defenses—protect against threats to the principles of continuity, distinctiveness, and self-esteem which constitute the structure of a person's identity. When one or more of these principles of identity is threatened, the person responds with coping strategies to eliminate or modify the threat, strategies such as denial, passing, conforming, and finding a support group.

Defenses are the psychological mechanisms people employ to shield the "self," the identity, from pain and perceived danger. Although defenses are generally considered to be unconscious psychological mechanisms, oftentimes they are only partially unconscious. That is, they are "pre-conscious"—able to be made accessible to the conscious mind through outside assistance (such as the guidance of a counselor). There are many different defenses, and usually more than one will be in operation at a time.

Defenses are, of course, familiar to anyone who knows about substance abuse, denial being perhaps the most familiar. Counselors need to know how to discriminate among the differing reasons LGBT substance abusers may have for utilizing various defenses at various times. Are these defenses being employed to protect the substance abuse (e.g., denial of any problems caused by alcohol/drug intake) or to ward off the assaults of homo/bi/transphobia (e.g., denial of sexual attractions toward people of the same sex or both sexes; denial of feeling conflicted about gender)? Or are the defenses being used to guard against the effects of both the substance abuse and the homo/bi/transphobia? Or perhaps to fend off other threats such as the feelings brought on by the trauma of sexual abuse?

These are delicate questions and require a certain amount of knowledge and skill to deal with them constructively. But they should be attended to and answered because counselors need to know when and how to address a defense. For example, the denial of substance abuse can be life-threatening, but the denial of a particular sexual orientation or gender identification may be life-saving for someone who is struggling to recover from addiction and does not yet have the inner resources to deal with anything beyond simply recovering.

Everyone raised in this culture is taught that "it's not all right to be lesbian, gay, bisexual, or transgendered" and in fact that being so is "disgusting, shameful, immoral, sick." It follows that people who even faintly suspect they might be LGBT will develop defenses against the danger that is perceived as and is actually inherent in being homosexual, bisexual, or transgendered in this culture. People who have even the slightest inkling they might be "different" (though many are not even sure in what way) will establish ways to protect themselves against knowing or at least against others' knowing.

Many lesbians, gay men, bisexuals, and transgendered people have highly developed defensive systems long before they start to drink or use other drugs. If, in the process of drinking and using other drugs in order to not know, not feel, or not care, they then get addicted, their already established defenses interlock with those engendered by their substance abuse. This interlock creates extra strong defenses which can all too effectively get in the way of LGBT substance abusers' treatment and recovery.

While this powerful defense system can make treatment difficult, it is often something counselors can readily understand because of their experience with substance abusers' defense systems. It is important that counselors draw on, yet go beyond, this understanding in order to make distinctions which are critical to the treatment process. They need to be aware of the even greater power of LGBT substance abusers' defenses. They need to distinguish between confronting the tough yet brittle defenses that protect the substance abuse and respecting those defenses that actually help LGBT individuals survive the onslaughts of homo/bi/transphobia.

Yet, such matters are not always clear-cut. Being able to make accurate evaluations and skillful judgments depends on counselors having a good grasp of the major defenses that lesbians, gay men, bisexuals, and transgendered people use in order to maintain their stability.

Counselors will also need to do a lot of self-monitoring of their own feelings and reactions in order to prevent themselves from colluding and/or colliding with clients' defenses. For example, if counselors are in denial of their own homo/bi/transphobia, they may respond to clients who fearfully relate having same-sex experiences or cross-dressing while drinking alcohol or taking drugs by strongly assuring clients they are not gay. Or suppose a client is filled with rage at an unjust homo/bi/transphobic society and turns that anger on people around him or her. The counselor may interpret the client's angry behavior as indication of a "poor attitude toward treatment," respond with anger, and treat the patient in a punitive way.

Suppose clients do not want to disclose their sexual orientation and/or gender identity to other clients on a unit. Counselors may collude by too readily agreeing to the clients' resistance, not exploring the matter further, and thereby joining the conspiracy of silence. Or counselors may collide with clients' appropriate defenses by insisting that clients "come out" in group when it is not safe to do so because the other clients are very prejudiced and the counselor cannot provide adequate protection from their homo/bi/transphobia.

Obviously, it is extremely important for counselors to know about and understand the major defenses that lesbians, gay men, bisexuals, and transgendered people utilize in order to deal with the external and internalized homo/bi/transphobia which constantly confronts them. The five primary defenses to be discussed are denial, rationalization, reaction formation, hostility and anger, and "passing."

Denial

Probably the most powerful defense of all is denial—a process by which people unconsciously change reality so that it suits their needs. In effect, they unknowingly create a subjective reality by reversing or significantly changing the facts of objective reality. In this manner, people are able to prevent themselves from knowing something that—if they did know about it—would be a threat to their self-esteem, to their identity as they know it, and thereby create unbearable anxiety. For example, suppose a man is married, loves his wife, and has sex occasionally with her. But he also has sex with a male friend every chance he gets. He believes they have sex only because this man is his drinking buddy and when they get drunk together they "find" themselves having sex. He absolutely believes this behavior has nothing to do with who he is or his marriage or his heterosexual identity. Through denial, he fends off any possible threat to the continuity or distinctiveness of his identity.

Denial produces that phenomenon wherein a person can behave in a way which might be obvious to or be interpreted differently by others but which he or she is unable to see or own. The ways substance abusers employ denial to prevent themselves from knowing what they cannot bear to know and the primal power of the defense is well known in the substance abuse field. Counselors need to draw on that knowledge to understand LGBT people's use of this defense against external and internalized homo/bi/transphobia.

The objective reality in a homo/bi/transphobic culture is that it can be dangerous to be lesbian, gay, bisexual, or transgendered, where the dangers range from insults to bodily harm. For many people, even to contemplate the slightest possibility that they might have any feelings of attraction for someone of the same sex or that their gender identity might not match their birth sex is so dangerous, so terrifying, they will unconsciously shut down their self-perceptions and literally "not know" they might have such "unacceptable" feelings. Thus it is entirely possible and not so uncommon for a person to engage, or to have engaged, in homosexual behavior and not see that behavior as even a hint they might possibly be gay or bisexual. It is equally possible for someone to hate his or her genitalia and cross dress and not see those feelings or that behavior as even a hint of gender conflict.

These are examples of what counselors need to sort out with clients—the one person may or may not be gay, the other person may or may not be transsexual. Each person's reaction may be denial or actual reality. Other people may be asexual or celibate and not know they have homosexual feelings. People may live and see themselves as heterosexuals and respond unconsciously with denial whenever anything occurs that even whispers of difference. A girl might grow up longing to be a man but marry, have children, and not know her feelings or give them meaning.

Our culture encourages people to deny the existence of homosexuality, bisexuality, and transgenderism. And the culture itself denies their existence whenever possible. It demands and rewards invisibility, for the most part tolerating LGBT people as long as they remain quiet, docile, and hidden in their closets. LGBT peoples' most total form of invisibility is denial, both to others and to themselves.

But this defense exacts a high price of unconscious, inner stress. It is maintained only by expending enormous amounts of psychic energy. Because this culture sanctions the use of alcohol and, tacitly, other drugs as a means of relaxing, it is not unusual that people in denial about their sexual orientation and/or their gender identity might use alcohol/other drugs to help them not to know who they are.

If the use of alcohol and/or other drugs to help block out threats to identity develops into problem usage and substance abuse, then the denial system becomes enormously powerful as the denial of addiction swirls together with the denial of sexual orientation and/or gender identity. The significance of this phenomenon is that removing the drug may throw people into crisis because they are left with a weakened defensive system and because they are confronted with the stresses of their raw, newly-recovering selves.

Basically, people who are in denial of their sexual feelings or orientation and/or their feelings about their gender and gender identity will unconsciously shore up their denial system. But there may be moments of crisis when the defensive system does not work well enough and people panic. Counselors can be extremely helpful at such junctures simply by reassuring, accepting, and supporting clients. It is possible and desirable to plant seeds of acceptance which may take root and blossom at a much later time.

For example, counselors may reassure their clients that fears and confusion about sexual orientation and/or gender identity commonly occur in early recovery and that one option is to put such considerations "on the shelf" for a while. Counselors can also indicate that whatever clients eventually determine about their sexual orientation and/or gender identity will be okay. Counselors may give clients books to read about sexual orientation and gender identity or may simply assure clients that they can come and talk about their feelings without fear of judgment. Regardless of counselors' specific actions, it is most important that they convey a caring and accepting attitude.

Reaction Formation

Another very powerful defense is that of reaction formation. People defend against what they fear they are or might be by identifying with, acting like, or becoming the opposite. It is not uncommon for people who are motivated in this way to identify with and become like the aggressors who attack the feared group (or characteristic). Thus people who fear they might be homosexual or bisexual might join a religious group which is especially vocal about its homo/biphobia and become an outspoken opponent of all lesbians, gays, and bisexuals. Or they might seek therapy that promised the possibility of changing sexual orientation or join a "conversion group" which promises that belief in Jesus Christ will enable them to choose heterosexuality.

Or they might just be those who tell or laugh the loudest at antibi or antilesbian/gay jokes. Or they might dress and act in exaggeratedly stereotyped ways—men acting and dressing in ultramasculine ways; women dressing and behaving in ultrafeminine ways. By these means, people who fear they might be lesbian, gay, or bisexual protect themselves against either knowing or owning the possibility of having a sexual orientation seen by society as deviant or against being identified with this hated group. Through this defense, they try to counteract the devaluation of their self-concept, the threat to their identity as heterosexual.

Transgendered people employ this defense of reaction formation, also. The primary manifestation of this defense is that of playing the gender role that conforms to their anatomical gender. If a transgendered person is born male but knows she is truly female, her reaction formation would be to overemphasize her masculine characteristics. She might work out, grow a mustache, and dress in a macho style. In this way, she defends against being female. In like manner, an anatomical female who knows he is truly male would overemphasize his feminine characteristics, wearing lots of makeup and jewelry, wearing ultrafeminine styles, and acting in stereotypical ways. In this way, he defends against being male (Brown and Rounsley, 1996).

This particular defense may pose difficult questions for counselors because it is possible that the transgendered person is consciously using another defense—passing—rather than the unconscious one of reaction formation. In trying to sort out such matters, counselors need to rely primarily on what their clients say, because what clients say is far more important than anything counselors may guess about people's identity.

Knowing about this particular defense can help counselors when confronted by exaggerated behavior. People who join antigay campaigns or who tell offensive jokes do seem, on the face of it, to be homo/biphobic heterosexuals. But that may be protective coloration which hides lesbians, gays, and bisexuals from themselves or others and that channels their self-hatred outward. People who present themselves as ultra masculine or feminine do seem merely to be somewhat extreme representatives of their gender. They may just be that, they may be lesbians, gay men, or bisexuals struggling not to be what they are afraid of—or they may be transgendered people trying to convince the world and themselves that they are their birth gender.

By recognizing how this defense works, counselors can listen to clients who bad-mouth lesbians, gays, bisexuals, and transgendered people or who belong to antigay or antitransgender organizations with a better perspective. Such clients may be heterosexual, but destructively homo/bi/transphobic; they may be lesbian, gay, bisexual, or transgendered (or terrified of being or becoming so) and unable to deal with it. With this recognition, counselors can appreciate the possibility that ultra masculine or feminine presentations can cloak fears of homosexuality or bisexuality or fears of being transgendered.

If counselors confront the homo/bi/transphobia, they may either help a heterosexual client begin to look at attitudes which can undermine recovery, or they may help a client who is possibly lesbian, gay, bisexual, or transgendered feel a little more at ease. By addressing the homo/bi/transphobia, counselors will assist people with their sexual and gender identity issues, whatever they may be. In this manner, counselors can convey a sense of safety and acceptance to clients who are struggling to find a place for themselves in this world.

Rationalization

This defense is especially familiar to those who work with substance abusers. It is the process by which people explain away an event, behavior, thought, or feeling they cannot bear to become aware of. By their explanation, they make it "not so" or at least different from reality. People tend to rationalize when threatened by the discovery that they are unacceptable (e.g., homosexual, transgendered, alcoholic, drug addict). Rather than suffer a devalued self-concept, they employ a coping strategy of altering reality. In this way, they remove the threat to their identity.

Examples of some rationalizations are thoughts and statements like, "I only did those things because I was drunk"; "I'm really bisexual"; "That's not like me. It's not my fault—I was seduced"; "I only did it because I was curious. I'm a free spirit, willing to experience everything"; "It was just a phase." Perceiving things through this kind of distorted filter makes reality less threatening.

Rationalizing results in further turmoil for those who are already confused or conflicted about their sexual orientation or their gender identity. Eventually they may not even know what reality is. If substance abuse becomes part of this muddle, more confusion is created as people rationalize their substance abuse. Thus alcohol and/or drugs can help maintain—and in fact intensify—people's mind-tricks and illusions.

When alcohol and/or other drugs are removed, people who are confused and conflicted about their sexual orientation and/or their gender identity become extraordinarily vulnerable, and their stress levels increase greatly. They need gentle care. Substance abuse has made their nerves raw, and removing the sedative exposes these nerves to the searing cold of reality. Abstinence has taken away part of the shield that helped protect them from facing their sexual orientation and/or gender identity issues, whatever those issues might be.

If there are other issues in their life like a history of sexual abuse, their vulnerability is heightened. This is a fragile state, indeed; and challenging clients' rationalizations about sexual orientation and/or gender identity is ordinarily not a wise move. Rather, counselors need to be aware of how fragile people in this state can be and to approach them with care, restraint, and support. Counselors need to convey the assurance that sexual orientation and gender identity require time to work out; that clients are safe with the counselor; and that clients are free to proceed at their own pace.

Hostility and Anger

Another defensive reaction is that of acting in hostile and angry ways. Being enraged at injustice is certainly a healthier reaction to homo/bi/transphobia than falling into despair, but when the defense hardens into an automatic, uncontrolled response that keeps others away, it creates problems with intimacy, honesty, and trust. Rage is a dragon guarding the treasure trove of self. If anyone approaches too close by asking questions or perhaps just by showing concern, the dragon may breathe fire and drive off the intruder.

It is especially important for counselors to recognize the possibility of this defense because it often appears during treatment. For example, LGBT clients may lash out at others with hostile and sarcastic comments, may be argumentative, may angrily withdraw from others, or may challenge everyone and everything.

Counselors should be prepared for the challenge to possibly take the form of clients' "flaunting" their sexual orientation or gender identity. Clients may engage in behavior which is intended to provoke others. For example, they may act out in ultrastereotypical ways: e.g., gay or bisexual males speaking in falsetto voices; lesbians or bisexual females acting very aggressive, talking tough and swearing; transgendered people cross-dressing.

Clients who are behaving in these ways are difficult to work with. What may be particularly upsetting to counselors is that this kind of rage reaction may be evoked by kindness. Out of concern, a counselor may question the patient with great sensitivity and thereby discover the client's sexual orientation or true gender identity. The client may become hostile and challenge the counselor's right to ask such personal questions. The LGBT client may then act mistrustful and suspicious and accuse the counselor of hostile motives, of wanting to know in order to share it with the staff as a hot piece of gossip.

THE COUNSELOR'S ROLE

Some patients (perhaps all patients at some point) will look toward the analyst for authentication of their gender organization and sexual orientation. Analysts can never be free of their biases and ought to be constantly searching for them in their own experience and in their patients' reactions. The pursuit of a bias-free ideal seems futile and disingenuous; analysts serve their patients better by an openness to discovering and rediscovering their own prejudices, affinities, and fears as an inevitable and interesting feature of analytic inquiry.

S. Mitchell (1997, p. 260)

Keeping in mind the painful sources of such rage and hostility, counselors can be better prepared to deal calmly and firmly with this defensive reaction and not take the matter personally. By meeting such outpourings of rage, suspicion, mistrust, and hostility with a certain therapeutic balance, counselors can help clients gain some control of their anger. By not reacting negatively to the client's "I'll reject you before you reject me" stance, counselors can often disarm the fury and help clients begin to get past their defensive anger and rage and deal with the terrible pain underneath. They can also help clients draw boundaries around their rageful behavior so they can remain in treatment.

Counselor Strategy

Counselors might say, "I realize that you're extremely angry. Apparently you feel safe enough here to allow your anger to show. And that's important. But you also must recognize that there are certain rules here that have to be followed—for example, not verbally assaulting others; not acting in sexually provocative ways; not deliberately provoking others' anger. In light of these rules, what do you think the way you have been acting means? What kind of messages do you think your behavior sends to others? Perhaps you can work on expressing your anger more directly—either to staff or to other clients or both. It is important, though, that you respect other people's boundaries, that you not pour out your anger onto other people, that you not provoke them. If you start feeling overwhelmed by your rage, talk to someone—do not act on it. It is a lot like learning not to take a drink or a drug. Instead of acting on your impulse, talk to someone."

The specific words may vary, but most important is that counselors accept clients and their pain, refuse to tolerate abusive and/or self-destructive behavior, draw clear boundaries, and help clients do the same.

PASSING

No person, for any considerable period, can wear one face to himself, and another to the multitude without finally getting bewildered as to which may be true.

Nathaniel Hawthorne
The Scarlet Letter

The most common strategy lesbians, gay men, bisexuals, and trans-gendered people use is *passing* (Bohan, 1996; Brown and Rounsley, 1996). Lesbians and gay men assume a mask of heterosexuality to make their homosexuality invisible. Bisexuals present as heterosex-ual to pass in mainstream society and as homosexual to pass in les-bian and gay male cultures.

Transgendered people who are homosexual or bisexual assume the same masks as their lesbian, gay male, and bisexual counterparts. Transgendered people also pass in regard to gender identity. In order to fit into the mainstream of society, they take "the gender role that is consistent with their anatomy" and thus deny their true self (Brown and Rounsley, 1996, p. 79). Or, if they want to be perceived as the gender they know themselves to be and want to fit into the main-stream as that gender, they will pass—act in accordance with the gen-der role that matches their self-identification (Brown and Rounsley, 1996).

It is especially important for counselors to understand this defense of passing because it is such a primary and often necessary strategy used by lesbians, gay men, bisexuals and transgendered people against the assaults of homo/bi/transphobia. While this is mainly a conscious defense, controlled by choice, it is also possible that people may use it so often that it becomes automatic and they are no longer conscious of doing so.

Three basic factors relate to the creation of this defense:

- Homosexuality, bisexuality, and transgender identity are, for the most part, hidden, stigmatized aspects of self.
- Society encourages and demands invisibility.
- The danger perceived as inherent in revealing a homosexual, bi-sexual, transgendered identity is often very real. In response to these factors, lesbians, gay men, bisexuals, and transgendered people learn to defend themselves by passing.

In light of these realities of homo/bi/transphobia, passing is a valid, healthy, adaptive defense required to protect such things as one's safety, self-esteem, job, or family. What is not healthy about passing is that it makes people feel bad about themselves because they are not free to self-disclose and be who they really are. Many LGBT people are forced by society's homo/bi/transphobia to make themselves invisible and be someone they are not. In effect, because they are not visible, they do not exist. Passing extracts an extremely high psychological price (Bohan, 1996; Brown and Rounsley, 1996; Klein, 1993; Weinberg, Williams, and Pryor, 1994).

Like any other defense, if passing becomes rigid, inflexible, and automatic, then it can be destructive. Some lesbian, gay, bisexual, and transgendered people cannot seem to drop the mask and be who they really are even around other LGBT people. Some LGBTs hide their sexual orientation all their lives, never telling even their closest friends. Some transgendered people cannot risk living in the role of their identified gender and live all their lives chained to the role dictated by their anatomical gender. In effect, they live and die as someone they are not. Even when it is clear that there would be minimal repercussions, some LGBTs cannot free themselves from their rigid defense to share their identity with others. That is the psychological price of internalized homo/bi/transphobia; it is paid in the coin of shame, guilt, fear, rage, despair.

Different Ways of Passing

There are many ways of passing, from the subtle to the obvious; different people pass in different ways. Although lesbians and gay men, bisexuals, and transgendered people share the basic motive for passing—to fit into the mainstream—the ways they do so vary enough so that they need to be considered separately from one another.

Lesbians and Gay Men and Passing

> Some of us are afraid to speak. We are afraid to speak out to parents, afraid to speak back to lovers, afraid to speak up in support groups. We are afraid because we worry about how we will sound, what we should say, or what others will think. In our fear, we remain silent and powerless.
>
> E. Nealy
> *Amazon Spirit* (1995)

The tactics used by lesbians and gay men can include taking a friend of the opposite sex to family functions; referring to lovers only by the pronoun "they"; and rarely, if ever, talking about their personal lives. Many lesbians and gay men force themselves into heterosexual dating patterns in their adolescence and early adulthood. A number of them enter heterosexual marriages and then either have extramarital affairs or do not acknowledge or act on their lesbian/gay/bisexual orientation and feelings.

The most common form of passing is dressing, talking, and acting as much as possible like a "straight" person whenever interacting with the heterosexual, heterosexist world. The majority of lesbians and gay men in our society pass most of the time and take off their masks only when they can feel safe with lovers, friends, or other known lesbians and gays. For a number of lesbians and gay men, this seems to be a relatively comfortable way of living, even though it means hiding—in effect, denying—an important part of the self.

Bisexual Women and Men and Passing

Although bisexual women and men share the burden of homophobia with their lesbian and gay sisters and brothers, they face additional problems. As Klein (1993) notes, "until now, bisexuality has been largely a negative, a *non*-state" (p. 11) and thus invisible to everyone, both lesbians and gays and heterosexuals. In a sense, this invisibility makes it easy for bisexuals to blend in, but at the cost of invisibility, nonexistence.

Weinberg, Williams, and Pryor (1994) describe the problems that bisexuals face when deciding whether or not (and how) to pass:

> Being out as a "bisexual" carries a unique type of social status, one that can most aptly be termed "double marginality." Bisexuals always risk being stigmatized from two directions: by heterosexuals for their homosexual inclinations and by homosexuals for their heterosexual inclinations. (p. 190)

It is no wonder, therefore, that bisexuals experience "apprehension about disclosure of their bisexuality to other people in their lives" (Fox, 1995, p. 72) and often deal with the biphobia directed at them by passing. As Klein (1993) adds,

The stigma of homosexual behavior in the heterosexual world and the equal intolerance for heterosexual behavior in the homosexual world have left most bisexuals feeling they have no choice but to pose as one or the other, in accordance with the values of whichever camp they are presently in. (p. 109)

Thus bisexuals often feel the need to pass in both worlds. Because the homosexual world tends to reject bisexuality (Eadie, 1993; Hemmings, 1995), if bisexuals wish to be accepted they must pass as lesbian or gay by hiding any hint or mention of their bisexual feelings, behavior, or attractions. Most bisexuals tend to move "primarily in the heterosexual world" (Klein, 1993, p. 121). As Weinberg, Williams, and Pryor (1994) add, "most of the bisexuals we knew were predominantly heterosexual in their sexual feelings, sexual behaviors, and romantic attractions." Therefore, they tend to "manage the stigma of being bisexual by passing as heterosexual" (p. 188). Passing as heterosexual takes much the same forms as do the passing techniques of lesbians and gay men.

The price of passing to avoid the biphobia of *both* the heterosexual and homosexual worlds is very high. Klein (1993) describes the deception required by passing as a "black cloud hanging over the heads of many bisexuals" (p. 125). Eadie (1993) speaks of the "purging" of those lesbians and gay men who are seen as "straight" by other lesbians and gay men (p. 128). Klein (1993) describes how the majority of bisexuals he surveyed "felt the pressures of the heterosexual and homosexual communities, which tended to create confusion, doubt, and fear about themselves and their sexual inclinations" (p. 127). What can happen is that, in a sense, bisexuals do not exist because they are invisible in both worlds.

Transgendered People and Passing

I was born into a world that tells people like me to be silent, to not reveal that I'm transsexual, to not reveal my truth. It's the therapeutic lie that eventually causes us to go mad: it's hiding, passing, and being silent that makes us crazy. Silence does equal death—that principle applies to any situation involving a culturally-mandated silence.

K. Bornstein (1994, p. 94)

The issues transgendered people face in regard to homo/bi/transphobia are numerous and, in part, different from those faced by lesbians, gay men, and bisexuals.

One difference results from the fact that transgendered people do not adhere to the gender roles that society stipulates as appropriate for males and females. But, as Bohan (1996) points out, "deviations from prescribed gender roles [are seen] as an indication of homosexuality" (p. 51). In effect, *all* transgendered people—whether hetero-, bi-, or homosexual—are subject to homophobia if they do not pass.

Another difference has to do with what passing means. In order to belong to the mainstream, to pass as "normal," people who cross-dress must either hide the fact totally or be so accomplished that others cannot guess their secret. For example, a heterosexual cross-dresser must exercise extreme caution about where and when he cross-dresses and must safely hide his accoutrements.

Brown and Rounsley (1996) describe another form of passing:

> *By playing the gender role that is consistent with their anatomy,* [our italics] transsexuals attempt to fit into the mainstream of society. They dress the part, develop their body, join groups, immerse themselves in careers, date the opposite sex, get married, have children—in short, they do everything they possibly can to live a "normal" life. (p. 79)

In this manner, transsexuals who cannot bring themselves to risk being seen as not belonging to their birth gender pass as "normal."

A different meaning of passing has to do with the behavior of transsexuals who are making the transition to the gender they know themselves to be. As Brown and Rounsley (1996) explain,

> The ability of transsexuals to "pass"—that is, *to be unquestioningly perceived by others as the gender with which they self-identify* [our italics]—is of primary concern for them, particularly prior to and during the initial stages of transition. (p. 135)

Unfortunately, these are the times when it is most difficult to pass because usually their bodies still display signs of their original gender.

Brown and Rounsley (1996) go on to explain that "Passing is very important to transsexuals. They want others to . . . relate to them as their true self, their true gender" (p. 136). Ironically, passing in this sense means being true to one's real self by hiding the outward signs that are false to the self.

The costs of passing are varied and numerous. Those transsexuals who live and pass as their anatomical gender usually experience great gender dysphoria—gender conflict—and feelings of anxiety, frustration, shame, depression, and despair. Ultimately they need to resolve this conflict so they can live a life worth living (Brown and Rounsley, 1996; Bullough, Bullough, and Elias, 1997; Israel and Tarver, 1997).

Those transsexuals who transition to the gender they self-identify with experience ongoing anxiety about "being read"—having others question their gender or actually realize they are transsexual (Brown and Rounsley, 1996). Bockting (1997) describes another cost—"the shame that many transsexuals struggle with as a result of the[ir] expectation to 'pass' as a nontranssexual woman or man and start a new life as such" (p. 50). Other sources note that "feelings of shame, self-doubt, and rejection" are built into the TS/TG community due to the pressures to conform to "acceptable" gender roles (Marcel, 1998, p. 8).

The Price of Passing for All LGBTs

The walls of the closet are guarded by the dogs of terror, and the inside of the closet is a house of mirrors.

Judy Grahn
Another Mother Tongue, 1984

Although many LGBT people have developed tough egos in the course of their fight against homo/bi/transphobia, that does not completely protect them from the high price of leading a double life. Creating and maintaining a believable mask in order to be invisible, to pass as "acceptable," requires much energy, skill, vigilance, and a certain sacrifice of self. To live as two people can engender great stress. For some lesbians, gay men, bisexuals, and transgendered people this stress becomes too great and causes serious problems. The split between inner and outer self, occurring over a long period of time, can gradually create strong feelings of confusion, fragmentation, disjunction, and emptiness. It may be difficult to retain a clear sense of self and self-worth when one must always hide or deny one's true self.

Unfortunately, many LGBT people try to mend the split and sedate the pain with alcohol and/or other drugs. These may be helpful in assuaging the pain and filling up the empty places—for a while. But if they become addicted, people experience even more feelings of confusion, fragmentation, and emptiness since these are also responses engendered by the disease process of addiction. When this occurs, responses to the disease of substance abuse and to the assaults of homo/bi/transphobia intermingle and intensify each other.

The tendency of substance abusers to pass as social drinkers and/or recreational drug users is well known, as is their tendency to develop masks of denial and rationalization to hide their substance abuse, even from themselves. When these people stop drinking and/or using drugs, the terrifying split between their frightened, vulnerable, true inner selves and their falsely brave outer selves often haunts their early recovery (Denzin, 1987). When LGBT substance abusers stop abusing drugs and/or alcohol, they face not only the terror of the splits created by their addiction, but also the agonizing reality of the gulf between their societally acceptable mask of heterosexuality and/or gender conformity and their true inner selves. They must come face to face with their marginalized, stigmatized selves and begin to deal with who they truly are.

In order to get help with their addiction and be able to come to terms with it, substance abusers must stop passing as social drinkers/users, drop their social drinker/user mask, and start dealing with their new identity of substance abuser. To assume—by some tenuous analogy—that substance abusers who are LGBT must also *necessarily* stop passing, drop their mask, and start dealing with their LGBT identity through self-disclosure is a mistake. To assume that unless they do so, these LGBT substance abusers will somehow not recover properly (if at all) is an even greater mistake. Some will recover and never come out. For those who do come out, the process of disclosing self is a long and sometimes perilous one which should not be forced or rushed.

It is especially important to respect this slowness of pace in the early stages of recovery. To pressure or force LGBT substance abusers to drop their masks at the same time they are also required to drop their masks of social drinking/use is often more than fragile egos have the strength to manage. That many LGBT substance abusers survive and recover in the face of such demands is a testament to their individual toughness of spirit. Others never enter treatment or else flee from it and often relapse. Some find help; some do not survive.

THE ROLE OF COUNSELORS IN THE EARLY RECOVERY PROCESS

Finding that voice, finding our voice, is part of recovery. Our voice is one of the gifts of sobriety . . . and it deserves to be cherished. Learning to use our voice clearly and appropriately in recovery is one way to reclaim our power in recovery.

E. Nealy
Amazon Spirit, 1995

The role of counselors in the early recovery of LGBT substance abusers is a very important and sometimes rather delicate one. Oftentimes, counselors may need to serve as buffers between their clients and the homo/bi/transphobia present in the treatment environment and process. They may need to interpret the "rules of recovery" which are sometimes put forth as the only way to get and stay clean and sober.

· For example, one "rule" states that unless people are completely honest and open about themselves they will not be able to establish or maintain recovery. The dictum is that in order to achieve stable recovery, substance abusers must practice rigorous honesty, take responsibility for their feelings and behavior, and not blame others for what is happening in their lives. Over and over, the message is repeated—no masks, no hiding of self—"We are as sick as our secrets." These premises present obvious difficulties for LGBT substance abusers, and it is critically important that counselors understand those difficulties and be prepared to assist their clients to make crucially important distinctions about the premises.

The reality for most LGBT people is that they must continue to pass in the outside world. If, for example, they are teachers, firefighters, clergy, police officers, or employees of many large corporations, they run a high risk of losing their jobs by coming out. If LGBT people are married and do not wish to break up that relationship, then they may choose to continue passing. If LGBT people's families are likely to disown them if the families find out, then passing would seem to be an appropriate response to that threat. If, in spite of AA's and NA's policies and traditions, the LGBT substance abuser runs the risk of being rejected by a particular group for coming out, then passing is most certainly the better part of valor.

What counselors can do if they can win their clients' trust is help them make some important distinctions. Counselors can reassure clients that they can choose not to disclose their sexual orientation and/or their gender identity and still get clean and sober. Counselors may need to help clients see that they need to get clean and sober first before they even begin to deal with issues of sexual orientation or gender identity. They can help clients understand that, as with all substance abusers, they must be rigorously honest about their alcohol and drug abuse and its effects on them, must start taking responsibility for their behavior and feelings, and must avoid blaming others for their addiction problems.

At the same time, counselors can assist their clients to begin addressing the homo/bi/transphobia that can pose a major threat to their recovery. Part of coming to healthy terms with homo/bi/transphobia is for LGBTs to realize that society has the problem, not them. It is healthy and necessary to their mental health for lesbians, gay men, bisexuals, and transgendered people to place the responsibility where it belongs—not on themselves for being who they are but on society which attacks those who do not conform to its moralistic views. As Cerbone (1997) states, "It seems that the ruptures engendered by prejudice begin to heal when damaged individuals recognize that the ruptures are not inherent in themselves but reside in the culture" (p. 130).

The extent of homo/bi/transphobia in this culture underscores the importance of LGBT people being able to find safety—accepting AA, NA, Al-Anon, and Nar-Anon meetings; open-minded sponsors; knowledgeable and empathic counselors; and treatment centers where it is safe for both clients and staff members to be open. These are extremely important factors because they provide LGBT substance abusers with safe opportunities to be open and honest in a world that frequently refuses to permit it.

The possibilities for safety are somewhat different for lesbians and gay men, bisexuals, and transgendered people. Lesbian and gay clients often report that when they speak at special interest meetings of AA/NA, they experience a wonderful feeling of freedom to tell their "real" story, to share their true selves. Often their stories include a generous and accepting sponsor who gave them hope and held out a nonhomophobic hand or an understanding and accepting counselor who listened, cared, and supported them in their struggle not to hate themselves and to accept both their substance abuse and their being a lesbian or gay man. These relationships are often especially important because many lesbian and gay people do not have their families' support—either because they are afraid to tell them or have done so and been rejected.

Safety is not so easily come by for bisexual substance abusers. They may run into biphobia from both heterosexual and lesbian/gay AA/NA meetings and sponsors. Counselors need to advise clients to proceed slowly and with caution about coming out. Transgendered people also need to proceed with care. Probably the safest places are urban centers specifically for transgenders or lesbian/gay centers that provide services for transgenders. Passing and being selective about where, when, and with whom to be honest and open about sexual orientation and/or gender identity are, therefore, legitimate activities for LGBT substance abusers in their recovery.

Although coming to terms with the possibility of being lesbian, gay, bisexual, or transgendered can be very difficult and painful, it does give people a certain advantage. As people become aware of their sexual orientation and/or their gender identity, the battleground changes. Whereas before, much of the fight was an inner one with heterosexist and homo/bi/transphobic attacks primarily directed at self, now people can focus their fight on the proper target—the forces of heterosexism and homo/bi/transphobia which originate and reside in society.

Chapter 6

Direct Treatment Issues

The most important initial task of the therapeutic process is to create a place for being, knowing, and experiencing oneself anew in an environment of recognition and acceptance.

J. Glassgold and S. Iasenza (1995, p. 207)

Perhaps the most important thing we can do as therapists who work with trans people and their partners is to help them name their own journey, and not try to box them into our preordained categories.

A. I. Lev (1998, p. 10)

This chapter is intended to provide some useful concepts, different perspectives, and practical techniques. There are, however, no hard and fast rules about how this information should be applied. The only sure statement is that "it all depends"—on the setting, the client, the stage of the substance abuse, the timing, and the counselor. This chapter offers guidelines and suggestions that counselors can incorporate into their counseling repertoire and use according to their needs and skills.

THE SETTING

In order to be most effective and helpful, counselors must know the strengths and limitations of the setting in which they are providing service. It is important to know what the administration's attitudes and policies about sexual orientation and gender identity are. Is the administration supportive of quality care for *all* sexual and gender minority patients? Does the administration covertly tolerate negative attitudes and behaviors toward LGBT people among its staff, administrators, and clients? What policies and procedures does it have to ensure provision of good treatment for all LGBT substance abusers?

It is equally important to know the attitudes of other staff members. Are they heterosexist? Homo/bi/transphobic? Are they well-informed about lesbian, gay, bisexual, and transgender issues or ignorant about them? Do they gossip about clients? Or do all staff treat all clients and their confidential, personal issues with respect and sensitivity? Are there any openly LGBT people on staff? If not, would a qualified openly lesbian, gay, bisexual, or transgendered person be hired if he or she applied for an opening? Is it safe for an LGBT person to have his or her sexual orientation and/or gender identity known to this staff? Is it safe for a non-LGBT person to advocate for LGBTs without being stigmatized in some way?

Are staff members comfortable discussing gender and sexuality issues, e.g., transgenderism, homosexuality, bisexuality in particular? Is in-service training provided to help staff deal with gender identity and sexual orientation issues? Does the treatment facility or agency have LGBT contacts in the community? Does it have access to consultants who can provide needed information, guidance, and support? The answers to these and other questions help assess and evaluate the setting and the degree of safety provided for the LGBT client (see Appendix B).

Specific Treatment Settings

Other questions need to be asked about each type of treatment setting. What are the length, intensity, type and goal of treatment?

In a *detoxification facility* where the length of stay is short and clients are often physically ill, the primary reason for asking about sexual orientation and gender identity is to be able to provide support to clients and to facilitate appropriate referral. Counselors need to know the patients they are treating because that knowledge will govern their treatment decisions. For instance, what kind of population does the detox serve? What risks do patients face? For example, if the detox serves a primarily revolving-door clientele, mostly street people who know one another, then it might be dangerous for clients to reveal their gender identity or sexual orientation to others. Knowing the client also enables counselors to provide more safety in the facility itself.

On *inpatient units*, some issues (e.g., the need for safety) are the same, but some are different. More time for treatment, stronger bonds among clients and staff, and a staff with more advanced training work to the clients' advantage. On a reasonably non-homo/bi/transphobic rehabilitation unit it is often possible for clients to talk about their sexual orientation and gender identity with counselors and in group therapy and to receive support from the group. Counselors need to know, also, how their unit regards and treats transgendered people in terms of, for example, bathroom use, room assignments, and use of pronouns.

The same conditions may be present in an *outpatient setting*. Counselors need to take into account the length, intensity, type, and goal of treatment, the population served, and the cultural context of the program (e.g., is the program in a large city or a rural setting?) Depending on many factors, an outpatient program may well provide a nurturing atmosphere to LGBT clients. For example, if the population served is fairly stable and serious about recovery, then it is probably possible to create a relatively safe environment. If, however, the program is situated in a rural area, homo/bi/transphobia in the community may preclude safety for an out lesbian, gay man, bisexual, or transgendered person. Or if the outpatient program serves DWI clients and has a high rate of turnover, it becomes more difficult to deal effectively with homo/bi/transphobia among clients and provide safety for LGBT clients if they come out.

Obviously, it is crucially important that counselors know their settings, the cultural context of those settings, and the populations they serve. Such knowledge is what makes it possible to protect and serve their LGBT clients.

Creating a Safe Treatment Environment

A treatment environment that is not homo/bi/transphobic has far-reaching effects because it is safe for both staff and clients. Such an atmosphere obviously works to the advantage of all clients. It provides an environment in which people are free to disclose secrets that might, if not shared with a supportive other, hinder their recovery.

Numerous factors can help to create this kind of non-homo/bi/ transphobic, accepting atmosphere. One of the best ways is to regularly and frequently schedule lectures on sexuality which include discussing lesbian, gay, bisexual, and transgender issues in a sensitive, direct manner. It is also helpful for staff to handle clients' responses to this lecture in a relaxed manner. Staff members who are direct and at ease when discussing gender and sexuality give all clients, whether LGBT or not, tacit permission to talk about their feelings and raise specific issues when they are ready to do so. It also identifies staff persons who are safe resources for clients.

Another way to help make the environment feel more secure is for administration and staff not to tolerate homo/bi/transphobic remarks by clients or other staff and to challenge them as directly and publicly as feasible. Having openly LGBT staff members can also send powerful messages that it is safe to be lesbian, gay, bisexual, or transgendered. In addition, these staff people can serve as excellent role models of the freedom to be oneself. Having LGBT recovering substance abusers available to serve as AA/NA contacts for clients is another way to send safety messages. They also serve as role models for both the LGBT clients and the non-LGBT clients, many of whom have never known a lesbian, gay, bisexual, or transgendered person, much less one who has successfully recovered from substance abuse.

An additional way to help create a safer, more affirming atmosphere is to make sure that the literature on the unit is written in LGBT-sensitive language. For example, pamphlets describing the program should not exclusively use the terms spouse or husband/wife. These references ignore the existence of same-sex and trans-sex partners and significant others and send a negative message to the LGBT reader. It is important that the language acknowledge *lovers* or *partners* or use some other term which is not limited to heterosexuals or nontransgendered people. In addition, having pamphlets and other literature that directly address lesbian, gay, bisexual, and transgendered people's concerns acknowledges their existence and contributes to a safer environment.

In the same sense, the concept of family and programs for the family needs to include same-sex and trans-sex partners and friends. For example, if an inpatient program is not inclusive, a "roommate" of thirty years might be ignored while a distant, alienated relative is made official next-of-kin, is given visiting privileges at family times, and is chosen to be invited to the family program. Or if the program is homo/bi/transphobic, staff might bar a transsexual friend from the family program because he or she is "too obvious" and staff fears the friend will make other participants uncomfortable. One problem with this (in addition to transphobia) might be that this person is the only family the client has. Obviously, treatment planning and outreach efforts need to be sensitive to the often-overlooked issues of the LGBT client or family member.

The *halfway house* setting is similar yet different from in- and out-patient programs. Because of the length of time people stay and because staff are frequently more closely involved with day-to-day living issues, strong bonds often develop among staff and clients. In many ways, because of the longer time period, this may be a good setting for lesbian, gay, bisexual, and transgendered clients to begin clarifying their sexual and/or gender identity issues, if necessary. They can go to lesbian/gay AA/NA meetings if they choose to and establish firmer bonds with the lesbian, gay, bisexual, and transgendered AA/NA communities.

Bisexual clients may choose a different path. They may feel safer attending mainstream AA/NA meetings where they can fit in as heterosexual if they so choose. Transgendered people may feel more comfortable in lesbian/gay AA/NA ("we're all queer together") if those groups are tolerant of transgendered people. They may need, however, to find specific transgender-affirming environments to deal with recovery and gender identity. This may require going to a large urban area in order to find such an environment.

The halfway house can provide either a valuable or a miserable experience for lesbian, gay, bisexual, and transgendered substance abusers. The quality of the experience depends on the quality of the staff. The experience can indeed be a powerfully positive one if staff members learn about working with lesbian, gay, bisexual, and transgendered clients, if they are willing to support them, draw reasonable boundaries for them, and challenge and refuse to tolerate homo/bi/transphobia in their house. If, however, the staff will not support the lesbian, gay, bisexual, and transgendered client, tolerates homo/bi/

transphobia either in themselves or in the house members, or denies the existence or possibility of LGBT clients, these clients are likely to leave early and not get the help they need.

Counselors need to assess how well their particular treatment setting lends itself to helping LGBT clients. One major consideration about placing transgendered clients in halfway house settings needs to be considered. The intake and psychosocialsexual histories must be thorough and must be taken into close account in the referral process. For example, a MTF transsexual who clearly identifies as female should be referred to a female halfway house where staff need to deal sensitively with such matters as bathroom use, room assignments, and personal pronoun usage. Such a referral, however, must be evaluated in light of the staff's attitudes toward transsexuals. If staff is transphobic, perhaps the client would do better to go home. If a halfway house tends to be homophobic, then counselors should not refer a lesbian, gay, or bisexual transgender client to that house. Obviously, knowing both the client and the setting is crucially important to good, ethical treatment.

How counselors work with their LGBT clients will depend on this assessment (see Appendix B). If the treatment setting is homo/bi/ transphobic, gossipy, insensitive, and therefore not very safe, then competent counselors will not reveal certain pieces of information even to other staff. They can provide clients with a sensitive ear but may have to advise them not to come out to others. If, however, the environment is safe, counselors can assure clients that if they wish to self-disclose, the staff will be supportive and helpful with peer responses. Clearly, much depends on the nature and atmosphere of the setting.

GATHERING INFORMATION

A question counselors frequently ask is, "Why should we question clients about their sexual orientation or their gender identity? Isn't it an invasion of privacy? Is it anyone's business?" If these questions are not asked, clients may read the omission as a signal that they are assumed to be heterosexual and non-transgendered and very likely LGBT people are not acceptable or are not visible in this setting. These omissions may suggest that this treatment facility or this counselor is not sensitive to lesbians, gay men, bisexuals, and transgendered people. Asking about gender identity and sexual orientation at least presents a choice. It says that the agency acknowledges that LGBT people exist, that the counselor is comfortable enough to ask.

Asking such questions of all new clients can provide the first ray of hope that nonjudgmental help is perhaps available. These messages are powerful motivators for frightened lesbian, gay, bisexual, and transgendered substance abusers and indeed for any client (LGBT or not) who is confused or frightened about any sexual and/or gender identity issue. In addition, asking permits clients to be less worried about when "they" (counselors, staff, other clients) will find out. Anxiety about being "found out" is often a constant, underlying fear that many LGBTs live with and can easily be evoked in a mainstream treatment setting. If clients are asked about their sexual orientation and gender identity as a matter of course, they at least have the opportunity to confront their fears directly. Such inquiries give clients a choice about disclosing and send a message that sexual orientation and gender identity are legitimate issues, relevant and important to the individual's identity.

Such a message is important not only for lesbian, gay, bisexual, and transgendered clients but for all clients: many non-LGBT clients worry about their sexual identity, about their sexual adequacy, and about issues related to their gender. If the atmosphere is opened to all issues, these clients may feel safer about asking any questions about themselves and about sexual orientation and/or gender identity. If sexual orientation and gender identity are not asked about, the anxiety will remain, perhaps increase, and will in some way interfere with and detract from the recovery process. Asking these questions also addresses the issue of secret pain which, if not shared, may result in clients' feeling alienated, alone, and unique.

Thus, counselors need to take a thorough psychosocialsexual-medical history in a caring, relaxed manner. The most reassuring message that can be conveyed is, "This is routine. We ask everybody these questions as a matter of course. We're okay with the answers, whatever they may be." If this message gets across, lesbian, gay, bisexual, and transgendered clients may not feel so frightened and may begin to develop some trust as a result. If counselors have trouble feeling relaxed and routine in asking questions about sexual orientation and gender identity specifically, they need to de-sensitize themselves. One helpful technique is to practice by role-playing both the counselor's and the client's role. It is a powerful and helpful exercise in empathy to experience the client's feelings and viewpoint. It may also help to talk with a supervisor and to obtain some more specific training about working with lesbian, gay, bisexual, and transgendered clients.

Some "How-To's"

Asking About Sexual Orientation

There are various ways to ask clients about their sexual orientation and their sexual experiences. One is to explain the Kinsey Scale and then ask clients to indicate their place on it. Another is to have clients fill out the Klein Grid (see Chapter 2, Figure 2.2) and discuss it. Oftentimes questions using the Kinsey Scale and the Klein Grid can form the basis for talking about fears or problems or orientation. Another method is to ask indirect questions such as, "Has sex ever been a problem for you?" or, "If you could have your choice of any counselor at all and could choose from male/female, LGBT/straight, African American/white/Hispanic, who would you choose?"

Other more direct questions include, "How often do you have sexual relations? Are they satisfactory, or have alcohol and drugs caused problems? Is (are) your partner(s) male or female, or do you have both?" "Who is your main sex partner? (with a list of potential candidates such as girlfriend/boyfriend, male/female partner or lover, husband/wife)?" Most direct of all are questions such as, "What is your sexual orientation?" or "Do you consider yourself to be homosexual, bisexual, heterosexual?" or "How would you describe your sexual orientation?" or "How do you identify yourself—lesbian, gay, bisexual, straight, asexual?"

Asking About Gender Identity

There are a variety of ways to ask clients about their gender identity. Using the Gender Identity Continuum Chart (see Chapter 2, Figure 2.3), counselors could ask clients where they place themselves in reference to the chart's descriptions. Another approach is to provide the basic definitions of such concepts as gender, gender identity, transgender, transsexual, cross-dresser and then ask clients how they relate to any or all of these definitions and how they self-identify. Another way to ask is to have the definitions listed on a form and ask clients to identify their gender identity in relation to them.

More direct questions might include, "Do you ever dress in the clothing of the opposite gender? If so, for what reasons? How does that make you feel?" "Is your primary partner male or female or transsexual?" "Do you identify as a woman or a man?" "Have you ever wanted to be the gender opposite to your anatomical gender?" "Are you unhappy living as a woman (man)?"

Asking About Sexual Behavior

Another standard part of taking the history is to ask about the person's sexual behavior while drinking and/or using drugs. Often the more direct the question, the easier it is to answer. Thus it may be best to ask, "While you were using alcohol and/or drugs, did you have sexual relations with someone of your own sex?" Counselors need, of course, to very carefully observe the response, whether it be shock, annoyance, embarrassment, or confusion, no reply, or too quick a reply. By asking and perhaps speculating about clients' responses to the question, counselors may be able to help clients (whether lesbian, gay, bisexual, or not) talk about painful material.

It is important to avoid rushing in and reassuring clients that same-sex behavior while drinking does not mean they are lesbian, gay, or bisexual. First, the client may or may not be lesbian, gay, or bisexual. Second, clients could interpret such a response as insulting or at least indicative of some homo/biphobia. Third, clients may be testing for safety by making an initial partial admission to engaging in same-sex behavior when drunk. To reassure prematurely can slam the door on any further exploration of feelings and questions. Instead, inviting and assisting clients to explore the meanings of their experiences for themselves is far more helpful. In the long run, this latter approach is often far more reassuring.

Asking About Sexual Abuse

It is also essential to ask clients whether they have ever been sexually abused—and by whom. It is important to ask both men and women because a number of men have been sexually abused, sometimes by women, more usually by male acquaintances, friends of the family, or relatives. Many women have been abused by fathers, brothers, grandfathers, friends of the family, neighbors, acquaintances, strangers. Some women have been abused by their mothers or other women.

Many of these abused men and women have lived for years with the fear that they are or will become lesbian, gay, or bisexual because of early same-sex experiences. They may or may not be lesbian, gay, or bisexual; but they need reassurance that sexual abuse does not *cause* sexual orientation because their unexplored fears may have contributed significantly to their use and abuse of alcohol and/or other drugs to gain relief. Certainly, if they are able, they need to be free to talk about such fears and to explore their sexual identity issues within a caring and safe atmosphere. Clients also need permission, however, to put stuff on the shelf and not talk about material that is deeply disturbing to them. As Herman (1992) notes, focusing on sexual abuse trauma early in recovery can be dangerously overwhelming to clients. In many ways, what and how much to explore or even give voice to becomes a matter of delicate timing, discerning judgment calls, and sensitive restraint on the part of the counselor.

Whatever way any of these questions are asked—either on forms the clients fill out or from forms the counselors ask from—the questions must be presented in a routine manner, they must be presented as routine questions, and they must be asked with sensitivity.

Learning the Truth

Although counselors may ask all the "right questions in the right way," lesbian, gay, bisexual, and transgendered clients may not answer them truthfully—for any number of reasons. It is important, therefore, that counselors listen with sensitive radar for other clues— depression (even though it may have many sources, it needs to be checked out against other clues); never using the singular pronouns "she" or "he," only "they"; confused and confusing answers or vagueness about close relationships, dating patterns, significant others, socializing, and sexual behavior. If counselors get a sense that the client may be hiding or not answering honestly, then they need to assess their own attitudes and delivery, the client's situation, and whether or not pressing for greater openness is advisable.

Clients may or may not answer frankly, but it is important that questions be asked. Over and over, LGBTs who have been in treatment reported they felt better when their counselors asked questions that gave positive signals. Some said they answered honestly, some said they lied, but almost all said they felt better because they believed the counselors cared and they could go to these counselors if they absolutely *had* to talk to someone.

The Importance of Asking

The importance of asking these questions is underscored by the many lesbian, gay, bisexual, and transgendered substance abusers who report they were never asked about their sexual orientation or gender identity during treatment. As they explained, the subject of their sexual orientation or gender identity was never raised, and they slipped through without receiving appropriate counseling, support, or referrals.

The following example illustrates the destructive effects of such negligence. A young man called NALGAP for help during a relapse which occurred shortly after he had completed a fourteen-day inpatient rehabilitation program. He explained that his sexual orientation never came up during the fourteen days, and he had not felt safe to raise the issue himself. So he left this rehab without knowing there were local gay men's AA meetings. Although he might have relapsed whether or not he knew about the gay meetings, the issue is one of counselors knowing their patients well enough to provide competent treatment. No one assisted this patient with viable aftercare plans.

Another example is that of a young woman who dressed in men's clothing, acted very macho, and bristled with anger. The other clients in her group were afraid of her, and the counselors tended to avoid her when possible. Everyone assumed she was a kind of "diesel dyke." Because no one asked her who she really was, no one learned that she was a lesbian who was terrified she was a transsexual. Thus no one talked to her about or gave her any information or support for this issue. She left treatment as invisible as she was the day she staggered in, vulnerable to relapse.

It is unethical for treatment professionals not to ask questions whose answers will enable them to provide appropriate care. Unless counselors ask, they cannot know who the client is. In effect, they end up treating the client's "false self." It is both ethical and compassionate to ask, support, listen, and respond.

Basic Treatment Information

> When each of us breaks the silence about the pain and suffering we have endured as lesbian and gay people living in a hostile world, the face of inhumanity is exposed. By sharing our stories and telling others what it was like growing up gay, our reality is voiced and validated.
>
> J. Neisen
> *Reclaiming Pride* (1994b)

Certain issues are particular to lesbian, gay, bisexual, and transgendered substance abusers and require specific attention. The question of *community* is often relevant to the recovery process and frequently arises when counseling LGBT substance abusers. It is important, therefore, that counselors have information about this matter and know something about how to utilize this information.

COMMUNITY

Lesbian, gay, bisexual, and transgendered people have journeyed to their time in treatment from diverse backgrounds, experiences and lifestyles, carrying with them differing needs for community. The client sitting across from the counselor may have been passing as heterosexual, living as a part of the larger culture, and wanting to continue to do so. Or the client may have been living as a member of the mainstream culture, but confused about or struggling with sexual identity, not knowing where he or she belongs. Or the client may have been living in a lesbian or gay male subculture with its own norms, mores, and activities which differ from those of the larger culture.

The client may be bisexual and claiming membership in either the lesbian or gay subcultures or in heterosexual culture. Or this bisexual client may be seeking to find some kind of bisexual community. Or the client may be a transgendered person who is heterosexual and wants to find an accepting community. Or the client may be a transgendered person who is lesbian, gay, or bisexual and is searching for an LGB community to which he or she can belong. Or the client may be transgendered and wanting to find a community that does not require its members to label themselves at all. Or the client may be a transsexual searching for others like him or her. The client may be LGB or T and describe himself or herself as "queer" in order to claim membership in the broadest nonheterosexual group possible.

LGBT Communities

Counselors need to have some sense of what communities their clients may come from and/or what communities they may go out to when they leave treatment. Such knowledge is especially important because these communities will constitute the environments, supportive or otherwise, that their clients will live in as they try to establish and maintain their recovery.

What Is Community?

When the term "community" is used in reference to LGBT people, its meanings need to be specified. Community, here, does not refer so much to a physical environment (such as a small town) as to a network of "affiliative links" that people "develop to kindred others without regard to proximity" (D'Augelli and Garnets, 1995, p. 293). Thus it is possible for LGBTs to feel, in some ways, that they belong to a community which may be national or international. Community also may be defined as kinship systems created by choice, based on emotional bonds, social interests, and/or sexual attractions, and engendered by shared oppression.

It is important to understand that there is not really one monolithic entity, one single community to which all LGBT people necessarily belong. D'Augelli and Garnets (1995) explain that because "sexual orientation [is] the only common ground, lesbian, gay, and bisexual community life is highly heterogeneous" (p. 313). On the other hand, there *is* a concept of community and a notion of joining together in groups to fight against oppression, to give solace and support to one another, and to make a life together. Like most human beings, many LGBTs would like to have a community that, in Bohan's (1996) terms, "transcends diversity" (p. 217).

While lesbians, gay men, bisexuals, and transgendered people may claim membership in this large, diverse community, they also have their own communities and subgroups within them. There is not just one lesbian, one gay male, one bisexual, and one transgendered community. Instead, there are many smaller subcultures. Each tends to have its own books, magazines, newspapers, music, activities, and interests. Each tends to have separate and distinct mores and values.

Although there is a larger, more encompassing lesbian and gay community to which many bisexuals belong, it is necessary first to discuss lesbian and gay male cultures separately, especially because after Stonewall in 1969 and the liberation movement it set in motion, many lesbians and gay men went rather separate ways. As Bohan (1996) explains,

> for women, liberation meant freedom from the constraints of heterosexist expectations and provided the opportunity to establish and find validation for new forms of relationships. . . . For men, gay liberation meant sexual freedom and an end to harassment. The new gay identity was expressed by a celebration of gay male sexuality. . . . (pp. 213-214)

The Lesbian Community

In the 1970s, lesbians developed their community sparked by and based in part on feminist beliefs and values. But as Bohan (1996) notes,

> Whisman (1993) has drawn a distinction between lesbian feminists of the 1970s, who defined their lesbianism in terms of its social and political meaning, and the "new lesbians" of the 1980s and 1990s, who are more likely to align with gay men, identifying as "queer" and defining their lesbianism in more sexual terms. (p. 217)

These more recent lesbian attitudes are reflected in various ways, one of which is that of "polyamory" (the newer, more inclusive, less negative term than "nonmonogamy"). Polyamory refers to more sexual freedom and experimentation, but it also refers to a way of being that broadens people's relational possibilities and arrangements, e.g.. two women sharing their life with one of the women's ex-lovers (Munson and Stelboum, 1999).

Lesbian life takes many forms. Bars, discos, and clubs still retain an important role in some parts of lesbian culture, and drinking and marijuana use are common in this venue. There are also many other avenues for women to follow. Many are ardent feminists, many are not. Some lesbians are politically active—as feminists fighting for women's rights (e.g., pro-choice), as AIDS activists, as fighters for better lesbian health care. Some are radical, some are moderate.

Many lesbians are involved in the social community. They may belong to any number of different groups—e.g., "Dykes on Bikes," softball and volleyball teams, golf or tennis clubs, organizations for lesbian businesswomen, for lesbians wishing to adopt or have children, parenting groups. There are women's choruses, dance groups, computer groups, theater groups, and writers' groups.

There is also a large group of women in recovery which offers a different way of life from that of lesbians who frequent the bar, club, or social scenes which include drinking and recreational drug use. This recovery subculture is quite distinct from the non-recovery groups.

Within the larger lesbian community there are, naturally, divisions and differences. For example, lesbians who see themselves as *butch* (assuming male roles, clothing, and attitudes) are very different from *lipstick lesbians,* women who dress and act in very feminine (or *femmes*) way. Some women are totally out of the closet and active in the women's community, while others are closeted and live their lives without much involvement with other lesbians, though they may avail themselves of certain events within the community such as dances or concerts.

Even though there are many, diverse expressions of lesbianism within the larger culture, "The lesbian community has tried to define a uniquely lesbian cultural vision, which is expressed in music and literature, and disseminated at national and regional music festivals and conferences" (D'Augelli and Garnets, 1995, p. 299). Basically, the community has succeeded through, for example, the voices of Melissa Etheridge, Holly Near, K. D. Lang, Rita Mae Brown, Dorothy Allison, and many others.

The Gay Male Community

There is a difference within the current "gay community" between older and younger men. Older gay males tend to have more conservative views based on their experiences of terrible oppression and the great need for secrecy. Younger men have grown up in a very different climate and tend to be more politically active and more "out there" and thus far more visible and verbal (Grube, 1991). Bohan (1996) cites Herdt and Boxer (1992) who

> pointed to the radical impact of Stonewall [in 1969] on gay male culture, differentiating between the early "homosexual" culture, which focused on bar life and secrecy, and the post-Stonewall "gay" culture based on more public identity and a shared sense of community. For men, gay liberation was expressed by a celebration of gay male sexuality. . . . (p. 213)

Much of gay male social and sexual activity takes place within a context of bars, discos, clubs, and baths. Social and sexual action also occurs at circuit parties and raves (weekend dance parties where often heavy use of alcohol and drugs such as Ecstasy, GHB, Special K, crystal meth, speed, cocaine, and marijuana occurs) (Cabaj, 2001). Many gay men also socialize and make sexual contact at private parties and gatherings. But wherever the socializing and sexual contacts occur, it is important to know that alcohol and other drugs often play a prominent part in the scene, particularly because drugs such as cocaine and crystal meth heighten sexual feelings and performance. In addition, "poppers" (amyl nitrate) are used to heighten and intensify sex.

Of course, many other opportunities exist for gay men to socialize and express their different interests. These include political groups such as ACT UP, anti-violence groups, sports, social groups such as gay fathers, businessmen's groups, writers' groups, and so on. The range of activities and groups is great, at least in major urban areas.

There is a wide range of other groups in which gay men can pursue their different interests. For example, the lifestyle of gay male leathermen is different from that of gay men who dress in drag. AIDS political activists act differently (and travel in different circles) from Log Cabin Republicans (a conservative gay group). As is true in the lesbian community, gay men who are in recovery live very different lifestyles from their alcohol and other drug-using counterparts.

The Larger Lesbian, Gay, and Bisexual Community

Even though a larger LGB community is perhaps difficult to describe, there is one that to some degree "transcends diversity" (Bohan,

1996, p. 217). D'Augelli and Garnets (1995) capture the concept very well:

> Contemporary lesbian, gay, and bisexual communities are based on shared identity derived from sexual orientation. The most well-known communities exist in geographically bounded neighborhoods in several large cities and are characterized by high visibility, many formal and informal institutions, and considerable political clout. . . . The many . . . organizations and activities in these neighborhoods—for instance, bookstores, theaters, restaurants, community centers, and scores of political, recreational, and social groups—serve as cultural centers, gathering places, and forums for expression of lesbian/gay culture. They foster a powerful psychological sense of community. . . . (p. 299)

The Bisexual Community

> I think some very courageous people stepped out there and made the effort to build a visible, proud, and supportive community. This was really exciting, but for the most part bi and transgender people were left out. Even to this day, I think that some people are still in denial that bi and trans people are and have been a part of the community.
>
> R. Fox (2000, p. 8)

Even though a study by Billy et al. (1993) "as well as some international surveys in the early 1990s indicated that the bisexual population is between 2 and 3 times as large as the homosexual population" (Klein, 1993, p. 130), there are few bisexual communities in the culture and those that exist are relatively new and still occupy rather tenuous positions. Klein's (1993) explanation for this is that the biphobia emanating from both the heterosexual and the lesbian and gay communities has pushed bisexuals to align themselves with one group or the other. Bohan (1996) adds that "Very little has been written about bisexual communities, perhaps because the biphobia found in both lesbian and gay as well as heterosexual communities has precluded their evolution" (p. 218).

Weinberg, Williams, and Pryor (1994) state that "It appears that bisexuals are where homosexuals were in the early 1960s" (p. 298). D'Augelli and Garnets (1995) describe bisexual men and women as "a newly emerging political force" (p. 300). Various authors (Bohan, 1996; D'Augelli and Garnets, 1995; Fox, 1995; Weinberg, Williams, and Pryor, 1994) believe that the future development of a bisexual community lies within the "Queer Movement" which is much more inclusive of those who combine sex and gender in nonconforming ways. As Weinberg, Williams, and Pryor (1994) note, bisexuality "is an identity that includes swingers, transsexuals, and many others—all united by a desire to escape traditional boundaries of sex and gender" (p. 299).

The final outcome is difficult to determine. What is important is to recognize that bisexuals do not, as yet, have much community support. Perhaps the best contacts at this time are members of the Queer Nation and listings in *The International Directory of Bisexual Groups* (Ochs, 1994) and on the Internet (see Appendix C).

The Transgender Community

> Many of us have identities that we have no language for. "Are you a guy, or what?" We are the anvils, and that question hammers us daily. For us, the question requires more than a one-word answer.
>
> It seems as though everyone who questions the totality of who we are—whether they despise us or admire us—thinks that an answer to the question "Are you a woman or a man?" will illuminate our identities. But for some of us, the ground we have staked out in the space between those two poles is precious. There is no one word at this time that will put the question of our identities to rest.
>
> L. Feinberg (1998, p. 69)

Although not always clearly defined or easy to locate, there are a number of transgender communities (Allen, 1997; Clements, 1999; Gainor, 2000; Israel and Tarver, 1997; Lombardi and van Servellen, 2000; Marcel, 1998; Nemoto et al., 1998; Valentine, 1998; Xavier, 2000). They are, however, quite diverse, not homogeneous (Allen, 1997; Gainor, 2000; Lombardi and van Servellen, 2000; Xavier,

2000). As Marcel (1998) notes, "The transgender community is a diverse population consisting of different categories and bases for gender identity. . . . There are many different sub-populations within the community" (pp. 11-12). Xavier (2000) agrees: in Washington, DC, "There is actually not one community, but a collection of sub-populations" (p. 7). Because there is such great variety among those who make up these communities, probably the best way for them to build community is to adopt Faderman's (1991) principle of "diversity-within-unity."

A primary reason transgender communities are harder to describe accurately is that they are "young." Or as Allen (1997) points out, the transgender community lags "many years behind the Women's, the Gay, and the Civil Rights Movements in organizing for political change . . . [but] by forming alliances, is learning and growing quickly" (p. 313). Kammerer, Mason, and Connors (1999) note in their needs assessment that

> Both transgenders and service providers pointed to community building as the foundation not only for HIV/AIDS prevention but also for improved health and social services more generally for transgenders. Pointing to the model of the gay community, they stressed that without a strong sense of community and mutual responsibility transgenders cannot get the kind of support they need as individuals. (p. 12)

Nemoto et al. (1998) add that "The transgender community can empower itself by uniting across ethnic and age barriers, and advocating for their own health, social, and economic needs" (p. 3). Political activism has become one of the hallmarks of developing transgender communities. As Allen (1997) comments, "People who spent years working to define (and separate) themselves, now look for common goals and mutual benefits in allying with the whole transgender spectrum . . ." (p. 313).

In addition to political activism, transgender communities engage in such activities as seeking and creating new spiritual traditions, meeting with one another at conventions and conferences, sponsoring social events. The two most powerful resources for transgender communities are community centers (such as the NYC Lesbian and Gay Community Center—NYCLGCC) and the Internet. The community centers provide social services, support groups, and social

functions (see Warren, 1999, for an account of services and prevention efforts provided by the NYCLGCC's Gender Identity Project).
The Internet provides a wealth of national and international resources—chat rooms, forums, access to books and articles, information of all kinds, including videos and music, lists of conferences and
conventions, and health resources.

Some Words of Caution

When considering the various communities their clients come
from and may return to, counselors need to keep in mind that some
people who would logically seem to belong to a group or community
may be rejected and not allowed to belong. Perhaps their belonging
may require them to conform to limiting rules and mores, or they may
feel they do not fit in. For example, racism, ageism, classism, sexism,
and biphobia (Bohan, 1996) are present in the "mainstream" LGB
communities, plus considerable transphobia. Thus, an older bisexual
man might well feel that he does not fit in to the "younger" gay male
culture. A Latina lesbian may feel she must deny her race in order to
fit in to the predominantly white lesbian culture. A lesbian may feel
excluded from mixed groups by gay men's sexism. A blue-collar gay
man may feel out of place among more corporate types. A transwoman who identifies as lesbian may feel rejected (and may *be* rejected) by the lesbian community. Where do heterosexual transgender
people turn to find community? Often they are rejected by the LGB
communities and must look elsewhere to find other kindred souls.

In addition, counselors need to keep in mind that the LGBT communities may pose a threat to early recovering LGBT people because
of the presence and sometimes an emphasis on alcohol and other
drugs. Fortunately, at least in major urban areas, there are large
LGBT recovery communities. But counselors need to have contacts
with these people and must know how to help clients find their way to
such groups.

It is also important to recognize that many people cannot avail
themselves of the communities discussed here. As Bohan (1996)
points out,

> Those who live in rural areas, for instance, typically have diffi-
> culty locating each other and form only small—and usually very

secretive—networks. These can reduce the sense of isolation, but they cannot provide the range of opportunities and support possible in the vast communities of large urban areas. (p. 220)

Bohan (1996) goes on to note that even many people in urban areas cannot avail themselves of the LGBT communities because they are not out (either not out enough or not at all) or because of language or cultural barriers.

SUMMARY

It helps to keep in mind that the terms "lesbian community," "gay community," "bisexual community," and "transgender community" do not refer to unified, sharply definable entities. Nor do they refer to all lesbians, gay men, bisexuals, or transgendered people since not all of them consider themselves a part of a larger community. Rather, these terms refer to loose aggregates of people who are diverse in character, values, attitudes, and behaviors. Some members of these communities may not tend to mix, while some may share and work together on common social and political goals.

Nevertheless, these groups, no matter how diverse or loosely organized, do tend to offer one or more of the things that people want from community. Some seek political action; some seek a culture; some seek ways to establish contacts with others like themselves; some seek a social support network; most seek a sense of belonging, of fitting in. Hopefully, their particular communities can fulfill those hopes and desires. To do so they need to follow the prescription described by D'Augelli and Garnets (1995):

> to create a safe setting for people to be open about their identity requires adhering to the principle of "diversity-within-unity" (Faderman, 1991). This model of community building encourages lesbian, gay, and bisexual people who differ in race, socioeconomic status, gender, age, religion, and so on to find a place within the same social collective, however large and diverse. (p. 313)

Hopefully, the LGBT communities will more and more frequently follow this model of community building.

Chapter 7

Special Issues in Treatment

In order to work with those who are marginalized, we need to help individuals comprehend their situations. Only then can we help the client assume the responsibility that understanding implies: facing the pain and fear implicit in a stigmatized identity. Thus, consciousness of one's situation demands courage—the courage to bear feelings of pain, fear, and shame. Finally, psychotherapy must aid the client to develop the internal resources and strength to act in spite of apparent risks—to act despite fear, shame, and danger.

J. Glassgold and S. Iasenza
(1995, p. 207)

Any consideration of treatment for lesbian, gay, bisexual, and transgendered substance abusers must take into account issues specific to this population. In addition, as Ratner (1993) points out, providing quality treatment for substance-abusing lesbians and gay men requires an awareness of their particular issues and problems. The same can be said, of course, for bisexuals and transgendered people.

SOCIALIZING AND SEX IN RECOVERY

One of the key issues in the process of recovery is that of clean and sober socializing and clean and sober sex. Because many lesbian, gay, bisexual, and transgendered people have used alcohol and other drugs as a part of their being sexual, they may be afraid to have sex, fearing that sexual contact will upset their equilibrium and they will drink and/or take drugs. Counselors can be helpful by talking about internalized homo/bi/transphobia, the part that the use of alcohol and other drugs has played in making it possible to have sexual contact, and the possibility of putting sexual activity "on the shelf" for a while. In fact, counselors may need to give clients permission to do so.

Because of the frequent links between sex and alcohol/drugs, counselors will need to explore various matters with clients. One that needs investigation is whether clients have been into hustling, prostituting, or using their bodies as a way to earn a living and to get alcohol/drugs. A number of LGBT youth, especially those who are runaways, hustle as a way to get money for alcohol and drugs. A number of transgendered people are or have been commercial sex workers. Because many transgendered people are so marginalized, that may be the one way they could earn money to live and/or to support their habit (Marcel, 1998). Nemoto et al. (1998) report that "about half (48%) [of the TGs of color in their study] were currently commercial sex workers" and "most (89%) participants had exchanged sex for money" (p. 2).

Counselors need to explore these matters with clients so they can help them with aftercare plans, make appropriate referrals, and help them deal with the feelings attached to their behaviors. If these behaviors are not discussed and explored, clients may be at a greater risk of relapse.

In addition, counselors can help clients explore ways to socialize and be sexual without jeopardizing their recovery. They will need to address the whole issue of going to bars and clubs in a way that is very different from addressing the matter with heterosexual substance abusers. It is important to understand the function of bars and clubs in some of the LGBT subcultures. LGBT bars and clubs are much more than bars or clubs; oftentimes they are the one place where lesbian, gay, bisexual, or transgendered people can go and be reasonably sure that most of the others in that bar are like them. This assurance of the other people's similar sexual orientation and/or gender identity is critically important because these are primarily invisible identities, mainly because of successful passing. Contrary to the mythology, it is not usually possible to know who is LGBT just by looking at a person. They do not "all look alike."

Traditionally, then, LGBT bars and clubs have been the places where people could go and feel relatively safe in making social and/or sexual overtures to others of the same sex and/or gender identity. These bars and clubs have also traditionally been the places where people would go to make contact—they were the places to meet others like themselves. Thus it just does not work to flatly state, "Look, if you don't want to get hit by the train, don't sit on the tracks. So don't go to bars/clubs." For many LGBTs, that is like telling them their social life is over—that they can no longer go to what is often the only place available to meet other LGBTs in a relatively safe atmosphere.

While it seems reasonable to strongly urge newly recovering clients to stay away from bars and clubs altogether for *at least* ninety days, they may resist such urgings. If clients are adamant about going to bars or clubs, it does not work to hit such resistance head on. Instead, counselors can help by being realistic. For instance, they can continue to caution about the dangers while at the same time assisting their clients in figuring out ways to make going to these places safer—such as going with a group of other recovering substance abusers, perhaps after an AA or NA meeting. Whatever the outcome, counselors should not engage in a so-called "knee-jerk reaction" of saying to lesbian, gay, bisexual, and transgendered clients, "Don't go to the bars and clubs." Such reactions elicit resistance and indicate the counselors' lack of knowledge about an important issue, something that will tend to undermine counselor credibility.

One other issue relating to sex and socializing in recovery needs to be mentioned. As is true for some heterosexuals, some lesbian, gay, bisexual, and transgendered people are caught up in compulsive sexual behavior. Depending on how people feel about themselves and their behavior, it is possible their sexual addiction puts them at high risk of relapse if they do not deal with it. Although most counselors are not equipped to work with this issue in any depth, they may have to recognize and acknowledge it if clients' compulsive sexual behavior puts them at risk. Probably the best course of action is to refer the client to an LGBT-affirming therapist who knows about substance abuse and sexual addiction. There are also a number of sexual addiction self-help groups, some of which are not homo/bi/transphobic.

At the very least, even if counselors just speak the words, i.e., acknowledge the existence of these sensitive issues, they will be able to signal clients that these matters can be discussed and that acceptance of sexuality is a part of recovery.

SIGNIFICANT OTHERS AND FAMILY ISSUES

In recent years, the substance abuse field has become increasingly aware of the need to treat not only the substance abuser but also the significant other (the person closest to the substance abuser) and other family members as well. Many facilities and agencies have created specific programs to provide such treatment. But a number of them do not provide specific outreach to or include lesbian, gay, bisexual, and transgendered substance abusers' significant others (SO) and family members.

Thus counselors need to consider several factors. They need to think creatively about who may be the client's SO and who may constitute the lesbian, gay, bisexual, or transgendered person's family. For example, the LGBT person and his/her lover do not live together and may even live far apart. Or the SO may be an ex-lover with whom the client lives and maintains a long-term friendship. Lesbian, gay, bisexual, and transgendered clients' extended families may well consist of their friends rather than blood relatives, so counselors need to learn what friends or acquaintances (such as landladies, bosses, storekeepers, colleagues, barbers, even bartenders) are involved with their clients. By doing so, counselors can determine who makes up the clients' support systems and encourage that support. Counselors may also be able to determine who the enablers are, what the clients' environments are like, and what will assist clients with re-entry issues.

Counselors need to be sensitive to another issue. It is quite possible that a person's lover, significant other, or close friend is closeted and does not feel safe coming to the treatment program or is not willing to risk disclosure by becoming involved in a group. Counselors may need to see the substance abuser and his or her SO as a couple or possibly refer them elsewhere for couples counseling. Or counselors may be able to help clients help their lovers or friends to come into the family treatment program. Such a program would of course need to be sensitive to and aware of the special issues regarding lesbian, gay, bisexual, and transgendered people. Most important, counselors need to realize that LGBTs' ties with others can be just as powerful, just as significant and influential as the blood and marriage ties of non-LGBT people.

Counselors also need to be aware of potential problems and issues in regard to lesbian, gay, bisexual, and transgendered clients' families of origin. If the program is not sensitive to these matters, it might push for contacting the family of origin without discovering that the client has been rejected by them. Or clients may have good reason for not wanting the family to become involved because they are not out and the risk of exposure is too great. For example, the shock of a family's suddenly learning that their daughter or son is a substance abuser, let alone that he or she is lesbian, gay, bisexual, or transgendered, may be more than a family's bonds can withstand. They might react with denial—"Just get clean and sober and you'll get over it." Or they might reject their child outright. Such reactions could well set clients up for relapse.

Or clients may feel they have let their family down by being LGB or T so that facing their family may stir up powerful feelings of guilt and shame. Clients may be unable to deal with the rejection if the family will not attend the family program if asked. In all these situations, counselors need to make therapeutic judgments (in consultation with the client) about what is best for the client's recovery. But those judgments must be based on an appreciation of the delicate nature of these matters.

Another sensitive issue may arise at times. It is quite possible that the lesbian, gay male, bisexual, or transgendered client is married, perhaps has children, and is also involved with another person or persons of the same sex or is a closeted transsexual. Counselors must then deal with knowing about a situation which they are not free to reveal to the husband or wife, but which clearly affects that person. Counselors also need to monitor their feelings and attitudes about such extra-marital relationships, about bisexual feelings and behavior, or about transsexual "secrets" to make sure any personal biases do not negatively affect the counseling.

For example, does the counselor feel strongly that the client should stay in the marriage, no matter what? Or is there a subtle belief that the client should tell the spouse, no matter what? Does the counselor believe that the client should give up the same-sex partner(s) or behavior? Are counselors willing to consider a same-sex lover as an SO worthy of respect and in need of treatment, just like the spouse? Can counselors entertain the possibility that bisexuality may be a perfectly comfortable choice for their clients? Are counselors willing to see the transsexual's choices as valid? Because these issues are so delicate and sensitive, counselors need to monitor their attitudes and act with great care, basing their treatment plans and actions on the most objective and unbiased perspectives they can muster.

It is possible that some clients will have no one. Then, it becomes especially important to find supportive contacts for them—to help them create a "family of choice," as it were. But it should be noted that all clients need assistance in forming links with outside groups and the larger community. If lesbian, gay, bisexual, and transgendered AA/NA members are available, they can help serve as support people. At the very least, counselors should contact hotlines and national organizations that can steer these client to others who can be helpful and supportive. Bibliotherapy can also help clients feel less alone. Thus it is important to supply LGBTs with books, articles, newspapers that speak to their sexual orientation and/or gender identity. Clients also should be informed about the vast number of LGBT resources available on the Internet (see Appendix C).

PARENTS OR CHILDREN OF LGBT PEOPLE

An often overlooked matter concerns those who are either parents or children of LGBT people. From time to time, the substance abuser in treatment is the parent or the child of a LGBT person. In order to assist such a parent or child, they first have to be identified. Thus counselors need to ask *every* client as a routine matter whether or not they have a lesbian, gay male, bisexual, or transgendered child or parent. As stated earlier, asking sends messages that counselors know such relationships exist and that it is possible to talk about them with a degree of safety. Many have never told anyone and feel unique and isolated.

Parents of LGBT people may be struggling with terrible guilt, feeling that somehow they caused their child's sexual orientation and/or gender identity. Often the first questions parents ask when they discover their child is lesbian, gay male, bisexual, or transgendered is, "Where did I go wrong? What did I do wrong?" The burden of such guilt can be extremely destructive to substance abusers struggling to recover. The same is true of the burden of anger, disappointment, shame, and confusion.

Substance abusers in treatment who are the children of LGBT people are also likely to be struggling with their feelings toward their parents. They may be experiencing pain, fear, confusion, shame, rage, and guilt—which can be destructive to recovery efforts if they are not worked through. They may feel overwhelmed by the fear that "Someone will discover my secret and will know how terrible I am." The double shame of their own substance abuse and their parent's LGBT identity is more than doubly painful. These clients may also fear others will think they are lesbian, gay, bisexual, or transgendered like their parents. For any or all of these reasons, most parents or children of LGBT people are not likely to volunteer this information and may indeed have kept their identity as someone related to an LGBT person secret.

When counselors create a safe space by asking in a caring and accepting manner, then it may become possible for clients troubled about these issues to get assistance. Basically, counselors can provide the same help to parents and children as to LGBT clients—assisting them to deal with their feelings, accepting them, reassuring them, educating them that no one *causes* homosexuality or gender identity conflicts and, when appropriate, referring them to organizations such as Parents of Lesbians and Gays or other support groups. The appropriateness of such referrals and of any particular counseling interventions needs to be determined on the basis of what stage clients (whether LGB or T, whether parent or child) have reached in the process of coming to terms with these issues (see Chapters 8 and 9).

RELIGIOUS GUILT

When first beginning to entertain the possibility of being lesbian, gay, bisexual, or transgendered or later when trying to come to terms with being so, many people feel great guilt and shame. These feelings often result from the conflict they experience between the terrible things their religion says about homosexuality, bisexuality, and transgenderism and the truth of who they are. Many LGBTs experience a "loss of God" and feel cast into spiritual darkness. They may be especially vulnerable in early recovery because the buffer of alcohol/drugs that was between them and their feelings has been removed.

Counselors can help with this partly through their attitudes. If they do not accept the view that being lesbian, gay, bisexual, or transgendered is a sin but instead view it as an acceptable alternative lifestyle, then clients can at least feel supported in their struggle to resolve some of their guilt, shame, and loss. Another means of helping is by putting lesbian, gay, bisexual, and transgendered clients in touch with religious organizations such as Dignity (Catholic), Integrity (Episcopal), the International Conference of Gay and Lesbian Jews, the Conference of Catholic Lesbians, the Metropolitan Community Church (Protestant), Unity, the United Church of Christ, the Quakers, and the Unitarian Church (see Appendix C). Another way is to have a non-homo/bi/transphobic clergyperson come talk with clients.

As Kus (1995) states, recovery involves a need to develop or regain spiritual beliefs and a spiritual life (see also Booth, 1995 and Royce, 1995). By following these guidelines, counselors can support and assist their lesbian, gay male, bisexual, and transgendered clients in their recovery.

CONFIDENTIALITY

This issue is one that touches on all others. It is at the heart of all decisions about trust, disclosure, and protection of sensitive information. Very few states, cities, or counties have laws which specifically protect lesbian, gay, bisexual, and transgendered people's rights (see Chapter 4). Too many LGBTs have lost jobs, children, places to live, and/or friends and family because their sexual orientation and/or gender identity was revealed. Thus knowledge about the laws of each state, city, and county is important for the creation of an informed and appropriate treatment plan.

But the question of confidentiality reaches beyond knowledge of the law because homo/bi/transphobia runs deep and often operates beyond the law. It becomes, therefore, necessary for counselors to make sure their clients' sexual orientation and/or gender identity is carefully shielded from potential danger.

Counselors need to be particularly sensitive about confidentiality issues when dealing with lesbian, gay, bisexual, and transgendered people who are parents because of custody questions. LGBT parents are often at very high risk of losing their children in custody battles if their sexual orientation and/or gender identity become known. Added to that, if the lesbian, gay, bisexual, and transgendered parent is a substance abuser, the risks run even higher. Another very sensitive issue is the results of any HIV/AIDS testing of clients either before entering or during substance abuse treatment. The media have clearly documented the negative reactions accorded people even suspected of having HIV/AIDS—from children being barred from schools to people being evicted from their residences and fired from jobs.

Another aspect of confidentiality which needs careful attention is staff and agency attitudes. If the agency itself or other staff are homo/bi/transphobic and counselors are required to share client information with team members, then counselors need to listen to their LGBT clients "off the record." Or if that is not possible, then counselors need to warn clients that whatever is said to the counselor may be shared with other staff. Clients need the opportunity to make informed choices.

Another important aspect of confidentiality is that of charting. A client's chart may be seen by people other than staff such as insurance companies or the courts. Thus it is possible that information about a client will be known outside an agency, a matter which seriously affects confidentiality. Different facilities have various ways of dealing with this problem. One method is not to write sensitive information in the chart. Another is to have some kind of code for writing about sensitive material. Whatever way a particular facility deals with this matter, confidentiality has a special urgency to it when sexual orientation and/or gender identity are involved.

HIV/AIDS (ACQUIRED IMMUNE DEFICIENCY SYNDROME)

In the past few years much progress has been made in the prevention and treatment of HIV/AIDS, especially in the use of antiretroviral drugs which have made it possible for a number of people with HIV/AIDS to live for long periods of time with the disease as a chronic rather than a fatal illness (see Dean et al., 2000; Israel and Tarver, 1997). Drawing on the Centers for Disease Control and Prevention's (CDCP)1999 report, Dean et al. (2000) point out that "the advent of highly active antiretroviral treatments (HAART) has sharply reduced AIDS deaths and opportunistic infections" (p. 114). However, the Center for Disease Control's (CDC) National Center for HIV, STD, and TB Prevention (NCHSTP) (2001) warns that "Despite medical advances, HIV remains a serious, usually fatal disease that requires complex, costly, and difficult treatment regimens that do not work for everyone" (CDC/NCHSTP: Internet).

Yet, not all is progress. Glionna (2001) reports on the San Francisco Department of Public Health's findings that "The rate of HIV infection among gay men in San Francisco has more than doubled since 1997 . . . suggesting a breakdown in safe-sex practices that for years had helped stabilize the city's HIV rate . . ." (*The Los Angeles Times* Archives: Internet).

In addition, the NCHSTP (2001) notes that

> Recent data on HIV prevalence and risk behaviors suggest that young gay and bisexual men continue to place themselves at considerable risk for infection with HIV and other sexually transmitted diseases (STDs). (CDC:NCHSTP: Internet)

Obviously, HIV/AIDS is a special issue that cannot be ignored. Not only gay men, but also injection drug users (IDU), bisexuals, heterosexuals, and transgendered people get HIV/AIDS. Some lesbians get HIV/AIDS. Whatever their sexual orientation and/or gender identity may be, substance abusers tend to be in a high risk group as a result of their sexual experiences while drinking and/or taking drugs and the effects of alcohol and other drugs on their immune systems, especially if combined with hormones in the case of many transgendered people (Ghindia et al., 2001; Gomez, 1995).

HIV/AIDS cannot be ignored because it affects *everyone* in some way—physically, emotionally, and spiritually. Perhaps most important, HIV/AIDS cannot be ignored by people committed to providing treatment to those suffering the ravages of substance abuse because to ignore it would be to violate their trust as caregivers and their responsibility as human beings.

It is axiomatic that substance abuse counselors must know and understand the basics about HIV/AIDS. They also need to be informed about safer sex practices, risk factors, prevention strategies, the effects of major medications, and ways to strengthen the immune system. Most important, perhaps, is the role of counselors in helping substance abuse clients to become better at self-care.

Self-Care

> During our addiction, we were strangers to ourselves. Drugs and alcohol functioned to hide ourselves from ourselves. We lost touch with our likes and dislikes, our thoughts and emotions, and even those things that mattered most to us.
>
> E. Nealy
> *Amazon Spirit,* 1995

One of the most destructive effects of substance abuse is that people's capacity for self-care is seriously compromised by their addiction (Khantzian, 1981; 1998). Their difficulties with taking adequate care of themselves range on a continuum from mild to extremely self-destructive, from being late to appointments or forgetting to eat a meal to relapse or suicide. Anyone afflicted by addiction is at risk, but for those in populations specifically at high risk for HIV/AIDS, self-care can be a life-or-death issue.

Gay and Bisexual Men

As Ghindia et al. (2001) note, "Substance abuse clouds judgment and contributes to hazardous behaviors that can lead to illness, such as HIV/AIDS, sexually transmitted diseases (STDs), hepatitis, and injuries" (p.105). They go on to say that substance-abusing gay and bisexual men may be at high risk for HIV infection "if their substance abuse disinhibits safe sex practices" (p. 106).

Ryan, Huggins, and Beatty's study (1999) "found that those subjects who reported being intoxicated during sex were also more likely to engage in higher risk sexual activities" (p. 75). Three other studies reported similar findings (Mulry, Kalichman, and Kelly, 1994; Seage et al., 1992; Stall et al., 1986). Ryan, Huggins, and Beatty (1999) state that while they could not be certain, they think it is likely that "intoxication and high-risk sex are both manifestations of a risk-taking or sensation-seeking personality style" (p. 75). Stall, Paul, et al. (1999) noted that HIV-risk sexual behavior (e.g., anal sex without protection) was more likely to occur among men whose sexual behavior was combined with substance abuse.

Lesbians and Bisexual Women

Lesbians and bisexual women are also at risk. As three studies of this population revealed (SFDPH, 1993a,b; Stevens, 1993), between 2 percent and 6 percent were injection drug users. The 1993 study (SFDPH) found that 7.69 percent of IDUs were HIV positive. Another, earlier study (SFDPH, 1991) of self-identified lesbians coming into methadone treatment backs up this finding. It showed that 8.8 percent of them were HIV positive. Furthermore, Gomez (1995) notes there is "data suggesting that . . . [self-identified bisexual women and lesbians] may be more likely to inject drugs than are exclusively heterosexual women" (p. 24). Gomez also summarizes the results of two studies by Cohen (1993) and Weiss (1993):

> Women who report at least one female partner *(regardless of self-identified sexual identity)* [our italics] are more likely to have injected drugs, more likely to have engaged in anal sex with men, and have higher HIV seroprevalence rates than do the exclusively heterosexual women. (Gomez, 1995, pp. 24-25)

In addition, a number of lesbians have sex with men. Gomez (1995) reports on four studies which showed that 16 to 34 percent of the lesbians and bisexual women questioned "reported having sex with men who had had sex with other men" (p. 25). Gomez (1995) goes on to note that "Reinisch et al. (1990) also reported that lesbians who had engaged in sex with bisexual men were more likely to have engaged in anal intercourse than were lesbians with heterosexual male partners" (p. 25).

Obviously, contrary to myths and stereotypes, lesbians *are* at risk of HIV infection because of unsafe sexual behaviors. And like their bisexual and gay male counterparts, if lesbians and bisexual women are substance abusers, their alcohol and other drug abuse can be a factor in that unsafe behavior. Thus lesbian and bisexual women substance abusers need the same education, the same prevention information, and the same kinds of counseling approaches to these matters as do gay and bisexual men and transgendered people.

Transgenders

The transgender population is at high risk for HIV/AIDS. A number of studies support this fact, among them a recent one (Clements, 1999) that studied 515 individuals of transgender experience (392 MTF; 123 FTM). The rates of HIV status were staggering: 35 percent of the MTF transgender individuals were HIV positive; 63 percent of the African-American MTF people of transgender experience were HIV positive. Although a smaller percentage (1.6 percent) of the FTM transgenders were HIV positive, many of them reported engaging in the same high risk behaviors as the MTF transgenders.

Clements' study (1999) also revealed very high levels of drug abuse in this population: of the non-injection drug users (IDU), 66 percent used cocaine, 48 percent used crack. Of the IDUs, 84 percent used speed, 58 percent used heroin, and 54 percent used cocaine. Such levels of substance abuse put the transgender population at very high risk.

Reback and Lombardi's study (1999) comparing the drug use of 209 MTF transgenders—76 sex workers, 133 non-sex workers— confirms these high rates. Those who engaged in sex work consistently reported higher AOD use than non-sex workers in the previous thirty days: alcohol use (51 percent versus 29 percent), crack use (25 percent versus 3 percent), crystal meth use (21 percent versus 5 percent), and cocaine use (12 percent versus 5 percent). Also, sex workers were more likely to be IDUs than non-sex workers (9 percent versus 2 percent). The ratio for injecting crystal meth was 8 percent versus 2 percent. Interestingly, the MTFs who did sex work knew about protection from HIV. They reported 95 percent condom use during sex work and 94.3 percent condom use with their nonpaying male partner as opposed to the non-sex workers' report of only 55.6 percent condom use with their male partner. Clearly, the transgendered people who did not engage in sex work were at much greater risk than the sex workers.

In the face of these terrible statistics, counselors need to be aware of the risk factors in their clients' lives and ways to lessen those risks. They need to teach clients about the effects of substance use and abuse on sexual practices, what constitutes high risk behavior, and ways to protect themselves from HIV infection.

For someone who is living with HIV/AIDS and is a substance abuser, the problem of self-care can also be a life or death issue. If people who have HIV/AIDS are impaired by substance abuse, they may choose not to or may not be able to follow the complicated drug regimen that keeps the disease under control. That puts them at serious risk of dying. In addition, if they keep on using or go back to it, they are at even greater risk because substance abuse can compromise the immune system.

As Dean et al. (2000) note,

> though data are not yet conclusive, research [Seage et al., 1992; Basgara and Pomerantz, 1993] suggests that a number of illicit substances may speed replication of HIV or have an immuno-suppressive effect. (p. 122)

They go on to say that

> adverse interactions have been documented between recreational drugs and other medications. Poppers, for example, cause potentially fatal drops in blood pressure when combined with the common erectile dysfunction medication sildenafil citrate (Viagra). . . . [There is also a] possibility that Ritonavir, a common anti-HIV medication, might inhibit the liver's ability to process the drug MDMA [Ecstasy], boosting levels of the recreational drug to potential fatal levels. (Wolfe, 2000, p. 122)

Obviously, it is extremely important for counselors to help clients, especially People with HIV/AIDS (PWAs), learn about the risks and about how to take care of themselves.

Prevention/Education

If counselors are going to provide good treatment for all clients—both LGBT and non-LGBT—they need to know enough about HIV/AIDS to be able to teach and reassure clients and other staff. The irrational fears held by the general public about HIV/AIDS are enormously powerful. Bachman (2000) reported on a Centers for Disease Control and Prevention "survey [2000] of what people know about AIDS [that] found that four out of ten mistakenly believe it is possible to get the disease by sharing a drinking glass or being coughed or sneezed on by an infected person" (*The Los Angeles Times* Archives: Internet).

Often this ignorance and these fears fuel other reactions—especially heterosexism and homo/bi/transphobia. For example, as Bachman (2000) reports, "Nearly 19% of those surveyed [5,600 participants] said they agreed with the statement 'People who got AIDS through sex or drug use have gotten what they deserve'" (*The Los Angeles Times* Archives: Internet). So it becomes crucially important that there be informed, level-headed staff people who can teach others and thereby allay some of their fears and temper some of their prejudices.

In addition, it is important for counselors to know enough about HIV/AIDS to address the fears of the "worried well," people in high risk groups (gay and bisexual men and women, men who have sex with men, transgendered sex workers, and injection drug users especially), who are often convinced that they have or soon will have HIV/AIDS.

Denial

It is especially important for counselors to address the denial and attendant complacency that some people have about the risks of unsafe sex practices. These attitudes are particularly strong among younger gay and bisexual men who apparently believe that older gay men are at risk, but they are not (Bohan, 1996). As the CDC:NCHSTP (2001) bulletin states,

> Abundant evidence shows a need to sustain prevention efforts for each generation of young gay and bisexual men. We cannot assume that the positive attitudinal and behavioral change seen among older men also applies to younger men. (CDC:NCHSTP: Internet)

The report goes on to say that "Research among gay and bisexual men suggests that individuals are now less concerned about becoming infected than in the past and may be inclined to take more risks" (CDC:NCHSTP: Internet).

One factor affecting this attitude seems, ironically, to be that of the progress in treating HIV/AIDS. As Dean et al. (2000) note, "One study . . . found that 18% of HIV-positive gay men were now practicing safe sex less often because of treatment advances" (p. 115). Maugh's (2001) report of the NCHSTP's latest study shows support for this view. He cites Dr. Harold Jaffee's statement that "The success of treatments using cocktails of anti-AIDS drugs apparently has seduced many young men into believing that the risks are not as severe as they used to be . . ." (*The Los Angeles Times* Archives: Internet).

Denial is also one of the deadly effects of homo/bi/transphobia. Maugh (2001) quotes Dr. Carlos del Rio of Emory University School of Medicine: "'In African-Americans, there is much greater stigma about being homosexual than there is among whites. . . .'" (*The Los Angeles Times* Archives: Internet). Another report from the CDC: NCHSTP (2000) states that

> researchers believe the stigma of homosexuality in communities of color may inhibit men of color from identifying themselves as gay or bisexual, despite having sex with other men. . . . this may prevent men of color from seeking or receiving the HIV prevention and treatment services they need. (CDC: NCHSTP: Internet: p. 2)

The CDC study (2001) of six U.S. cities reports that a staggering 30 percent of young gay and bisexual African-Americans and 15 percent of Latino men are HIV positive as opposed to 7 percent of the whites. The CDC:NCHSTP report (2001) cites 18 percent for Latino men.

Another alarming aspect of this epidemic is revealed by a CDC: NCHSTP report (2000):

> [These are] the results of a multi-site CDC survey of 8,780 HIV-positive men who have sex with men. Of those surveyed, 24 percent of African-American and 15 percent of Latino men who have sex with men identified themselves as being heterosexual. (CDC:NCHSTP: Internet)

The report goes on to note that "by not identifying as gay or bisexual, these men may not accept their own risk for HIV, and therefore, may unintentionally put their female partners and children at risk" (CDC:NCHSTP: 2001: Internet). Maugh (2001) cites CDC researchers' reports that "Three quarters of all newly diagnosed women are black . . ." (*The Los Angeles Times* Archives: Internet).

Information such as this underscores the great need for counselors to address HIV/AIDS in clients who are men and women of color. In addition, counselors must aim their prevention and education efforts at all clients, however those clients may identify themselves. If a narrower approach is taken (e.g., directing HIV/AIDS information primarily to identified LGBTs), many clients who do not or are not willing to identify themselves as gay or bisexual may be at high risk because they have sex with men, and women who may be heterosexual run the risk of being infected by these men who have sex with men.

The Need for Prevention Education

One approach to denial and complacency is to supply information. For instance, people at risk need to know that the

> long-term effects of the combination anti-HIV drug regimens are unknown. Recent years have seen increasing reports of high cholesterol, diabetes, and redistribution of body fat known as lipodystrophy. (Dean et al., 2000, p. 114)

They also need to be taught about the adverse interactions possible between recreational drugs and prescribed medications and about the immunosuppressive effects of many illicit substances (Dean et al., 2000).

Although not all fear, ignorance, denial, and complacency can be banished simply by teaching about HIV/AIDS, education is certainly a most effective weapon. When educating people, it helps to begin with the most basic information, especially how the disease is and is not transmitted because many people (including a number of LGBTs) are remarkably uninformed or ill-informed—e.g., believing such myths as HIV/AIDS can be caught by touching someone who has HIV/AIDS or that the penetrator in the sex act cannot get HIV/AIDS. Information about the ways that alcohol and other drugs can weaken the immune system should also be included in any lecture on the physical effects of substance abuse.

In addition, *everyone*—those who are lesbian, gay, bisexual, and transgendered and those who are not—should be taught about safer sex practices, about the risks of unsafe sex practices, and the relationship of substance use and abuse to those risks. As the CDC's National Center for HIV, STD, and TB Prevention (2000) emphasizes, prevention is the most important tool there is for dealing with HIV/AIDS.

Some useful tools for assessing risk factors for clients and for providing helpful information can be found in the SAMHSA:CSAT's publication, *Substance Abuse Treatment for Persons with HIV/AIDS* (2000). This book has chapters on many important topics such as mental health treatment, ethical issues, and counseling clients with HIV and substance abuse disorders. Included are helpful lists of such matters as Sexual Risk-Reduction Topics and HIV/AIDS Risk Assessment. In addition, the book discusses a public health model,

> sometimes called the risk-reduction model, [that] emphasizes incremental decreases in substance abuse or HIV risk behaviors as treatment goals and tries to keep clients in treatment even if complete abstinence is not achieved. (p. 107)

Counselors will find this whole book extremely valuable and very user-friendly in helping them to prepare prevention education and counseling strategies.

Other HIV/AIDS Issues

A related issue that counselors need to attend to and help their clients with is that of tremendous grief. Whether clients themselves have HIV/AIDS or are friends/lovers/relatives of PWAs, the grief brought on by the serial deaths and the specter of death is often overwhelming. The loss suffered by survivors is traumatic. Among the symptoms of that trauma may be "distressing emotional reactions such as anxiety, dread, horror, fear, shame, rage, sadness and depression . . . somatic complaints including sleep difficulties; substance abuse" (Shernoff, 1997, p. 148). Obviously these reactions can serve as fuel for the addiction fire or as a relapse trigger and need to be recognized, addressed, and treated.

Counselors need to know what their agency's policies are towards Persons with HIV/AIDS. Are PWAs acceptable for admission? Or does the agency (or institution) refuse to admit someone who has HIV/AIDS? What happens if someone has an HIV positive test reading? It is critically important to know these things about policy in order to anticipate events and attitudes if clients disclose information indicating that they are in a high risk group (such as being a gay or bisexual male substance abuser or an injection drug user) or if clients reveal a background of sexual activity while drinking and/or taking drugs which places them in a high risk group.

If a client was found to have HIV/AIDS, would he or she be forced to leave the program or be isolated? If the agency admits people with HIV/AIDS, then what policies and procedures have been established regarding PWAs? Are there lists of standard precautions? Are they posted so that all staff and all patients can read them? Is literature explaining HIV/AIDS available to all patients and staff? Do all staff receive thorough and ongoing inservice training?

Is a discussion of HIV/AIDS included as a standard part of lectures on sexuality? Are instructions about safer sex practices included in the sexuality lectures? What is the agency's policy about testing for HIV? How are the findings of this test handled regarding confidentiality and the particular state's laws? Do clients have the right to refuse to take the test? Or will they be asked (or pressured) to leave if they refuse?

One other matter needs to be considered. What attitudes about recovery do staff members and affected clients have in the face of an HIV/AIDS diagnosis? Any client coming into a substance abuse program who is diagnosed as having HIV/AIDS has to deal in some way with the question of what value recovery has in the face of this chronic, perhaps fatal disease. And other clients and staff may have to deal with that question, too.

It is especially important that all staff (from the cleaning people to the administrators to the psychiatrist) be trained in issues of death and dying and of living with a chronic, long-term illness. They also need training in the ways that the Twelve Steps and other belief systems relate to these matters. Staff people need also to be able to turn to one another when dealing with the inevitable stress involved with chronic illness and death and dying work.

In addition, staff need to monitor their own attitudes regarding HIV/AIDS and the ways people contract the disease to determine whether they may have feelings that gay and bisexual men are, after all, simply reaping the whirlwind of sexual promiscuity. If staff members have such attitudes, they need either to work them through or refer the client to someone else. Ultimately, the essentials of good counseling are what apply here: counselors need to be well-informed, aware of their own attitudes, and willing to assist clients in whatever ways they can.

OTHER ISSUES

Some other problems and issues counselors need to keep in mind are (1) the prejudice and violence that LGBTs are often exposed to (both from society and sometimes from their partners) and (2) the physical and mental health problems generated by the stigma visited upon LGBTs.

Counselors need to check out their clients' experiences with prejudice and violence and help them learn coping skills and self-care techniques. If there is partner violence, then counselors will need to address the matter, hopefully with both people.

Counselors also need to attend to their clients' health problems and assist them in getting good healthcare. These efforts may include getting lesbian, bisexual women, and transgender clients gynecological care; getting all LGBT clients screening and treatment for sexually transmitted diseases (STDs); arranging for transgender clients who are taking hormones to continue receiving them and have them monitored. These efforts may also need to include working with such mental health problems as PTSD, depression, and panic disorders.

Whatever the specific problem, counselors need to be alert to signs of difficulty and/or illness. They also need to take detailed, thorough histories and ask clients about these matters.

Acknowledging the Whole Person

Whatever specific issues may arise for any particular client, the essential truth is that failure to address and attend to them can be destructive to the client. There is, of course, no scientific way to measure the destructiveness of such negligence; but over and over, lesbian, gay, bisexual, and transgendered substance abusers report how terrible it felt to have counselors ignore obvious clues about sexual orientation or tell them that sexual orientation was not relevant to recovery. In addition, transgendered substance abusers report the pain they experienced having their gender identity denied or ignored or being told that they had to recover before they could attend to their gender identity issues.

Since being LGBT involves far more than sexual orientation and gender identity and raises many important life issues, not to be acknowledged as a whole person feels terrible. It also means that proper and appropriate treatment cannot be given. On the other hand, counselors' attending to these special issues with knowledge and sensitivity provides lesbian, gay, bisexual, and transgendered substance abusers with the quality of treatment that can help them recover from their substance abuse.

Chapter 8

Developing a Positive Lesbian, Gay, or Bisexual Identity

Until you learn to name your ghosts and baptize your hopes, you have not yet been born; you are still the creation of others.

M. Cardinal
The Words to Say It (1994)

INTRODUCTION TO THE STAGE MODEL

It is time, now, to consider a model of the process many LGBT people go through—in some manner or another—when they seek to discover who they are and redefine what their overall identity is in regard to their sexual orientation and/or their gender identity. Essentially, this model is about the process that is most often referred to as "coming out." Another term that Lev (in press) uses to describe this process as it applies to transgendered people is "emergence." Although it is common and frequently used, the term "coming out" does not adequately capture the enormous complexity and great diversity of this process. And perhaps no one term can.

This model is intended to provide a perspective on the ways many LGBT people take on, integrate, and learn to manage a stigmatized identity. The model also presents a view of how going through this process can enable people to accept who they are as lesbians, gay men, bisexuals, or transgendered people and develop a positive sense of self, a positive identity.

This model is a theoretical construct and as such cannot really do justice to the incredible complexity and variety of an individual's actual, specific journey to identity. It does, however, furnish a perspec-

tive of the process that can assist counselors in interpreting and clarifying what many clients may be experiencing. It is a perspective from
which counselors can ask and get answers to various important questions.

Some of these questions are—What am I seeing, hearing, experiencing with this client? What does this behavior mean? What do
these feelings signify? How can I help my client who is confused
about his or her sexual orientation? How can I help my client become
more comfortable with his or her sexual orientation? How can I help
my client who is struggling with his or her gender identity? How do I
know what intervention or what question or what information is appropriate for this client at this moment?

In addition, the model can be applied to the experiences that substance abusers go through when they stop using alcohol and/or drugs
and seek to discover and define their identity as a recovering person—oftentimes in twelve step programs and/or therapy. The model
furnishes ways to describe, explore, and understand the dynamics of
learning to manage and integrate issues of gender identity and/or sexual orientation and issues of recovery. It also provides a perspective
on the dynamics created by the interaction between the two processes. Furthermore, it describes some of the issues, problems, and
concerns that may arise as a person follows this course of action.
Thus, the model can be helpful in planning and guiding treatment
strategies.

The construct presented here is primarily a composite of two models (although with influences from numerous others). One was created in 1971 by William Cross, a black psychologist, in order to explore the process by which a "Negro" develops an identity as a black.
In essence, Cross (1971) describes how people "transform" their
identities from a negative, stigmatized state to a positive one in which
they refuse to accept the validity of the stigma and take pride in their
identity. As he notes: "The process should be viewed *as the Afro-
American model for self-actualization under conditions of oppression*" (p. 109). The other was constructed in 1979 by Vivienne Cass, an
Australian psychologist, on the basis of her empirical study of "how a
person acquires a homosexual identity . . ." (Cass, 1979, p. 219).

Some of the other studies and constructs that contribute to the
model used here are Ponse's (1978) research on lesbian identity is-

sues; Rudy's (1986) investigation of the process of "becoming alcoholic"; Kus's (1987, 1988) study of gay men in AA; and McNally's (1989) study of recovering lesbians in Alcoholics Anonymous.

The construct used here is based on Cross' five stage model. But it incorporates many of Cass' ideas, findings, and explanations and adds the names of her model's stages to the Cross model. This construct also uses ideas from many writers who discuss and study identity development, especially with regard to LGBT people, and draws on the substance abuse and trauma literature and on the writings and clinical experience of the authors.

Dynamics and Structure of the Model

Although this model contains five stages that suggest they are distinct entities, they are not. Almost unnoticed, one stage can merge into another. A person may move back and forth between stages or may, while in one stage, have an experience which ordinarily occurs in a different stage. A person may stand for long periods of time with one foot in one stage and the other foot in another. Movement within the model is much more fluid and non-linear than it is possible to indicate. Nevertheless, movement does tend to occur in a somewhat progressive manner.

Some writers have commented on what they see as the rigid, perhaps unrealistic and value-laden nature of a linear, progressive model (Bohan, 1996; Brown, 1995; Gonsiorek, 1995). Probably the best response is a statement from Cass (1992) herself:

> Stages are proceeded through in sequence. . . . Although some people have questioned me on this fixed order I believe that *once we make changes in cognitions, that is, how we think and process information, we can't simply return to a previous naive state* [our italics]. For example, if I come to the conclusion, "I'm probably gay," I can't then act as if I've never had that thought. However, if I don't like that view of myself I can adopt strategies that will allow me to play it down, put it in the back of my mind or find some acceptable explanation for why it happened [in effect, to rationalize or deny it]. In my model this would be called foreclosure. (p. 7)

As Fox (1995) also notes, "stage theories give a general rather than exact outline of events involved in the coming out process" (p. 52). Thus the model presented here describes stages of development as occurring in a basically linear and progressive fashion.

Application of the Model

Design

This two-chapter section on the stages is structured as follows:

1. Description of the stages of developing a positive identity as they pertain to lesbians/gay men.
2. Description of a stage model that applies to bisexuals.
3. Description of a stage model that pertains to transgendered people.
4. Discussion of the previous three descriptions in terms of (1) the interfaces between the processes that both LGBT people and substance abusers engage in to deal with stigmatized identities and (2) the treatment issues that are relevant to those processes.

Rationale for Design

The reason that the stages are applied first to lesbians and gay men is that they are the two groups most thoroughly studied and theorized about in the past thirty years. Therefore, lesbians and gay men's progress through these stages can serve as a helpful paradigm for other groups. Applications of stage models to bisexuals and transgendered people are of much more recent vintage, and much less has been written about them.

The reasons lesbians and gay men are discussed together are twofold. First, although there are distinct differences between them, there is enough similarity in regard to their navigation of these stages to allow discussing them together. Second, to discuss them separately would generate great repetition. Therefore, counselors need to take the information offered and apply it in a selective manner.

Bisexuals and transgendered people are discussed as separate groups. The differences between these two groups is too great to allow for discussing them as a single entity. The marked differences between these two groups and lesbians and gays preclude discussing them all together.

Some Cautionary Words

The development of identity does not necessarily follow a direct and predictable path. Furthermore, some people simply never engage in this process. For example, some people whose *behavior* is homosexual, bisexual, or transgendered do·not identify or see themselves as homosexual, bisexual, or transgendered. Therefore, they will not follow the path set forth by this, or other, identity development models. Also, there are many substance abusers who stop drinking and/or taking drugs but do not go through these stages either.

For those who do engage in the processes described in this model, the journey often takes place over a long period of time, sometimes over a whole lifetime. Some people may stay in one stage all their lives and do just fine. Others may slowly wend their way through the process; others may speed through. There is no one way to do this; no right or wrong way. The ways people experience this process of discovering and defining or redefining their identities are as complex, as varied, and as diverse as the people themselves.

It may be helpful, therefore, for counselors to recognize that they serve as just one small link in a long chain of events and experiences. For people to deal with the oppressing misery of substance abuse and become recovering substance abusers is a long and complex process. For people to contend with the grinding oppression of homo/bi/ transphobia and heterosexism and learn to accept and integrate their identity as lesbians, gay men, bisexuals, or transgendered people is also a long and complex process. But even though helping professionals can play only a small part in such lengthy and complicated processes, the part they do play is often critically important. To provide clients with warmth, acceptance, and safety is to provide them with sanctuary, with an opportunity to gather together their forces and choose life.

THE PROCESS OF DEVELOPING A POSITIVE LESBIAN/GAY IDENTITY

Also, we don't fit all the 'stages' that are in the books, so you should keep the door open for different experiences.

Anonymous lesbian
quoted by J. M. Hall (1992, p. 92)

Prior to Stage One

The process of developing a lesbian/gay identity cannot begin until people ascribe *personal meaning* to their encounter with information, behavior, feelings—whatever form that may take. Until the encounter takes on personal meaning, people essentially see themselves—their values, their perspectives, their identities—as congruent with the mainstream. The reference point for their values and the attitudes, ideas, and beliefs which shape and define those values is the mainstream. Thus the reference point for people who may be lesbian or gay is heterosexuality, and they see themselves as heterosexual. Similarly, the reference point for people who may be substance abusers is social drinking and/or recreational drug using, and they see themselves as social drinkers/drug users.

The key defense at this point is denial. For people who might possibly be lesbian or gay. internalized homophobia tends to be very strong, and most have a great need not to know, not to discover or encounter any information about their sexual orientation that might prove disconcerting. Many people dissociate or split off parts of themselves in order to deal with threatening information or knowledge. The same dynamics are true, of course, for those who might be substance abusers—they desperately need *not* to know that their drinking and/or drug-taking is different from that of mainstream social drinkers/drug-takers. Counselors need always to remember just how high an investment people have in "not knowing," in preventing others and particularly themselves from discovering the truth about Self.

Stage One: Preencounter (Discovery)— Identity Confusion

> I believe that a lot of my drinking was to keep me in the closet and I think a lot of women drank to stay out of the closet. Some drank to stay in it, and some drank because they didn't want to be lesbians, or "why, oh why can't I be normal, let me have another drink." I've heard many people say that a professional did not help them. My own professional denied my lesbianism. She believed it was a phase.
>
> Mary (research participant)
> quoted by E. McNally (1989, p. 92)

At some point, certain people begin to sense that something about them is different. Often this may be a subtle feeling that they are not quite like others, that other people seem at ease while they are not. There may be hints of homosexual feelings. These hints can and often do create a great deal of confusion and anxiety. Some people try to resolve these feelings by attempting to discover what these hints of difference might mean.

They may read something (e.g., the dictionary definition of homosexual or a pamphlet on substance abuse) or may ask another person about a "friend" who has homosexual feelings or a "friend" who may exhibit signs of drinking/drugging problems. If what they find is negative (e.g., "homosexuals are sick, unnatural people"; "substance abusers are weak and disgusting"), then they may slam the door on any further exploration and retreat into even greater denial. In effect, they deny that homosexuality (or substance abuse) has any personal meaning for them.

Cass' (1979) term for the ways people have of shutting down, of stopping the process from going any further, is "foreclosing." There are, of course, numerous strategies of foreclosure that will effectively block off any further information or action. Using alcohol and drugs is often a major one and if the use becomes problematic, then the denial in response to homophobia is joined by the denial of alcohol and drug problems. Other foreclosure tactics may be to refuse to "hear" any more information about the subject; inhibit sexual activity (become asexual); marry; pursue a course of hypersexual heterosexuality; pray; seek a "cure"; rationalize and redefine the feelings and behavior ("We're just friends"; "I was drunk and didn't know what I was doing").

Whatever the specific strategy for foreclosing, the power of the denial is tremendous. People have an enormously high investment in being okay in their own and the world's eyes. Their psychic survival depends, therefore, on denial and any other defense that will help them block off the terrifying knowledge of who they are or might be. It is not surprising that foreclosure strategies play an important role in the various stages of identity formation.

Treatment Issues

People in this stage may come to treatment still in denial of their substance abuse problem, sent there by an employer or a family's intervention. They may come because they have hit bottom with their alcohol and/or drug problem or they may have been forced into treatment by a DUI arrest or a drug charge.

Although something has challenged or broken through their denial of the substance abuse problem, their defenses against knowing they might be lesbian or gay are likely to be intact and remain so. Thus, even when not drinking and/or drugging, they do not see themselves as lesbians or gay men. If, for some reason, treatment staff strongly suspect that this client is lesbian or gay, push hard enough, and somehow manage to break through the defense system, they risk pushing an already frightened and vulnerable person over the brink into a pit of homophobic shame.

In effect, it is possible through such confrontation to elicit a homosexual panic in a person who is unconsciously terrified of his/her homosexual feelings. Lesbians and gays who have suffered this kind of treatment report going back out to drink and/or drug away the horror of this forced and unconscionable confrontation. Obviously, defenses exist for very important psychological reasons and need to be regarded with respect.

Counselors' Role

If counselors shouldn't push, what should they do? They should routinely ask all clients what their sexual orientation is, but should accept the answer, whatever it may be. This action sends positive messages that the facility relates to sexual orientation issues in an affirming and matter of fact manner. Having open lesbians and gay men on the staff sends messages that it is safe to be who you are. It is also very helpful to have lesbian/gay recovering substance abusers visit the agency on a regular basis and to have them, as a matter of course, speak regularly at in-house AA/NA meetings.

These actions are important for two particular reasons. One is that they signify the agency's acceptance of sexual orientations other than heterosexuality. The other reason is that positive role models are extremely helpful. The importance of this becomes evident if one tries to imagine a substance abuser attempting to get sober without ever meeting any successfully recovering substance abusers. Even if the worst is so, that no lesbian/gay people are available, heterosexual counselors can serve as positive role models of nonhomophobic attitudes.

It is also possible to sow seeds directly. Counselors can make sure that books on homosexuality and bisexuality are clearly visible among other books in their offices. A list of lesbian/gay meetings of AA and NA should be posted along with the list of other AA/NA meetings; and a good, clear lecture on sexuality which includes homosexuality and bisexuality as acceptable lifestyles provides positive messages. Also, having openly lesbian/gay substance abusers speak regularly at in-house AA/NA meetings can be reassuring to clients who are confused and frightened. It is also likely to smoke out homophobia among the other clients and thereby give counselors a chance to deal with it openly (just as they would racism). To see counselors deal openly and firmly with homophobia can be very reassuring to those who may be struggling with feelings of differentness.

Just as counselors should not confront clients about their sexual orientation, they should not tell clients in this stage to go to a lesbian/gay meeting of AA or NA. In effect, such a recommendation implies to clients that they are seen as homosexual. Such an implication can be terrifying to a person in Stage One because their investment is in being seen (and seeing themselves) as heterosexual. In addition, people whose counselors sent them to such meetings while they were in this stage later reported they felt overwhelmed and extremely threatened by the experience.

There are exceptions. If clients exhibit confusion, conflict, or guilt when discussing their behavior while drinking and/or drugging or express great doubt about their ability to get sober but can't specify the reasons, counselors might suspect the possibility of conflict about sexual orientation issues and try either to help clients disclose or at least entertain the possibility that their conflict is what keeps getting them to relapse. If counselors feel the need for assistance in doing this or feel inadequate to the task, they might ask a lesbian/gay recovering substance abuser to come in and talk with the client. Such sessions are risky and must be handled with delicacy and skill and sensitivity.

But sometimes taking such risks can help save a life if clients keep relapsing for no visible reason other than their feelings. Counselors need, however, to be very clear with themselves about their reasons for pushing or confronting a client, and it is usually a good idea for counselors to discuss such a proposed action with another professional skilled in lesbian/gay treatment or with a lesbian/gay person before carrying it out. If counselors do carry out some kind of confrontation, it is critically important that they be able to effect some closure and provide a good deal of reassurance to clients. Perhaps one of the most helpful methods is to assure clients that once having taken even a brief look at their behavior and/or feelings they are free to "put matters on the shelf" for a while if they want to until they are able to achieve some longer term recovery and consequent stability.

Perhaps the most significant aspect of Stage One, and the one that needs always to be kept in mind, is that it is a stage of not-knowing. Furthermore, via their denial and dissociation, some people remain in this stage throughout their lives, never consciously questioning or knowing what their sexual orientation really is, never acknowledging their feelings of attraction toward same-sex others, foreclosing on directly facing and accepting who they really are. Some others move on to the second and subsequent stages. It is important for counselors to realize that while some of their clients may move into Stage Two while they are in treatment, many will probably not do so until they have been clean and sober for several years. Thus it is especially helpful to make sure clients have good aftercare treatment, that they be referred to therapists who are not homophobic. The importance of good referrals cannot be overstressed.

If and when people do make the transition to the second stage, others may be puzzled by what appears to be a sudden, often inexplicable shift. Seemingly these people have suddenly "become" lesbian or gay. Familiarity with this model and with substance abuse recovery provides a more reasonable explanation for this phenomenon. As people get and remain clean and sober, they begin to come out of the fog. They gradually become aware of their surroundings and themselves in relation to those surroundings. They begin getting in touch with their feelings. Their awareness of themselves and their reality and their ability to deal with their reality tend to increase. Thus as recovering substance abusers who are in Stage One begin encountering hints about their sexuality, they may start being able to face and explore these hints rather than run from them.

Stage Two: Encounter (Discovery)—Identity Comparison

When we change how we view ourselves and the world, we open ourselves up to new possibilities. When we learn to act on these possibilities, despite the risks, we change our lives and our futures.

J. Glassgold and S. Iasenza (1995, p. 226)

People enter Stage Two when they encounter somebody or something that breaks through their denial and prompts them to consider that being lesbian or gay might have personal meaning for them. This may occur as an accumulated result of their reading and conversation if the clues they come upon are positive, such as discovering a reassuring book like *Accepting Ourselves and Others* (Kominars and Kominars, 1996) or *Loving Someone Gay* (Clark, 1997). Or they may have an emotional encounter or experience with a book, a play, a TV show, a movie, a person which leads them to look at the world and their place in it a little differently.

Coming to this awareness may occur gradually, over a long period of time, or the discovery may jolt or shock people. It may be thrilling. It may be a shattering experience. It is always an important one. It has the capacity to turn people's worlds upside down. One reaction might be "Oh, my God, maybe I am one!" Another might be, "What will happen to me now? What will my life be like now? How will I deal with these changes in my life?" Another might be, "Hmm—this is interesting."

The encounter or discovery introduces people to a different reality in which they often have to contend with intense feelings of alienation, fear, and confusion and must struggle to learn how to live within this new reality. The primary task is to reinterpret reality in light of the new information. The basic defensive postures that people assume in response to these events and feelings are "bargaining" and rationalizing in order to put off or alter reality to make it bearable. Substance abusers in this stage may bargain with themselves by saying, "I'll only take drugs on weekends" or "I'll change brands of what I drink." Or they may rationalize their drinking and/or drug-taking by thinking, "Well, I'm not that bad" or "I can stop any time I want to. I just don't want to right now."

Lesbians and gay men at this point may bargain with themselves by viewing their feelings or behavior as only temporary, a "phase" that will pass. Or they may think, "Maybe I'm bisexual." (It should be noted here that this person may well *be* a bisexual. But what is referred to here is a bargaining that somehow the person's feelings and behavior are not really homosexual.) Or, they rationalize: "I was drunk and didn't know what I was doing"; "I didn't initiate what happened; the other person 'came on' to me"; "I'm different—I (Mary) just happen to love Sally who just happens to be a woman."

While people may be experiencing exciting new feelings and behaviors, because of society's and their own, internalized homophobia they cannot easily accept the notion of their new possible identity. For some people, the process of working through the feelings and coming to terms with the new identity can be a relatively brief, fairly mild, and somewhat positive one (as is the process for some substance abusers who have minimal trouble accepting their substance abuse).

But for many, the process of accepting even the idea of this new identity entails an often protracted and painful struggle with self and society. In the course of these struggles, people may experience strong feelings of alienation ("Where do I belong if I am this way?"), fear ("How will I learn to live with this new identity?"), and confusion ("Who am I anyway?").

In reaction to the pain and difficulty they may be experiencing, people may foreclose in a variety of ways. They may go back into the denial and dissociation of Stage One, or they may stop their progress by continuing to bargain and rationalize. Substance abusers may keep changing brands and vowing to quit tomorrow. People struggling with their sexual orientation may continue to see themselves as really heterosexual or view their behavior as constituting a "special case." They may seek professional help in order to get "cured." They may isolate themselves by having nothing to do with anyone who is or even appears to be lesbian or gay. In any event, what happens to people who foreclose in this stage is that they do not progress or develop their sense of self-identity as a lesbian or gay man. They cannot integrate who they may really be, but they cannot fully be at ease with who they may wish they could be (a "normal" heterosexual).

Treatment Issues

People in this stage who are struggling with their sexual orientation are probably the most vulnerable to rejection and humiliation. Thus if they enter treatment at this point, they may protect themselves against any perceived threats to their old "heterosexual identity" by all means available. They may lie, deliberately mislead others, retreat behind a cloud of confusion, or rationalize every attempt by others to get at their real experience. They may isolate themselves from others.

These are people who have a sexual orientation "secret" which they are hiding and are fearful of revealing to others. These people may come across as being very "together," high-functioning, and aloof. Or many in this stage tend to be withdrawn, depressed, frightened, and extremely troubled.

If clients admit to having concerns about sexual identity when they are questioned at intake or some later time, then counselors can be directly supportive and helpful in a number of ways. Counselors need to be guided by the same sensitivity they use with substance abusers in this stage who are often unable to accept the label and the identity of substance abuser; they do not push recovering people to label themselves before they can tolerate such an action.

When discussing matters with clients in this stage, it is important to use language like "feelings of attraction" rather than "lesbian" or "gay." Helpful also are those gentle methods of encouraging clients such as: "It must be hard for you to talk about this"; "What would it mean to you if you were to discover that you are attracted to someone of your own sex?" "Could you explain a little more about what you're feeling?"

Obviously, the techniques counselors use to help people discuss whatever is difficult for them are appropriate in this situation. So, too, are all the other considerations like timing and joining clients' resistance. In terms of timing, the most help a counselor can sometimes give is to be a safe person to talk to and to advise that feelings about affectional/sexual attraction take time and often benefit from being put on the shelf for a while. Joining the resistance may also involve agreeing that this subject is difficult to discuss and perhaps should be put aside for the time being. If counselors and clients do, in fact, put these issues aside, counselors need to emphasize that they are open to talking with clients at another time. It is important that clients receive appropriate referrals for their aftercare treatment.

Of greater concern are those who do not admit to any problems or worries about sexual identity issues but who seem troubled by some kind of secret (perhaps feelings of attraction for someone of the same sex). The majority of people in Stage Two probably fall into this category, burdened by secrets they do not feel able to disclose. Direct confrontation is not likely to get at these secrets, and it is counter-indicated.

If the intake process and an in-depth psychosocial-sexual history do not elicit information about what is troubling these clients, counselors should be supportive in a general way and not press for information. The ways of reaching and helping these clients will tend instead to be indirect, such as sexuality lectures, visitors and speakers from lesbian/gay AA/NA groups, prominently displayed lists of lesbian/gay AA/NA meetings, openly displayed and available literature on gender identity and sexual identity issues, and an overall nonhomophobic attitude in the treatment setting. Of course, referral to non-homophobic aftercare becomes especially important.

In addition to these indirect ways of signaling clients about the safety of their surroundings, counselors need to directly address issues of confidentiality and, therefore, trust. Because people in Stage Two feel so vulnerable and so uncertain about both their identity and their safety, it is critical to reassure them that if they do risk disclosing their secrets to the counselor their confidentiality will be respected and indeed actively protected. Confidentiality is especially important because many people in this stage are still involved, at least partly, in heterosexual lifestyles and many may still be married, with or without children.

One approach is simply to tell a client that the counselor will keep confidential whatever is said in one-to-one sessions (if the counselor is able to do so). Certainly, counselors should make clear to all clients what the boundaries of confidentiality are. Is material shared with other staff? Just with the immediate supervisor? Only with the medical director? A helpful technique is to tell clients, "If you want to discuss this issue, I will not put it in the notes." Counselors can underscore this statement by putting their pen down on the table. At the very least, counselors need to be clear and direct with clients about the issues of confidentiality and to convey to clients that they understand the importance of it to anyone dealing with sexual identity issues. For instance, it is important that a married woman or man know that the counselor appreciates the possible dangers and complications inherent in their situation.

In this stage, as men and women begin to encounter or discover their sexual identity, even if only to themselves and even if only very tentatively, they have begun the process of "coming out," the process of admitting to and owning their gay or lesbian orientation. Some of them will never "come out of the closet" any further than to acknowledge hints or possibilities. Many will come out in selected places and with selected others but will remain primarily closeted. What is important to realize is that coming out is a process, that it may take a lifetime, and that coming out in treatment may be the worst (or the best) thing a client can do—depending on the client, the staff, and the circumstances.

The Encounter/Discovery Stage is critical to early movement toward developing a more positive lesbian or gay male identity by beginning recovery from external and internalized homophobia. This same stage is critical to substance abusers' beginning their road to recovery. Substance abusers must encounter something that breaks through their denial, discover their feelings, and admit to their experiences and what those experiences mean for their lives. This is the First Step. If people, whether lesbians and gays and/or substance abusers, have some sense of hope (as in the Second Step), if they can accept—even a little—who they really are, then they can move ahead to Stage Three. If they do not, they may go back into the denial/dissociation of Stage One or stay in the isolated and fearful position of Stage Two.

Above all else, counselors need to understand and remember that people who are in Stage Two are perhaps more frightened and certainly more vulnerable than in any other stage. They have just tentatively entered into an unfamiliar country, but they have no map. This is even more threatening because the majority of people in society do not want them to go there and do not speak the language. People in this stage often feel threatened, frightened, confused, alienated, and terribly vulnerable to rejection and humiliation. They need support, protection, understanding, compassion, and acceptance. They do not need to be and should not be confronted, pressured into self-disclosure, gossiped about, pushed to disclose in group, or in any way forced to expose themselves to others. People in Stage Two are ripe for leaving treatment prematurely; many do so because they feel pressured or because they are not receiving the support they need. Kindness and compassion can make all the difference; by enabling a person to stay in treatment and get the help he or she needs.

Stage Three: Immersion/Emersion—Identity Comparison/Tolerance

> Oh, brave new world,
> That has such people in't!

> W. Shakespeare
> *The Tempest.* V.1.183-184

A Two-Part Stage

This stage has two parts to it—immersion and emersion (emergence from)—each with distinct features. Basically the first part, *immersion,* consists of embracing and joining with, submerging oneself in, the lesbian or gay male world, whatever form that immersion may take. This experience is very similar to what adolescents do as a part of forming their identities. The second part, *emersion,* is an emerging from this state, a coming out of the total submersion of self in the larger group of those similar to oneself. In effect, involvement in both parts of this stage are what enable people to compare themselves to others, reject what does not define them, and move on.

Part One: Immersion

Reactions. The need to be with similar others draws people into this stage. In some fashion, they discover others like themselves. They may not like being around similar others or may be frightened by them. They may reject lesbians and gay men as a defense against identifying with them. Or they may either be enchanted by this discovery or at least heartened by it. One common reaction is, "Maybe it's okay to be lesbian or gay." With these feelings, they enter into the first of the two parts of this stage. Many, if not most, plunge into the lesbian or gay male world, whether an actual world or community or one constructed from books, movies, music, and/or the Internet. They tend to explore the meanings and behaviors of these new worlds by surrounding themselves with everything that is lesbian or gay.

This immersion can take many forms. For example, one woman in McNally's (1989) study reported that when she began to see herself as lesbian she threw out all books and recordings by male writers and performers and replaced them with works only by women. Some gay men immerse themselves in a sexually active gay life. Many men and women submerge themselves in the bar scene or attend raves and circuit parties. Women and men in this stage who are already in recovery may surround themselves with groups, AA/NA meetings, and other recovering people who are specifically lesbian and gay.

There is also a tendency to denigrate what is heterosexual. Many lesbians and gay men in this part of Stage Three are likely to dehumanize heterosexuals (for example, call them "breeders") and view the "straight" world as inferior (e.g., insensitive, power-hungry, cruel). These actions are part of a complete or partial withdrawing from the mainstream; a splitting of the world into *us* and *them;* a turning inward and to peers. These steps help them begin sorting out and reshaping values and finding new reference points for the self. This tendency to withdraw may also be contradicted at times by a need to confront the mainstream "other." Whatever form it may take, much of this process is geared toward labeling others in an either/or fashion in order to clarify personal identity. Counselors may note a striking similarity both to the experiences of substance abusers who immerse themselves in AA or NA and look down on "Earth People" and to the experiences of adolescents forming their identities.

People in this first part of Stage Three tend to experience two major feeling states—pride bordering on arrogance and great anger. The arrogance helps protect them against the tremendous pain of rejection. It is also a way of proclaiming the validity of a new identity. In addition, many lesbians and gay men begin to feel great rage against the heterosexual world for oppressing them and for demanding that lesbians/gays hide and feel ashamed of their sexual orientation. Their anger is most certainly a response to both external and internalized homophobia.

Forms of Immersion. Immersion can take many forms. Often the very tentative and confused "trying out" of the possibility of being lesbian or gay (Stage Two) gives way to active investigation of what being a lesbian or gay man can mean. A number of people in this stage may get involved in a great deal of sexual experimentation and many relationships. Many people seek places where other lesbian/gay people congregate. Although these may include social or political clubs, often the most common, if not the only available place, are the lesbian or gay bars. If lesbians and gay males in this stage already have problems with drinking and/or taking drugs, immersing themselves in the lesbian or gay bar scene or in raves or circuit parties can have potentially devastating consequences (see *Socializing and Sex in Recovery* in Chapter 7).

In this stage many lesbians and gay men leave their hometowns and move to lesbian/gay "ghettoes" in urban areas, surrounding themselves with other lesbian and gay people and isolating themselves from the heterosexual world. Another form of immersion is adopting, indeed heightening, the stereotypical behavior ascribed to gay men or lesbians. Men may assume more feminine mannerisms and women may adopt more masculine mannerisms in order to identify themselves by stereotypes and to belong to the subculture. This behavior is often an assertion of self—"I'm queer; I'm here. I'm different. I'm proud of it!"—and a challenge of mainstream values.

This behavior is often viewed by heterosexuals as lesbians and gays flaunting their sexual orientation. It may be much more associated with an assertion of self. Somewhat opposite behavior can also occur. If people are already in stable relationships, they may choose to immerse themselves even more in the relationship and their existing social circle and simply isolate themselves from their families and the larger society.

Whatever behavior occurs during this stage, the essence of immersion is an attitude, a perspective. It is the filter through which everything is viewed and measured: *Is the other person gay or lesbian? Are others committed to being lesbian or gay? Will heterosexuals be present at social functions? Who among us is gay or lesbian, who is not?* In similar fashion, substance abusers who are in this part of the stage tend to evaluate all facets of life in relation to their addiction: Is the other person recovering? Are other people in the program? Will they serve alcohol, will there be drugs at this function?

The immersion part of this stage serves an extremely significant function. During this time, people gather the information and acquire the attitudes and feelings that enable them to start integrating their being lesbian or gay and their recovery identity. It is the crucible in which they are able to test and learn about their developing identities—to the point where they are able to say with some assurance and certainty, *I am lesbian or I am gay. I am* not *heterosexual* or *I am recovering.*

If people foreclose in this stage, they may define themselves as gay or lesbian but stay immersed in a small, rigidly defined subculture and/or ghetto and thus isolate from the larger culture. This behavior can be compared to that of some substance abusers who foreclose at this stage of their recovery; they may be clean and sober for many years, but they still attend eight to ten AA or NA meetings a week and center their lives around AA/NA, excluding other activities. Such foreclosure may keep them safe, but it tends to limit their worlds.

Treatment Issues. Certain problems may arise if lesbians or gay men enter treatment while in this stage. Many of them are struggling with a double dose of anger: the defensive anger of the substance abuser, and the defensive anger of the lesbian/gay person who has become sharply aware of the pain and injustice of homophobia and oppression. Although they may admit to counselors that they are lesbian or gay, they may act sullen and refuse to talk about the matter. They may be aggressive and tell counselors to mind their own business. They may make statements such as, "What do you know? You could never understand me because you're not lesbian or gay!" or "You'd drink or use drugs too, if you were lesbian or gay!"

Even seasoned counselors report they sometimes feel thrown off by such challenges. It is helpful to note the similarity to other resistant statements common to substance abusers such as, "You can't understand me because you're not an addict/alcoholic" or "You'd drink/take drugs too if you had a job (a spouse) (a life) like mine." Essentially, the same kinds of therapeutic responses work in these situations. Counselors can join the resistance. They can agree they probably don't fully understand but are willing to listen and will try to understand. At the same time, they can offer empathy and assistance.

Some lesbians and gay men in this stage may act out in ultra stereotypical ways, using exaggerated mannerisms and attitudes—limp wrists, lisping, acting tough. In this way, they throw down the gauntlet to those around them, daring others to accept them. (It should be noted, however, that such mannerisms and behaviors could well be an integral part of this person's way of being. It is important to distinguish between acting out and being who one is.) Another client may throw a group into an uproar by describing sexual experiences in great detail. Another may act seductive and make provocative remarks to other clients.

In the face of such defiant behavior, it is important for the staff to keep cool and recognize that this is simply one way resistant, defensive alcoholics/addicts may express their feelings. Counselors need to remember to not take it personally. Nevertheless, such behavior is irritating and may stir up the homophobia of even the staunchest supporter of lesbian/gay rights.

Tolerance and understanding are the watchwords here, but firmness and a refusal to be bullied are also necessary so that counselors can help clients set limits on their behavior. The best approach is to face clients head-on about boundaries and about what is and is not acceptable in the particular program. Most important, counselors should help clients see that acting out their rage and defiance in self-destructive ways may result in serious harm to themselves and may keep them from continuing in treatment.

Another reaction and form of behavior common to this part of the stage is the "pink cloud syndrome": some lesbian/gay people who have discovered "being lesbian or gay is great" and have immersed themselves in being lesbian or gay may want to announce this news to everyone they know. This may or may not be a good idea.

The desire to share their news with everyone may be motivated by any number of different feelings—joy or anger or impulsive pouring out of anxiety. But whatever the motive, the action needs to be examined for its self-destructive potential. A number of lesbian/gay people in this stage want to tell their families, their friends, their fellow-workers, and indeed the whole world they are lesbian or gay. They need help in looking at the consequences of such disclosures, especially early in their recovery when their judgment may not be very sound.

The lesbian/gay person's wanting to share all is strikingly similar to newly recovering substance abusers who suddenly want the whole world to know they are in recovery. Such decisions often reflect poor judgment and poor reality testing about the possible consequences. Since substance abusers in early recovery tend to be confused and not to exercise good judgment, counselors need to help them evaluate their decisions to tell all. Acting as advocates and guides, counselors may also have to counsel their lesbian/gay clients to plan and carefully pace their coming out of the closet and help them think through the consequences and risks.

Part Two: Emersion

If people do not foreclose in the first part of this stage and manage to move forward, they gradually begin to come to terms with their feelings and circumstances. They begin to *emerge* from their oversimplified, either/or view of the world. In addition, as Cross (1971) puts it, they are able to begin "synthesizing . . . rage with reason" (p. 104).

In the immersion part of Stage Three, people's feelings tend to run them; in the emersion part, people gain increasing awareness of and control over their feelings and behavior. If they enter treatment while in the emersion part, they are likely to still be angry, but more controlled in their expression of that anger and less likely to be defiant and confrontive. Thus they are usually more amenable to treatment.

The Interface Between the Stages and Substance Abuse

Before moving on to a discussion of Stage Four, it is necessary here to note two particular findings of McNally's (1989) research. She found that none of the lesbians she interviewed were able to go beyond Stage Three while they were active in their addiction. Kus (1987, 1988) found the same results in his studies of gay men in recovery. The reasons seem to be that people's active addiction impairs their cognitive and affective abilities and their judgment, all of which are skills necessary to the process of self-actualization.

However, McNally and Finnegan (1992) also noted that once recovery began, it aided in the coming out process:

> There was a powerful *circular* interaction between the women's transformation of their alcoholic and their lesbian identities. Accepting and internalizing their alcoholic identities enabled them to explore, accept, and internalize their lesbian identities which, in turn, enabled them to continue to transform and strengthen their alcoholic identities. (p. 96)

Stage Four: Internalization—Identity Acceptance/Pride

> Individuals who successfully affiliate with AA have not merely found a technique which helps them stop drinking; they have also found a new life style and philosophy, a new perspective from which to view the world, a new identity.

> D. Rudy (1986, p. 19)

People who move into this stage have begun to accept rather than just acknowledge or tolerate their being lesbian or gay. They have begun to internalize, to own, their lesbian or gay male identity, just as recovering substance abusers who are in this stage have begun to accept their identity as substance abusers. Essentially, people in this stage must perform three major tasks:

1. Come to terms with the reality of their new identity
2. Recognize and acknowledge that they do not belong to the mainstream
3. Evaluate and reinterpret their values, roles, and interpersonal environment

Oftentimes this stage is characterized in part by a feeling of disenchantment: "Okay, so I'm a lesbian or a gay man. Now what?" The pink cloud disappears and they come back down to earth and reality. Different people react in different ways. Some lesbians and gays reject the mainstream and pull back from it because they feel they can never belong as accepted members. Others may stay immersed in lesbian or gay subcultures because they are afraid, or because they are caught up in contempt and hatred for the heterosexual world, or because they are stuck in a simplistic, either/or, "them or us" frame of mind.

Others, however, grow as a result of their experiences and become more satisfied with, more accepting of, themselves. They progress to a psychological state of being lesbian or gay, but do not go beyond that to reintegrate themselves in the larger world. Some lesbians and gay men internalize their acceptance of who they are, make a commitment to their new life, and move on to Stage Five.

Emotions Common to This Stage

People who are in Stage Four are likely to experience a wide range of emotions: depression, guilt, delight, grief, rage, relief. They may have been feeling these emotions before, but they are likely to experience them more deeply in this stage. This is a time of greater self-reflection. And it is a time of working through the feelings and coming to terms with who one is.

Some people raised in formal religions may feel guilty because homosexuality is viewed as a sin by the larger culture and by most churches. Others may feel guilty for their sexual behavior while drinking and/or using drugs. They may feel guilty for disappointing their parents by not being heterosexual, by not providing grandchildren, by not being acceptable. They may be experiencing a loss of closeness with their family and/or friends if they have decided not to come out to them. Or they may be experiencing an actual loss of their family and/or friends if they have been rejected because of their sexual orientation. Or if lesbians or gay males are parents, they may feel guilt for "inflicting this burden" on their children. If guilt about addiction accompanies these feelings, their force is compounded and people may end up feeling guilt and shame just for "being."

People may also feel great anger at the unfairness of experiencing such guilt simply because of who they are. Many continue to feel rage at being a stigmatized person in a harsh and unaccepting world. Some people get stuck in their rage. Many people, however, channel their anger into political and social activism and fight the injustices and cruelties of a homophobic system. Such activism is often a source of pride that can serve to motivate people in their growth process.

Some lesbians and gay men experience much grief and sadness over the loss of the great American dream of "normality," of belonging to the mainstream. At this stage, lesbians and gay men are coming to terms with the truth that they are, in fact, homosexuals and as such can never fully belong to the larger society of heterosexuals. They cannot even hold hands with a same-sex partner in a public place without evoking raised eyebrows or worse. And no matter how closeted, no matter how invisible they may choose to be, lesbians and gay men are always aware of their difference and what that may expose them to in the outer, homophobic world.

The process of mourning, the recognition that by claiming one's sexual orientation, one loses membership in the mainstream, occurs for lesbians and gay men in much the same way it does for substance abusers who mourn the loss of "normal" social drinking and recreational drug-taking and the loss of being "normal" social drinkers/drug takers. Lesbian/gay substance abusers must contend with a double dose of grief, and counselors need to recognize this, acknowledge it, and try to help clients deal with it. For lesbian/gay substance abusers, sometimes just knowing that another person has some sense of these losses can be incredibly helpful.

Although most people in this stage experience feelings of guilt, grief, and rage, often these feelings are tempered by delight and relief. Realizing who they are and having come this far in the process, people are frequently pleased by what they find about themselves and their lives. Many of them discover an emotional freedom to live their lives as they choose. They may opt for monogamy, nonmonogamy, polyamory; they may come out or choose not to; they may live among the larger society or in lesbian/gay sections of cities; they may mix with heterosexuals in their social lives or may socialize exclusively with other lesbians or gay men.

The point is that people who reach this stage of development must come to terms with what they feel, what their values will be, how they will live their lives. They must internalize these components of their identity and decide for themselves what kind of life they will live as a lesbian or gay man. These decisions and the identities chosen are incredibly diverse.

This process of coming to terms with self is often a difficult, complex, and slow one, but it can also be a highly rewarding one. People often confront truths about self and the world that enable them to grow beyond their original boundaries. This phenomenon is true both for lesbians and gay men and for recovering substance abusers. For many people, the struggles with the hardships of addiction and oppression bring about a transformation of spirit and allow them to develop a positive identity.

Treatment Issues

If lesbians or gay men are in this stage when they are in treatment, they may (like those in Stage Three) hurl such challenges as, "You can't possibly understand—you're not lesbian/gay!" Or they may be burdened by guilt over unresolved conflicts about the unacceptability of being lesbian or gay. Some may have escaped into socially sanctioned behavior such as marriage, but feel guilty because when they drank, they acted upon their homosexual desires.

Much of what counselors can do for lesbian/gay clients in this stage is to not take the anger personally, to be supportive in regard to the guilt, and to respect and assist with the mourning. If lesbian/gay-affirming clergypeople are available, they may be helpful to clients. Counselors may be able to help clients work through some of the guilt and anger by pointing out the promise of being "lesbian/gay, proud, and recovering." Giving lesbian/gay clients appropriate information to read may help and assisting them to meet healthy recovering lesbian/gay substance abusers can give them hope by providing role models for being both lesbian or gay and successfully recovering. Such role models convey the positive message that by being clean and sober, people can find their way. It is especially important at this stage to refer clients (if possible) to lesbian/gay AA/NA meetings.

Much has been said about grief, loss, and anger in this stage. But this is also a time of developing and getting in touch with a growing sense of pride which is often strongly flavored by anger. This pride frequently serves as a force that motivates people to become active in lesbian and gay causes. This activism tends to be healing because people are beginning to learn to channel their anger into constructive, positive efforts. Stage Four is a time of internalization of new, more positive values based on working through grief, loss, and guilt, and on the claiming of a newly developing self.

Stage Five: Synthesis/Commitment—Identity Synthesis

After successfully dealing with such difficult emotions as guilt, grief, and rage and such major issues as stigma and self-esteem, people in Stage Five basically accept themselves as lesbian or gay. They are able to feel pride about their identity. They have synthesized their experiences, worked through much of their internalized homophobia, and integrated being lesbian or gay into their personalities. That is, they have reached a point where being lesbian or gay is one part, albeit a very important part, of their overall, larger identity; it is one aspect of their Self. Their perspective tends to be, "Society has a problem because it's homophobic. But I am who I am, and I'm okay."

By this stage, people have usually worked through much of their guilt and grief. Many of them have channeled their anger into a commitment to work for the betterment of other lesbians and gays or into some other constructive activity. They have developed a positive sense of their lesbian or gay male identity and tend to see the world as divided less into lesbians/gays versus heterosexuals, more into supportive/nonsupportive people. For the most part, lesbians and gay men at this stage are out of the closet in most places and can generally permit who they really are to be seen and known.

They have reached a state of "self-actualization under conditions of oppression" (Cross, 1971, p. 109) which is quite different from that of Stage Three. This contrast may be compared to the difference between the often frantic quality of early recovery from addictions and the serenity of later recovery achieved by working the AA or NA program and working through issues in counseling or therapy. People tend to be more balanced, more centered, and more at peace with themselves.

Treatment Issues

When lesbians or gay males are in this stage, usually their addiction is what requires primary attention. Certainly, their being lesbian or gay is relevant to their treatment plan or their aftercare planning (e.g., getting in touch with the significant other; discussing sex and socializing in recovery; determining the best kinds of AA/NA meetings to attend). But when they tell counselors that being lesbian or gay does not constitute a particular problem or is not a major concern for them, they mean it. Even so, counselors should keep in mind McNally's (1989) and Kus' (1987, 1988) findings that lesbians and gay men were not able to progress past Stage Three while drinking or using drugs. Thus, while lesbians and gay men may feel like and believe they are in Stage Five (and may in fact exhibit many of the characteristics of this stage), many of them will probably need to go back and come out again in recovery.

A word of caution is in order here. It is tempting sometimes to draw on the ease and expertise of lesbians and gays who have accepted themselves and developed a positive identity. They can be great teachers for counselors to learn more about what being lesbian or gay means and great role models for other lesbians and gays who may be struggling with their sexual identity. While a little of this may be all right, gays and lesbians in Stage Five should not be used as teachers or "counselors" for others who are not so far along in their identity development process. Counselors always need to keep in mind that Stage Five people are really novices with regard to their addiction and need to be treated like the vulnerable beginners they are.

The Importance of the Model

We have presented a five-stage model of the formation of a positive lesbian or gay male identity. Primarily, we have done so to provide counselors with a logical, understandable perspective on what it means to be a lesbian or gay male in a homophobic/heterosexist society and to have to struggle with substance abuse.

THE PROCESS OF DEVELOPING
A POSITIVE BISEXUAL IDENTITY

Some say the dream of sexual liberation that took hold in the '60s is starting to be realized, and that the new bisexual movement is the beginning of an age of sexual identities that are as diverse and complicated and rich as the human beings they are describing.

L. Markowitz (1995, p. 23)

Introduction

One basic premise that underlies this discussion is that, like lesbians and gay men, bisexual women and men *do* come out, they need to come out (at least selectively), and they need to develop a sense of who they are (Bohan, 1996; Cass, 1990; Fox, 1995; Klein, 1993; Weinberg, Williams, and Pryor, 1994). Although bisexuals' processes of coming out and of developing a positive identity are in some ways similar to those that lesbians and gay men engage in, there are also important differences (Bohan, 1996; Fox, 1995; Klein, 1993). As Fox (1995) reports, Cass (1990), in a shift from her earlier position, describes "bisexual identity . . . as a viable sexual identity, with a *separate developmental pathway distinct from that characteristic of a homosexual identity*" [our italics] (pp. 52-53).

Some Considerations

Perhaps one of the most important differences is that bisexual people face not just homophobia, but *biphobia* (Bohan, 1996; Fox, 1995; Klein, 1993). Weinberg, Williams, and Pryor (1994) describe what bisexuals face as " 'double marginality.' Bisexuals always risk being stigmatized from two directions: by heterosexuals for their homosexual inclinations and by homosexuals for their heterosexual inclinations" (p. 190).

Bisexuals face a double set of tasks—they need to acknowledge and accept their homosexual feelings and attractions as an integral part of their identity, but they also need to acknowledge and accept their heterosexual feelings and attractions, no matter how they may act upon these two attractions (Fox, 1995). As Weinberg, Williams, and Pryor (1994) note, "Bisexuals found it impossible to make sense of their sexuality by adopting either a heterosexual or homosexual identity" (p. 291). In order to come to terms with their *bisexual identity*, bisexual women and men must come to terms with both the homosexual and the heterosexual components of that identity.

The difficulties inherent in these tasks are formidable. To come out as having homosexual attractions means to deal with all the homophobia lesbians and gay men must contend with. Thus, the models of lesbian/gay identity development can be helpful in understanding this process. However, to come out to lesbians and gay men as having heterosexual attractions may elicit heterophobic remarks and reactions and accusations of betrayal. Part of the hostility springs from some people's notion that bisexuals are carriers of AIDS (Weinberg, Williams, and Pryor, 1994), part from the fact that bisexuals can easily pass as and claim citizenship in the world of heterosexuals and thus can seek and receive "heterosexual privilege" (Bohan, 1996; Weinberg, Williams, and Pryor, 1994).

Three other differences should be noted here. Bisexuals tend to be older than lesbians or gay men when they come out, and they are less likely to be out than are lesbians or gay men (Bohan, 1996; Weinberg, Williams, and Pryor, 1994). In addition, bisexuals do not have the benefit of a large, powerful, well-established community in which they can find safety, encouragement, and role models to help them in developing their identity (Fox, 1995; Weinberg, Williams, and Pryor, 1994).

A Stage Model of Bisexual Identity Development

> We only become what we are by the radical and deep-seated refusal of that which others have made of us.
>
> Jean Paul Sartre

For all the flaws inherent in a linear, progressive stage model, it is still a helpful construct. It provides a perspective on the tasks and issues faced by people as they come to terms with identity. When applying this particular model, it is important to keep in mind several ideas. One is that bisexual people are extremely diverse and heterogeneous (Bohan, 1996; Fox, 1995). Another is that there seems to be no one, typical pattern of identity development for bisexuals. As Fox (1995) notes,

> A multidimensional theoretical approach to bisexual identity formation has developed which acknowledges that individuals arrive at their sexual identities by several possible routes and that sexual identity may remain constant or change as a normal response to both personal and social influences. (p. 58)

With these ideas as background, it is time to consider a model of bisexual identity development proposed by Weinberg, Williams, and Pryor (1994), based on their study of bisexual women and men. Although this model, like others, is limited, it nevertheless provides a helpful perspective.

Stage One: Initial Confusion

Confusion, self-doubt, and wrestling with questions about their sexual identity mark the first stage in people's process of defining themselves as bisexual. The primary source of confusion is the task of facing and understanding their feelings of attraction which do not match with their prior sexual attractions and orientation. Inherent in this process are a number of difficulties. One is not knowing how to handle the sexual feelings they are experiencing; another is fearing the loss of their long-term heterosexuality or homosexuality. Another is not knowing about the term "bisexual" to help them classify and organize their experiences by having a helpful label; and another is having difficulty with their internalized homophobia.

This period of initial confusion often lasts a number of years, as people struggle to find their way through their confusion and doubt and lack of information. For many people, it is a time of stress and uncertainty and people may turn to alcohol and/or other drugs to help them cope.

Stage Two: Finding and Applying the Label

In some ways, this stage is similar to the second stage of lesbian and gay male identity development—the Encounter Stage. Common to this stage are encounters with information and/or people's first homosexual or heterosexual experience. Thus, when people learn about the term for (and concept of) bisexuality, this encounter with a label that explains them to themselves often frees them to move ahead and define themselves as bisexual. Often this encounter brings with it great relief. But even when people have discovered the label, it is usually the sexual experience that gives the label its personal meaning.

Other people may find and apply the label as a result of not being able to continue to deny their powerful sexual feelings for both sexes. Others may reach this turning point by receiving encouragement from a partner who has already defined him or herself as bisexual or from organizations that are bisexual-identified.

Whatever the particular source of the encounter and subsequent labeling, the time involved in this stage is often quite long and the process a slow one. But as people come to think of themselves as bisexual, they then move on to the next stage.

Stage Three: Settling into the Identity

This phase may be likened to Cross' (1971) fourth stage of internalization. In this stage, people more confidently label themselves as bisexual, and their transition to their bisexual identity brings with it much greater self-acceptance. Other people's negative attitudes toward them and their sexual orientation are far less important. However, it is important to note that it is difficult, if not impossible, to fully internalize and develop one's identity while in the throes of substance abuse.

Interestingly, Weinberg, Williams, and Pryor (1994) note that even those who seem most secure in the identity seem not to have a sense of completion. Many of their respondents reported they might stop their bisexual behavior at some time in the future if they were to get deeply involved in a serious monogamous relationship.

Stage Four: Continued Uncertainty

This stage is what Bohan (1996) calls "The hallmark of bisexual identity formation . . ." (p. 107). It is a stage that is perhaps unique to bisexuals. Weinberg, Williams, and Pryor (1994) note that when bisexuals in the study were asked to describe this stage, the primary response was that even after having discovered and applied the label "bisexual" to themselves, and having come to the point of apparent self-acceptance, they still experienced continued intermittent periods of doubt and uncertainty regarding their sexual identity. (pp. 34-35)

A major reason for this uncertainty is "the lack of social validation and support that came with being a self-identified bisexual" (p. 35). Another reason is the stresses exerted by both worlds. The heterosexual world is as adamantly homophobic toward bisexuals as it is toward homosexuals. The homosexual world tends to pressure bisexuals to label and identify themselves as lesbian or gay and to engage in exclusively same-sex activity. Such stresses may contribute to substance abuse or, if people are in recovery, may pose significant relapse risks.

Troiden (1988) sums up the dilemma of bisexuals who are struggling to establish and maintain a solid, integrated sexual identity:

The unwillingness of people in general, and significant others in particular, to acknowledge bisexual preferences makes it more difficult to maintain and validate these preferences than heterosexual identities, which are supported continuously by sociocultural institutions, or homosexual identities, which are recognized by institutional arrangements within the homosexual community. (p. 82)

Treatment Issues

This model and the other information presented here point to the difficulties bisexual women and men face in society. Counselors need to have a sense of what their clients must deal with and what resources are available to help them in their efforts.

Although there has been some progress in society, perhaps some slight increase in tolerance, it is clear from this stage model that bisexuals have specific problems and concerns unique to them. This situation has various effects. It may be difficult or risky for bisexual clients to come out as bisexual even in a lesbian/gay affirmative treatment program. Clients may be unwilling to label themselves as bisexual because they fear counselors will not understand them or their concerns. They may be painfully confused about who they are, and their confusion may be compounded by substance abuse. They themselves may think "It's just a phase." Or they may fear that counselors will think that. They may be terrified that they really are "AIDS carriers." They may feel that there is no community for them, anywhere.

Some treatment issues counselors need to attend to are such matters as what AA/NA meetings their bisexual clients should attend. Some bisexuals feel more comfortable in "straight" meetings; some feel more comfortable in lesbian/gay meetings. If there are bisexual AA/NA meetings available, then clients may want to attend these. Essentially, the best way to deal with this issue is to ask clients where they would feel most comfortable.

Another question that should be raised is who bisexual clients might ask to sponsor them. Common sense, of course, will determine the answer. Who will clients relate to and who will provide the safest harbor? Again, choices will depend on what clients say about their comfort levels.

If possible, counselors should try to get recovering bisexual people to serve as links to the recovery community and as role models. In addition, providing reading materials on bisexual identity and recovery will help.

Basically, the same techniques of counseling apply here. Counselors need to address issues of clean and sober sex and socializing with bisexual clients. If clients are married, counselors need to be careful about family meetings. If bisexual clients are involved in a relationship outside the marriage, counselors need to respect clients' confidentiality and not pass judgment on them. On the other hand, counselors need to address whether bisexual clients' relationships are stressful and therefore possible relapse factors.

Whatever the specifics, counselors need to reassure bisexual clients that their recovery is paramount and that counselors will help in any way possible. Counselors themselves can serve as part of the support network for these clients by offering acceptance and by demonstrating knowledge and empathy about bisexual identity issues. In addition, bisexual clients can be guided to Internet resources and to other support networks where available.

SUMMARY

These two sections on stages of lesbian/gay and bisexual identity formation are put forth as a way of understanding what it means to come to terms with one's sexual identity in a hostile world. As Bohan (1996) notes,

> The intertwined tasks of identity development, stigma management, and coming out lie at the very heart of LGB experience; this complex process creates who one is and negotiates a place for that identity in a painfully hostile world. . . . To understand a given individual's experience as she or he comes to an LGB identity, one must first understand that individual; LGB identity formation is an addition to and not a substitute for the developmental process we all pursue. (p. 121)

Counselors who wish to help their lesbian, gay, or bisexual clients need both accurate information and a sense of their clients as individuals.

Chapter 9

Developing a Positive
Transgender Identity

Academics, shrinks, and feminist theorists have traveled through
our lives and problems like tourists on a junket. Picnicking on
our identities like flies at a free lunch, they have selected the
tastiest tidbits with which to illustrate a theory or push a book.
The fact that we are a community under fire, a people at risk, is
irrelevant to them.

R. A. Wilchins (1997, p. 22)

Rather than wallow in self-pity or boil in some cauldron of rage
and injustice, I think it's time for transgendered people to come
together under our own banner: a banner that would include
anyone who cares to admit their own gender ambiguities, a banner that includes all sexualities, races, ethnicities, religions,
ages, classes, and states of body, a banner of the Third.

K. Bornstein (1994, p. 98)

INTRODUCTION

In an article on working with transgendered people, Lev (1998,
p. 10) asks, "What is it like to go through life in a body that doesn't reflect, in a fundamental way, one's inner experience of self?" Another
question that can be asked is, "What is it like to discover that one's
birth sex does not reflect or fit one's inner experience of self?" These
questions lie at the heart of any discussion about transgendered people's attempts to discover, define, and come to terms with their true

identity. This process of defining self, of coming out (to self, to others), is central to how transgendered people can transform a stigmatized identity into a positive one.

Some Considerations

> I always felt when I looked in the mirror
> There was someone looking back from there
> Somewhere beyond where I could see
> Awaited the one who was the real me
> She's the girl beyond the glass.
>
> Quoted in Brown and Rounsley (1996, p. 228)

Counselors need to know at least the basics about gender identity and the issues involved in coming to terms with one's gender identity in order to help their substance abusing clients who are transgendered. The material presented here is intended to provide a working knowledge of this most complex and complicated subject.

Diversity

As Lev (1998) states, the term *transgender* "is an umbrella term to describe people who do not identify with the gendered assumptions that are placed on their physiological bodies" (p. 9). Bolin (1997) notes that

> the term transgendered . . . is inclusive of all people who cross-dress. It incorporates those who self-identify as male-to-female transsexuals, female-to-males, male transvestites, cross-dressers, and those who lie between the traditional identity of transsexual and male transvestite . . . (p. 28)

The term also refers to those people who take a middle course. These are people who may modify their bodies with hormones or surgery but choose to keep certain characteristics of their original sex (e.g., an FTM with a vagina or an MTF with a penis). Many of these transgendered people live part-time as one gender, part-time as the other. Many of them adopt an androgynous appearance (Denny, 1991).

Because of this enormous diversity, it is necessary to consider many factors or options when describing the process(es) by which transgendered people come to terms with who they are and define and affirm their transgender identity. As Bockting (1997) comments, "Options for identity management are no longer limited to adjustment in one and/or the other gender role, but include the possibility of affirming a unique transgender identity and role" (p. 51).

Transphobia

The primary reason transgendered people have to struggle when they engage in the process of defining their identity is transphobia—the fear, hatred, and revulsion toward anyone who transgresses traditional gender roles and expectations. Many people strongly resist and sometimes attack transgenderism because it calls into question the established, clear-cut, rigid system of distinctions about gender roles and the patriarchal system that is built on those roles. People of all kinds seem to have great trouble even considering, much less talking about, transgenderism because there is so much ignorance about it, so many myths and stereotypes about it. People tend to be frightened by something so different, by something that calls into question what they are used to, and by something that requires tolerating ambiguity.

Transgenderism makes people anxious because it creates uncertainties and doubts: it calls into question long-held beliefs—e.g., there are two, and only two, genders—man and woman—and biology determines destiny. Because their very existence questions or challenges such eternal verities, transgendered people are seen as sick, as evil, as unnatural. Many people view them as the enemy and believe they should be controlled and made to conform. Some people believe transgenders should be eliminated. Transgenders are also subjected to the harsh effects of homophobia because most of society mistakenly assumes that anyone who does not conform to "proper" gender roles and behavior is homosexual.

Transgendered people must also struggle with their own internalized transphobia. Having grown up in this society, they have internalized its transphobic values. Thus when they discover they are transgendered, they often turn that transphobia (and homophobia) on themselves and see themselves as wrong, bad, sick, disturbed, at fault (Brown and Rounsley, 1996; Marcel, 1998).

Sexual Orientation

Another difficult issue transgendered people must deal with is that of sexual orientation. This is a complex matter that must be addressed. Some transgendered people identify their sexual identity as heterosexual; some as bisexual; some as homosexual. Those who identify as having a homosexual or bisexual sexual identity are of course subject to homphobia and biphobia. But so too are transgendered people whose sexual identity is heterosexual because of the powerful myth that anyone who transgresses gender roles is really homosexual.

Counselors need to recognize that part of developing a gender identity involves coming to terms with sexual orientation. For counselors to be helpful, they need to understand the complexity of these matters. For instance, transsexuals who alter their birth sex to match their gender identity may *look* like they are homosexual because they are attracted to someone of the same biological sex.

For example, an FTM who does not have a penis may appear to be a woman with another woman—and therefore a lesbian. But the FTM person may *know* perfectly well that his gender identity is that of a man; therefore, he is a man with a woman in a heterosexual relationship. Another example is that of a biological female who cross-dresses as a man and whose gender identity is that of a man. He may be attracted to other men and therefore would identify as gay.

Another example is as follows: suppose a transsexual who transitions to the gender identity of a man has a lesbian partner. Does this now make this partner a heterosexual? No, it does not, because sexual identity is not dependent on gender. The woman partner who in this case is lesbian does not change her sexual identity because her partner changes gender.

Ultimately, what counselors need to do is *ask* their clients how they identify their sexual identity—heterosexual, bisexual, homosexual. Then counselors need to respond according to what clients tell them—*not* according to what anybody else *thinks* is so.

Owning One's Gender Identity

I have no interest in being part of a transgender or transsexual movement whose sole purpose is to belly up to the Big Table and help ourselves to yet another serving of Identity Pie, leaving in our wake some other, more marginalized group to carry on its own struggle alone.

R. A. Wilchins (1997, p. 87)

Since being transgendered is so reviled in this society, why would any TG person disclose this information? Lev (in press) provides one answer:

> The majority of transgender and transsexual people seeking counseling for gender dysphoria present in the awareness stage in great emotional pain. . . . Some clients exhibit an almost psychotic presentation due to the intensity of their fear and shame . . . . The fear of social punishment for transgressing social norms and the life-long presentation of a false self can also *create* numerous mental health problems . . . [which] might be better understood as reactive symptomology, and post-trauma sequelae. It is literally "crazy-making" to live a false self.

Bockting's (1997) answer is that

> *Intrapsychically,* self-affirmation of one's identity as transgender or transsexual alleviates shame and is experienced as liberating. The never-ending pressure of trying to conform to how a man or woman is supposed to look and behave, the fear of being "read," the secrecy and isolation associated with hiding one's transsexual status, can form an incredible burden that can be released through coming out. (p. 51)

Coming out as transgendered, while in some ways similar to the process experienced by lesbian, gay, and bisexual people, is quite different in other significant ways. Coming out for all these groups means coming to terms with, owning, and integrating who one is. But the process is also very different for transgendered people. Lev's (in press) term for this process is that of *transgender emergence,* a term that highlights the difference between coming out of hiding (the closet) and developing a gender identity as a transgendered person.

Transgender emergence differs in a number of basic ways. (1) For an LGB person, coming out "does not challenge people's basic notions about human nature . . ." (Brown and Rounsley, 1996, p. 119);

(2) transgender emergence means that a person's appearance, gender, and social roles will change, often radically; (3) LGB people can pass if they so choose; transgendered people are not likely to be able to pass once they begin their transition. As Brown and Rounsley (1996) point out, "The change from female to male [or vice versa] can't be hidden" (p. 120).

Brown and Rounsley (1996) add that "Nobody but transsexuals find themselves in the position of having to acquire the identity and social skills of a whole other gender. Moreover, they must do so without the benefit of years of socialization" (p. 128). Their emergence as a differently gendered person is also beset by ongoing threats of premature discovery and of punishment for transgressing powerful social norms. Unlike lesbians, gay men, and bisexuals who can usually pass at will, transgendered people in transition must learn as they go and their learning often exposes them to scrutiny and discovery.

Other factors are different. Transsexuals who go through the whole process of altering their bodies to conform them to the gender opposite from their birth gender must choose whether they will "assimilate"—i.e., pass as not transsexual—or will come out as transsexual. Other transgendered people "define themselves . . . doing as little or as much as they wish to their bodies, but stopping short of genital surgery" (Denny, 1997, p. 39). They may live full time in their chosen gender identity or part time in both genders or may define themselves as being neither gender (Bolin, 1997). They may or may not come out as transgendered except to a few chosen people. They may come out and become visible and politically active. Obviously, there are many different paths people can follow while still engaging in a process of developing a positive gender identity.

Substance Abuse

Transgendered people face tremendous obstacles to being or becoming who they truly are. Before discussing the process of developing a transgender identity, it is important to consider some of those obstacles.

Substance abuse problems are rife in this population. Valentine's study (1998) of intake records at the Gender Identity Project in New York City showed high rates of substance abuse in the transgender population: 27.1 percent reported alcohol abuse; 23.6 percent reported drug abuse. Clements' study (1999) of 392 MTF transgenders revealed the following: 16 percent had received treatment for alcohol problems, 23 percent for drug problems. The reports of noninjection drug use were staggering: for example, marijuana, 90 percent; cocaine, 66 percent; crack, 48 percent; heroin, 24 percent. Of the injection drug users, 84 percent used speed; 58 percent heroin; 54 percent cocaine.

Xavier's Washington, DC, study (2000) elicited reports from 34 percent of the participants that alcohol was a problem for them; 36 percent reported drugs to be a problem. Furthermore, 46 percent reported having sex while drunk or high; 22 percent cited drug use as their reason for engaging in unsafe sex. Marcel (1998) states that the rate of substance abuse in Boston is high. A 1995 study showed that 80 percent of the transgendered people surveyed reported using crack. In 1999, Kammerer, Mason, and Connors found that in Boston there were no alcohol or drug treatment groups or facilities specifically for transgendered people. In addition, when transgenders went to lesbian and/or gay twelve step meetings, there was often friction about their presence.

Other Problems

In addition to (and often intertwined with) substance abuse issues are other obstacles and problems. Transgendered people are targets of incredible oppression. In some ways they are the last large minority group that it's "okay" to oppress. In Clements' (1999) study of 392 MTF transgenders in San Francisco, 85 percent reported verbal abuse directed at them; 57 percent lost jobs; 39 percent had trouble getting adequate health care; 30 percent reported physical abuse; and 21 percent had lost their place to live because they were transgendered. This report is of conditions in what is considered to be one of the most liberal cities in the country.

Accounts about Boston mirror the Clements study (1999). Marcel (1998) reports that transgendered people are subject to discrimination and social bias that engenders much shame and self-doubt. Valentine's (1998) report from New York City echoes those from San Francisco and Boston. He found that transgendered people face great obstacles—not so much from inner turmoil (gender dysphoria/discomfort) but from the tremendous outer pressures of discrimination against them. These are the transphobic views that people who do not conform to the sex and gender determined by their body are deviant and should be punished.

The results of this oppression are appalling. Thirty-five percent of the people in Xavier's study (2000) reported having suicidal ideation; almost half of them stated they had attempted suicide. Sixty-four percent attributed their suicidal ideation to gender issues. Other effects were that 30 percent in Xavier's study reported no income; 32 percent reported income under $10,000. Frequently, coming out as transgendered means loss of job and income. Brown and Rounsley (1996) note that for transsexuals, coming out may well lead to job loss.

One of the more terrible results of acknowledging one's gender identity can be a loss of jobs, families, friends and/or partners that make up one's social structure (see Israel and Tarver, 1997). As Marcel's Transgender Education Network study (1998) notes, "Without a social structure many TS/TG people, especially those from minority communities and low-income families, turn to the sex industry for financial survival and sexual relationships . . ." (p. 9).

Nemoto et al.'s (1998) findings, from their study of MTF transgenders of color, were similar: "Commercial sex work provided a common means for economic survival for participants" (p. 2). McGowan's (1999) needs assessment also notes "the economic necessity for . . . [some of the participants] to engage in sex work for income" (p. 30).

Being sex workers puts people at high risk. Nemoto et al. (1998) note that "Sex work offers a means to support drug use, and sex becomes riskier when using drugs" (p. 2). Marcel (1998) comments that "those who work in the sex industry are at high risk for substance abuse because of the prevalence of drugs and alcohol in this environment" (p. 9). Reback and Lombardi's study (1999) of Los Angeles TGs reveals that those engaged in sex work showed much higher percentages of alcohol/drug use than non-sex workers. For example, 51 percent of sex workers versus 29 percent of non-sex workers reported alcohol use; 25 percent versus 3 percent reported crack use. Reback and Lombardi (1999) also found that sex workers were more likely to inject drugs (8 percent versus 2 percent) and their crystal meth use was high.

Other risks involved in sex work are violence inflicted by customers (Marcel, 2000; Nemoto et al., 1998). In Clements' study (1999), 80 percent of the 392 MTF transgenders interviewed reported a history of sex work; 59 percent revealed a history of being raped. Furthermore, unprotected sex is common (Nemoto et al., 1998). One of the worst aspects of these conditions is that "Commercial sex and drug use usually start during adolescence or early adulthood" (Nemoto et al., 1998, p. 1). And Goodrum (2000) points out that "TG youth living on the streets are more likely than any other youth to engage in prostitution or consensual sex with a variety of partners without using safe sex techniques" (Internet). Valentine's findings (1998) point to one possible contributor to the youth of participants: 80 percent of the 357 clients became aware they were transgendered when they were between the ages of one and eleven; 13.2 percent became aware between twelve and eighteen. Many young people feel they have no recourse but to run away to large cities to escape the transphobia they face at home and in school, but such actions expose them to the drug and sex trades of the streets.

There are a number of other risks to which all transgenders (not just those who are sex workers) are vulnerable. For example, Xavier (2000) found that 58 percent of the transgenders surveyed reported getting hormones from non-medical sources. Eighty-five percent of Clements' (1999) respondents reported "unprotected receptive anal sex" (p. 1). Many report suicidal ideation and suicide attempts (Lev, in press; Marcel, 2000; Xavier, 2000). Brown and Rounsley (1996) note that at least 70 percent of Brown's transsexual patients reported suicidal ideation. Depression and PTSD resulting from such hate crimes as physical/sexual abuse (e.g., rape, beatings) and from transphobia are also frequent problems (Lev, in press; JSI Research and Training Institute, 2000).

Compounding these problems and issues is an overriding one—that transgendered people are usually given poor, transphobic treatment by the medical/psychiatric establishment or are frequently denied access to health care and substance abuse treatment altogether (Kammerer, Mason, and Connors, 1999; JSI Research and Training Institute, 2000).

With these obstacles, problems, and issues in mind, it is time to consider the process transgendered people can engage in to develop their transgender identity.

THE PROCESS OF DEVELOPING A POSITIVE TRANSGENDER IDENTITY

> I secretly believe that "transgender" is so popular because people are more comfortable saying it out loud than "transsexual," which—if you hold the word up in the mirror and read it backward—has sex cleverly embedded in it.
>
> R. A. Wilchins (1997, p. 16)

This discussion will draw on two models for viewing the process of developing a positive transgender identity. One is a model describing the "four major tasks underlying a full personal rebirth, a full sense of inner renewal, as a gender-transformed person" (Etscovitz, 1997, p. 486). The other is a stage model of transgender emergence developed by Lev (in press) based on her long-term clinical experience. The overarching reference for this whole discussion, however, is the identity model developed by Cross (1971).

The following should be noted: this discussion deals in some detail with complex and complicated matters and thus may seem overwhelming. However, it is not necessary to know all of this information in detail, but only to have some awareness of it and some sense of how it applies to clients. It is also important to keep in mind that it is difficult and problematic for anyone to navigate a social, emotional, developmental process of any kind when the person is drinking and/or taking drugs.

The Task Model

> It is useful to have the capacity for uncertainty and self-doubt built into true self feeling. It is a wonderful moment when one can say, "Aha, so that's who I really am." What a relief to catch on, to have a sense of knowing.
>
> M. Eigen (1996, p. 167)

Etscovitz (1997) presents a linear four-task model for developing the positive identity of a "gender-transformed" person. [As a reminder, the matching stages from Cross' (1971) model are appended after each task.]

The four tasks are:

1. *Self-Recognition (Naming It)* involves becoming aware of being transgendered, different. This task (as do all the others) takes a long time and requires giving up one's denial. Its central focus is on discovering and determining "just what kind of transgendered person one really is, whether transvestite, transgenderist, or transsexual" (p. 486). [Cross, Stages 1 and 2: Preencounter and Encounter]
2. *Self-Acceptance (Claiming It)* involves accepting the fact that one is different—truly transgendered—and coming to accept and affirm oneself as transgendered. Gradually the person works through and lessens negative feelings about self such as shame and self-loathing. [Cross, Stage 3: Immersion/Emersion]
3. *Self-Integration (Taming It)* This task is "more complicated and challenging" and involves "gaining meaningful control of one's life as a whole [which] constitute[s] the task of self-integration" (p. 487). Integration involves, for example, managing to keep one's cross-dressing secret, if necessary; or an FTM living and working as a male but retaining the legal and anatomical status of a female; or handling "the radical personal and social changes" (p. 487) brought on by reassignment surgery. [Cross, Stage 4: Internalization]
4. *Self-Transcendence (Framing It)* means that "one has to find, to create, to frame a larger reality within which the struggles take place and at the same time hold the potential for resolution" (p. 487). In effect, people need to find a spiritual and existential base for their identity. [Cross, Stage 5: Synthesis]

As Etscovitz (1997) explains, each task involves a three-part process: "reaching in"—looking within self; "reaching out"—relating to and sharing with others; and "reaching up"—finding "a wider purpose in life, a wider meaning" (p. 488). It should be noted that this process follows the steps necessary to reach the goals at the heart of all identity—"a sense both of internal coherence and meaningful relatedness to the real world" (Josselson, 1987, pp. 12-13).

Although this task model is not particularly detailed, it is helpful as a way of looking at the basic process that transgendered people go through in order to accept their gender identity and develop a positive sense of that identity.

TRANSGENDER EMERGENCE: A DEVELOPMENTAL MODEL

I do not know whether I was then a man dreaming I was a butterfly, or whether I am now a butterfly dreaming I am a man.

Chuang Tzu
The Tai Te Ching:
A New Translation with Commentary (1989)

On the basis of her clinical experience, Lev (in press) has formulated a six stage model of transgender emergence, what she calls "a general blueprint to describe the process of gender identity acceptance." This model is presented here. We thank her for her generosity in letting us cite from her work while it is still in manuscript form and in giving us such helpful feedback.

To make clear and to highlight the interrelationships among three paradigms, the equivalent tasks from the Etscovitzs task model and the corresponding stages from Cross' model are appended to Lev's stages which are discussed and presented here. In addition, where appropriate, we have added our own comments about substance abuse and what counselors can do to help.

The Six Stages of Lev's Emergence Model

Stage One: Awareness

In the early part of this stage, people are either unaware, not conscious of, or not attending to their gender incongruity or their difference. This lack of conscious awareness may be the result of people's dissociating from their feelings about their gender or their denying what they have "known" (on some level) for a long time. This point in the process corresponds to Cross' Stage 1: Preencounter, when people are in denial although there may well be hints of difference. Or as Cass (1979, 1984, 1992) puts it, people have not yet ascribed personal meaning to their experiences and feelings.

In order to avoid dealing with their possible differentness or to stay in a state of denial, people may foreclose (Cass, 1979) on awareness by doing a variety of things—joining a religion, getting married, trying aversion therapy or other forms of behavior modification, controlling their transgendered behaviors (e.g., cross-dressing in secret), purging opposite gender clothing (akin to throwing out all the liquor and/or drugs in one's possession), joining a hidden or secret community (e.g., cross-dressers).

A rather common method of foreclosure is that of using alcohol and/or other drugs as a bulwark against consciousness. As is well known, the denial and dissociation that travel with substance use and abuse tend to synergize with the denial and dissociation common to this stage.

If, however, something happens to push people into awareness of feeling and *being* different, then they are likely to experience great distress. This corresponds to Cross' Stage 2: Encounter, in which people encounter themselves because something has broken through their denial. Etscovitz's task here is, of course, Self-Recognition.

Because "the emergence process for differently gendered people" (Lev, in press) means going against societal (and familial) expectations, when people begin to encounter their true selves, they experience the shock of gender dysphoria. As Lev (in press) states, "For most people, awareness of their gender incongruity is experienced as a gender dysphoria, a profound discomfort with their birth sex and confusion over what this means."

Clearly, this part of this stage is a time of tremendous vulnerability, as is also true for LGB people who are in Cross' Stage Two: Encounter. It is often a terrifying psychic emergency that "can create chaos and upheaval" (Lev, in press) (much like the shocking discovery of one's addiction) and can cause emotional flooding (Khantzian, 1981; Krystal, 1988). The shock of discovery "mimics the symptomology present in a PTSD diagnosis" (Lev, in press). Although some people experience joy and some have known all along but not dealt with their truth, many experience tremendous emotional distress, some suffer psychotic breaks, some do not survive. If people are using alcohol and/or other drugs at this juncture, they may increase their use dangerously. If they are in recovery, they may be in grave danger of relapse.

Counselors need to be aware of the great vulnerability that people in this part of this stage experience and need to be supportive and help clients *consider* tapping into resources such as the Internet. But clients should not be pushed to do any of this because such contacts may raise anxiety to intolerable levels, thus putting people at risk of increased substance use or relapse if they are recovering. As Lev (in press) notes, "The therapist brings with him or her immense power of authority, and the modeling of acceptance, kindness and ease can help assuage the intensity of the dysphoria."

Stage Two: Seeking Information/Reaching Out

As Lev (in press) notes, in this stage of the emergence process,

> Transgender people begin seeking information about transgenderism and reaching out to find others like themselves. . . . Unlike Stage One, which is often overwhelming and exhausting, Stage Two is more emotionally exhilarating and transformative.

Etscovitz's matching task is still that of Self-Recognition.

Seeking Information. The biggest single source of transgender information, validation, affirmation, and support is the Internet. And many transgendered people in this stage immerse themselves in its resources such as articles, personal narratives, political discussions, professional journals, clinical/medical information, chat rooms, lists of conferences and meetings. In addition, there has been a flood of books about transgenderism in recent years which help people begin to understand and sort out their issues and find suggestions for further action. As Lev (in press) notes, "Amassing information is essential to the client emerging as transgender, and is the first step in the development of a fully integrated identity." This part of Lev's stage is similar to part one of Cross' Stage 3: Immersion.

Reaching Out. "Transgender people begin to reach out to others in this stage . . . [an action that] is the single most difficult task of their lives." This difficulty springs from the fear people feel about being "found out," a fear they have usually battled with for much of their lives.

They may reach out by joining chat rooms on the Internet or corresponding via e-mail. Some attend transgender meetings or support groups. Some may go to transgender bars or clubs. Some may attend conferences.

Whatever path people may take, they experience this part of this stage in various ways. When they meet and mix with others who are transgendered, some people are brought up short by their internalized transphobia. Unless they work it through, they will tend to reject other transgendered people, will not socialize or mix with them, or will feel hostile toward them. This rejection constitutes a foreclosure so that there need be no further exploration. Rejection is also a way of defending against identifying with others and thereby acknowledging one's transgendered state.

Some people, however, feel great relief upon finding others like them. It is as if they have found what they were seeking all their lives, even when they did not realize their quest. Lev (in press) observes that some people leap into their new life, totally immersing themselves in it:

> assimilating new information and making new friends—with vigor and speed. They embrace their new identity, and their new community, completely and thoroughly, separating themselves from their former lives.

Lev (in press) points out that people in this state may take great risks because they are caught up in the thrill and excitement of their discovery.

> Fathers may begin cross-dressing at home, in front of children who are confused and frightened. Husbands may begin discussing starting hormones with wives who are still bitter and angry over the disclosure. Some people agree to meet strangers from a chat room without adequate thought about safety. . . . Clients seek out black market hormones, trying to circumvent the system, potentially endangering their health.

Part One of Cross' Stage Three: Immersion accurately describes this phenomenon of impulsivity, overeagerness, and lack of caution. As people suddenly get free of what are often lifelong chains of oppression and repression, they frequently feel impelled to leap ahead, without much forethought.

The interfaces of alcohol/drug use with this tendency to leap without looking are clear. Substance use (and/or abuse) feeds impulsivity and poor judgment. Furthermore, people who are marginalized and stigmatized often use alcohol and/or other drugs as ways to connect with others. Thus transgendered people at this point may immerse themselves in the bar scenes or parties where substance use and abuse may be rampant.

The counselor's role is to counterbalance this lack of caution. Counselors need to help clients slow down, exercise caution, pace themselves, and move ahead with "deliberate speed." As Lev (in press) comments, "The clinician's role during this stage is to stabilize the process." They can help clients examine the possible consequences of their behavior and evaluate the possible risks. If there are alcohol/drug-free spaces and events available, counselors can recommend them. They might also help clients to connect with clean and sober transgendered people.

If counselors can win their clients' trust, they are in a position to advise moving slowly and to have clients perhaps heed that advice. It is important to remember, however, that some clients will not listen to anybody's words of caution and will impulsively plunge ahead. In that case, counselors can be helpful by being supportive and by providing clients with a fall-back position if their actions backfire.

Stage Three: Disclosure to Significant Others

This stage is akin to the second part of Cross' Stage Three: Emersion. People are emerging from their immersed, impulsive state and beginning to look around. Etscovitz's matching task is that of Self-Acceptance but broadened now to include seeking acceptance from others. Transgendered people in this stage are caught between wanting to share who they really are even though they know how great a risk that may be and knowing how painful this information may be for those they tell.

As Lev (in press) notes, this may well be the most difficult and painful part of people's emergence process. The prospect of disclosing is often terrifying, and some people avoid doing so. Some are "forced out" without their consent. Others choose to disclose who they truly are to others.

Obviously, one way people may choose to deal with stress is to use alcohol and/or other drugs. It is a major coping tool that supplies feelings of courage, soothes anxiety, and blurs sharp edges. Unfortunately, it also splits people's feelings off from their judgment and makes it difficult to evaluate the consequences of behavior. If people are in recovery at this point, the stress may put them at risk for relapse.

Significant others and family members react with a range of feelings when they are told. Almost always, disclosure shakes people up—even if they have suspected or known for a long time. They may experience shock, fear, rage, confusion, pain, love, caring. They may blame the transgendered person or themselves for what is happening. Counselors need to exercise great care in their interaction with Significant Others (SO). If there are counseling sessions with SOs or lectures/groups in a family program, counselors must be very careful to adopt an even-handed and non-aligning stance. Counselors need to check the possibility of countertransferential responses such as favoring their transgendered client and downplaying the SO's feelings or concerns or aligning themselves with SOs.

As Lev (in press) notes, at this stage, transgendered people are often extremely self-centered, obsessive, compulsive, impulsive, depressed, and sometimes suicidal. In terms of differential diagnosis, it helps to remember that substance abuse feeds and intensifies these emotional states and that these same states are generated by the addiction.

Although many transgendered people reach this stage in young or later adulthood, no matter what their chronological age may be, they tend to exhibit adolescent behavior and need guidance, support, and stabilizing from counselors. This will likely include help in containing impulsivity and support for slowing down their exploration of possibilities.

Stage Four: Exploration—Identity and Self-Labeling

This stage, like Cross' Stage Four: Internalization, is marked by exploration. Lev (in press) explains that

> transgender people begin to explore the meaning of their transgenderism and search for a label or identity that best explains who they are. The key issue . . . is the acceptance and resolution of their gender dysphoria and a developing comfort with the

gender identity. . . . This is the stage where transgender people come to terms with a great truth about who they are.

The matching basic task is one of Self-Integration (Etscovitz, 1997). This is, of course, both joyful and stressful. And once again, the demons of stress may call to people for relief through alcohol and/or other drugs.

As people work on integrating and consolidating their identity, they explore what this new life may involve. They begin to recognize that there are many ways to be transgendered, and they begin asking powerful questions such as, "Who am I?" and "What is the meaning of my life?"

As a part of this quest for meaning, people investigate what to call themselves—for example, transwoman/transman, queer transgender, transsexual, transvestite, gender variant, bigendered, transgendered lesbian or gay man or bisexual. Another part of this stage is the "exploration of roles, clothing, mannerisms in ways that are exciting but can also be frightening" (Lev, in press).

Transgendered people may begin exploring more cross-dressing and may experiment with public experiences with some version of cross-dressing. Transgenders may experiment with appearing more feminine or masculine without necessarily changing gender role. They may engage in living part-time in the other gender role.

As Lev (in press) notes, in this stage,

> transgender people begin to explore their future options for transition and its impact on loved ones and vocational/financial needs. Many people decide not to take hormones or transition full-time, although they may consider these options.

Counselors need to support their clients' choices. But they need to be aware that there can be pressures on people from within the transgender community to change and move ahead. Counselors may therefore need to help clients "slow down" or not yield to pressure and instead to explore carefully what clients want and what is best for them.

As transgenders begin to have these "real-life" experiences they "begin to understand the real life costs of changing gender" (Lev, in press). This can, of course, be a very difficult experience.

"All transsexuals lose something once they come out" (MTF patient quoted in Brown and Rounsley, 1996, p. 126). Often people experience terrible losses—jobs, homes, partners, children, families. Such losses can be destabilizing and destructive—leading possibly to substance abuse, possibly to relapse if people are in recovery, possibly to commercial sex work as a means of survival.

As Lev (in press) notes, "The consequences for exploring gender transition can be devastating . . . [such as] internalized hatred and confusion about their gender identity, the disappointment and criticisms of family and friends, or . . . concurrent mental health concerns . . ."

Because of these and other factors, this can be a very dangerous time. People may experience depression, intense guilt, suicidal ideation, and substance use may intensify into abuse. Like others suffering from PTSD, people may not adequately protect themselves or may be hypervigilant and thereby draw dangerous attention to themselves.

Counselors, of course, need to assist by being empathic and supportive of transgendered people's struggles to integrate and consolidate their new identity. In addition, counselors need to know where to refer clients and what resources are available. Obviously, this is a crucial time for many transgendered people in terms of substance abuse and recovery, and counselors need to address both substance abuse and the life issues their clients may be facing. ·

*Stage Five: Exploring Transition
and Possible Body Modification*

The corresponding stage of Cross' model is still his Stage Four: Internalization because this continues to be a time of self-integration and internalization of facets of identity. This is "a time of consolidating gender presentation and making decisions about body modification" (Lev, in press). As Brown and Rounsley (1996) note, transsexuals

> must create a new identity. . . . They cannot simply emerge "full blown" as the other gender. They must rebuild themselves psychologically, socially, and interpersonally by integrating elements of their old self into the new one. (p. 127)

Part of this process involves changes brought about by such measures as electrolysis, hormones, and the continued "real-life test."

For transsexuals and some transgenders, passing as the other gender becomes extremely important while at the same time difficult when people are new at it and are in an "in between" state. Particular issues arise in this stage because people are having to deal with definite restrictions placed on those who are transgendered.

Traditionally, the medical establishment would not give hormone or surgical assistance to people unless they were willing to alter their bodies completely. Yet a number of transgendered people wish to engage in mixed gender presentation. Some want hormones to make themselves more like the opposite gender but are unwilling to have sex reassignment surgery. But getting hormones without surgery has traditionally been legally not possible.

This often puts at risk people who urgently desire hormones to bring about their transformation. As Lombardi and van Servellen (2000) point out, this inability to obtain hormones legally drives many people to acquire them illegally. This can be dangerous because "the networks involved with illicit hormone use may overlap with illicit drugs and HIV risk behavior" (p. 294). In addition, self-injecting hormones mimics injection drug use.

Furthermore, hormones alter mood, so counselors need to warn clients to watch for this whether clients are still using alcohol/drugs or are in recovery. Certainly, research is needed to guide addiction professionals and gender identity specialists about the possible hazards of hormone use coupled with substance abuse or recovery. Counselors need to be aware of these issues because they are so tied to substance abuse and recovery.

Decisions about hormones, surgery, and how to live one's life are central to the choices people make. Some people choose to completely alter their physical bodies with sex reassignment surgery, some only partially (e.g., an FTM has a mastectomy but retains the vagina). But it is important to recognize that "Once body modifications begin, transgender people are forced out of the closet—a critical difference between coming out gay and emerging transgendered" (Lev, in press).

Some people choose not to alter their body, but cross-dress and at times present as the opposite gender. Some people choose to follow a middle way—neither female nor male, but both/and. As Lev (in press) notes, it is quite possible to have an integrated self without being one gender or the other. But all transgendered people need to be free to make choices. Counselors can help greatly by advocating for and supporting their clients during these difficult times.

Stage Six: Synthesis

This is the final stage of Lev's model and corresponds to Cross' Stage Five: Synthesis. Etscovitz's corresponding task is the fourth one of Self-Transcendence. In effect, transgendered people in this stage have integrated their gender identity into their overall identity. "They have become comfortable with who they are, and where they stand in the transgendered continuum" (Lev, in press).

What this means depends of course on each person's individual goal for self. The person may identify as woman or man, transwoman or transman; as transsexual, transvestite; as queer transgender; transgendered lesbian, gay man, or bisexual, or transgendered heterosexual. But whatever people name themselves, they are able to say, "I am who I am." As Lev (in press) puts it,

> They have synthesized this key element of their identity—their gender identity—into the greater whole of who they are. . . . The development of their gender identity . . . has finally caught up with the rest of their development.

A Word of Caution

If transgendered people have been actively substance abusing during their attempts to engage in this process of gender identity development, qualitative research on lesbians (McNally, 1989) and on gay men (Kus, 1987, 1988, 1990) suggests that substance abuse impairs the cognitive and affective skills utilized in developmental processes. Thus they would not have been able to fully develop a positive identity. As Kus (1990) notes, "self-acceptance of a gay or lesbian identity does not occur until sobriety is chosen and lived" (p. 41).

The primary reason for this finding is that substance abuse impairs the cognitive and affective skills needed to work through and come to terms with the ideas and emotions inherent in the process of developing a positive stigmatized identity. No research has been conducted regarding transgendered substance abusers' development of a positive identity, and much needs to be done in this area. But it seems likely that transgendered people who are substance abusers might need to go back to Lev's Stage Two (Cross' Stage Three: Immersion) and re-do and re-think their identity development when they are in recovery.

SUMMARY

The above description of Lev's (in press) stage model is intended as a suggested perspective on the process transgendered people engage in as they figure out and come to terms with who they are, as they emerge as transgendered. The model (and the other task model) is not a definitive one, but it is a good working one for counselors to be familiar with.

In considering this model, it may be helpful to relate back to the Cross model as it applies to lesbians and gay men. It is also helpful to remember that no matter how different and unfamiliar transgender issues may seem, counselors can draw on what they learn here and combine that knowledge with their substance abuse expertise to provide good treatment to their transgendered clients.

Epilogue

I wanted a perfect ending—Now I've learned, the hard way, that some poems don't rhyme, and some stories don't have a clear beginning, middle, and end. Life is about not knowing, having to change, taking the moment and making the best of it.

Gilda Radner
It's Always Something (1989)

As we look back over this book, we are struck by how rich and complex this whole subject truly is. But we are also very aware of how difficult it is to capture or to do justice to the glorious complexity, diversity, and infinite variety of human experience. At best, we hope that this book will serve to introduce the reader to some of the concerns and issues of lesbian, gay, bisexual, and transgendered people, particularly those who are trying to recover or who are recovering from substance abuse. In addition, hopefully it will provide the reader with some understanding of and some practical suggestions and guidelines for counseling lesbian, gay, bisexual, and transgendered substance abusers.

In conclusion, we wish to make some suggestions and comments.

1. This is just a book. It is just one book. It is a start, but in order to more fully comprehend the complex issues LGBT people face and to become more comfortable working with them, counselors need to read other books and articles. Even more important, perhaps, is getting to know some lesbians, gay men, bisexuals, and transgender people in order to begin to dissolve the many myths and stereotypes everyone in this culture has learned. In effect, it is important to look upon working in the substance abuse field as an on-going educational process.

2. Although this book has focused on difference and diversity, it is important to realize that in many ways lesbians, gay men, bisexuals, and transgenders are not so different from counselors or anybody else and there are many similarities among all people.

Counselors should keep in mind that they have many skills whose value and effectiveness do not lessen in the face of what are sometimes unfamiliar experiences or issues of LGBT clients. Furthermore, successful treatment relies much more on the constructive and accepting attitudes of the caregivers than on their technical abilities.

3. At the same time, however, it is important to remember that many people (both clients and treatment providers) confuse other problems with LGBT gender identity and sexual orientation. It is not uncommon for people to mistakenly view such matters as sexual compulsiveness, PTSD, intimacy problems, sexual abuse, and psychiatric problems as gender identity or sexual orientation issues. Thus it becomes critically important to be able to make clear, nonjudgmental, accurate diagnoses and treatment plans. For example, just because someone is lesbian, gay, bisexual, or transgendered does not mean that he or she will have emotional problems. Many of the symptoms people present may be related to their substance abuse and/or their struggles with oppression. Well-informed differential diagnoses are crucial.

4. Because of this need for proficient diagnostic skills and because such skills are always subject to bias and human error, it is imperative that counselors seek and receive good, nonhomo/bi/transphobic supervision and further training. It is also very important to have staff support.

5. Too often people in the substance abuse prevention/treatment field mistrust and resist other professionals' working with people affected by substance abuse. But these other professionals *can* learn about substance abuse and effectively treat people. Because lesbians, gay men, bisexuals, and transgendered people have often received (and often continue to receive) such poor treatment, professionals, especially those who are lesbian, gay male, bisexual, and transgendered, need to be encouraged to learn about substance abuse and ways to treat it. The field needs the expertise and the spirit of these professionals.

6. All counselors need to become advocates. They need to speak out against homo/bi/transphobia wherever they encounter it, and they need to advocate for their clients' best interests. Oftentimes the counselors are the only people who will stand by their clients in the face of terrible prejudice and oppression.

7. All counselors and administrators need to raise their consciousness about and to advocate for other minority groups. The substance abuse prevention/treatment field has tended to be a conservative, white, straight, middle class, often male field. But that does not adequately represent the people who are in need of the professionals in this field. The field needs many more African Americans; lesbians, gay men, bisexuals, and transgendered people; women; Latino/as, Native Americans, Asians. It needs them in every facet of the system—administration, treatment, prevention, education, training. In addition, there is a need to make sure that racism, classism, sexism, ageism, ethnocentrism, heterosexism, and homo/bi/transphobia are addressed, challenged, and hopefully eradicated *everywhere.*

8. Finally, it is important to keep in mind that there are many stories—not just one or two. Kinsey created his now-famous scale in order to describe and accommodate the tremendous diversity of people's experiences. Too often, however, this culture views people in destructively narrow and limiting ways because it is so afraid of diversity and difference. Unfortunately, psychiatry and psychology tend to support such narrow perspectives by classifying people as normal or abnormal. But the truth is that each of us has his or her own stories, and all people want to be accepted and responded to according to who they are as individuals. It is our responsibility, then, to make sure that we as treatment providers and concerned human beings recognize, respect, and celebrate every individual's particular story.

The need for good treatment and the results of receiving it are echoed in these recovering people's words:

> It took me maybe a year and a half to feel really comfortable with my alcoholism and my new identity and to start to build another identity from the scraps of the old one. (p. 165)

> I never liked myself before and during my drinking. I never wanted to be who I was or where I was from the time I was a child. I never liked myself at all, but I love myself today. I'm the only me I've got, and I'm glad I've got me. (p. 169)

Research participants
(Quoted in McNally, 1989)

Appendix A

Glossary

androgyny: A gender identity in which people adopt both male and female characteristics or neither. They may exhibit mannerisms of both genders, they may wear gender-neutral clothes, and/or they may wish to be identified as neither gender or as both. Their reasons for identifying themselves as androgynous may be to meet their identity needs or to take a political stand challenging society's stereotypes (Israel and Tarver, 1997; Marcel, 1998).

asexual: Someone who is not sexually attracted to anybody and is not involved in any sexual behavior.

biphobia: Fear, anger, contempt, hatred, mistrust directed at bisexuals—from both heterosexual *and* homosexual people.

bisexual: One whose sexual/affectional attractions are to persons of both genders.

circuit party: Weekend dance party ordinarily attended by gay and bisexual men. Substance use and abuse is a common feature. (*See* RAVE).

coming out: Process of revealing one's sexual orientation or gender identity, both to self and to others.

countertransference: All the counselors' responses to clients. Some of these responses are conscious ones in reaction to what clients do. These are considered forms of *objective* countertransference because there is an objective reality involved. *Subjective* countertransference involves preconscious or unconscious responses to clients which are based on unresolved issues from the counselors' past and which, therefore, are to some degree not appropriate to the current reality of the counseling relationship.

cross-dressers: Transvestites—although cross-dresser is the preferred term—are those who dress in the clothing of the opposite gender. They ordinarily do not want to change their bodies, but wish to express masculine/feminine (or both together) aspects of themselves through their clothing. People cross-dress for a variety of reasons: to become sexually aroused, to make political statements, to entertain, to liberate repressed feelings, to

224 COUNSELING LGBT SUBSTANCE ABUSERS

play (known among GBT men as "camp" and dressing in drag). Most cross-dressers do not experience their gender as incongruent with their expression. Many male-to-female cross-dressers are heterosexual; a number are gay and bisexual men. Some lesbians cross-dress, also.

crystal (crystal methamphetamine): Central nervous system stimulant that heightens mood and sexual feelings.

designer drugs: Drugs such as "E"—Ecstasy (MDMA), Special K, and GHB used to alter moods and heighten and enhance sexual feelings and sexual activity.

drag queens: Male cross-dressers who wear women's clothing but make no attempt to "pass" as women. **Drag kings** are females who dress as men but do not attempt to "pass" as men. Drag queens and drag kings generally cross-dress to express their gender identity for political or entertainment purposes or for personal reasons.

ethnicity: Refers to groups' common national, geographical, and/or cultural heritage marked by shared customs, language, beliefs, and history.

ethnocentrism: "The belief that one's own cultural approach is the normative lens through which to view a situation or experience" (Smith, 1997, p. 287).

eurocentrism: Adherence "to a set of white European-male-based cultural values which are often used by society to define what's perceived as 'normal'" (Woll, 1996, p. 71).

gay: Refers to men (and sometimes women) who are attracted to people of the same gender.

gender: Refers to what a culture determines (and dictates) are the behavioral, social, and psychological attributes of maleness and femaleness. "*Gender* is a social construct used to distinguish between male and female, masculine and feminine" (Brown and Rounsley, 1996, p. 20) and is based primarily on external genitalia. *Sex* is a part of gender.

gender bender (or gender blender): "Gender benders are males or females who challenge and cross traditional gender boundaries, often in outrageous ways" (Brown and Rounsley, 1996, p. 17).

gender dysphoria: Discomfort, pain, and conflict experienced when a person's gender identity does not match his or her biological or birth sex.

gender identity: Refers to an individual's personal sense of how he or she experiences his/her sex and gender and the psychosocial and cultural factors that influence that personal sense (Marcel, 1998). "It is an individual's identification with maleness and femaleness, as well as how those feelings (and their subsequent needs) are internalized and possibly presented to others" (Israel and Tarver, 1997, p. 44). Gender identity "is our own deeply held conviction and deeply felt inner awareness that we belong to one gender or the other," an awareness that "is firmly in place by the time we are five years old" (Brown and Rounsley, 1996, p. 21). Gender identity determines how a person sees, expresses, and presents him or herself as a man or a woman.

In recent years, however, there has been increasing controversy about the concept of just two genders. A number of people now argue that there are *many* genders and that to limit ourselves to just two genders (male and female) is to distort reality. Thus it becomes extremely important to recognize that gender identity refers most accurately to the way a person sees, expresses, and presents self as man, woman, or neither, or as a gender that falls on a continuum but is not either/or.

gender roles: Society's "rules" that prescribe the appropriate behavior and ways of being that govern a person's presentation of self as a man or a woman. Gender roles consist of those characteristics, activities, and behaviors which society says are proper for someone of that gender.

hermaphrodite: *See* INTERSEX.

heterosexism: "The ideological system that denies, denigrates, and stigmatizes any nonheterosexual form of behavior, identity, relationship, or community" (Herek, 1995, p. 321). It is the prevailing cultural belief that heterosexuality is the *only* normal mode of sexuality and sexual expression and experience. Thus, according to these beliefs, anyone who is heterosexual is normal; anyone whose sexuality, sexual expression, feelings, attractions, and experience are *not* heterosexual is abnormal and is to be despised.

heterosexual: One whose sexual/affectional attraction is to persons of the opposite gender.

homo/bi/transphobia: Cover term referring to fear, anger, contempt, hatred, mistrust directed at lesbians, gay, bisexuals, and transgendered people.

homophobia: Now means both irrational fear of and hatred and contempt for homosexuals and homosexuality and indeed any sexual orientation that varies from heterosexuality.

homosexual: One whose sexual/affectional attraction is to persons of the same gender.

intersex: People born with ambiguous or not clearly differentiated genitalia or "with medically established physical or hormonal attributes of both the male and female gender" (Israel and Tarver, 1997, p. 16). Traditionally, these people have been assigned (either socially and psychologically or, sometimes, surgically) to the female or male sex by the medical profession on the basis of their physical attributes and raised according to the gender roles of the designated sex.

lesbian: A woman who is sexually and/or affectionally and/or socially attracted to other women.

LGBT: An abbreviation referring to lesbians, gay men, bisexuals, and transgendered people.

MSM: Men who have sex with men and WSW (women who have sex with women)—applied to men and women whose behavior is *technically* homosexual (i.e., same-sex), but who do not see or identify themselves as homosexual. Ordinarily, these are people from cultures (e.g., Hispanic, Turkish) that allow for certain kinds of same-sex behaviors but do not ascribe sexual orientation meanings to them.

pansexual: A person whose sexual feelings and behaviors are fluid, ranging from heterosexual to bisexual to homosexual.

passing: For a lesbian or gay man, acting in ways that enable them to be seen as heterosexual. For bisexuals, acting in ways that enable them to be seen as either heterosexual or lesbian/gay. For transgenders, cross-dressing well enough so as to be seen as a member of the opposite gender.

polyamory: This term "usually implies sexual involvement with more than one person." Used in place of nonmonogamy. In a broader sense, "The term 'polyamory' includes many different styles of multiple intimate involvements, such as polyfidelity or group marriage; primary relationships open to secondary affairs; and casual sexual involvement with two or more people" (Munson and Stelboum, 1999, pp. 1-2).

poppers: Amylnitrite inhalants used by gay men to enhance and intensify sexual feelings and activity.

queer: Term used to refer to those who are not heterosexual or to those who refuse to be boxed in by restrictive gender and sexual orientation definitions. Originally a demeaning term, now reclaimed by many as a power term, especially by younger LGBTs.

race: Ordinarily defined as similar physical characteristics that distinguish groups of people.

rave: Type of dance party at which many of its patrons are involved in substance use and abuse.

sex: A biological term used to describe a person's chromosomal makeup and sexual anatomy—female, male, intersex. If a child is born with female sex organs (e.g., uterus, vagina), then she is female. If a child is born with male sex organs (e.g., penis, testes), he is male. As Stuart (1991) states, "Sex relates to . . . the genitals, the function the genitals perform, and how the genitals are used for reproduction or pleasure" (p. 5).

sexual identity: Refers not just to people's sexual behavior, but to who they are as complete human beings, including their sexuality.

sexual orientation: Refers to a person's sexual and/or affectional attractions to another person, including fantasy, behavior, and emotional/affectional needs.

she-male: A term sometimes used, but that tends to have demeaning connotations. "She-males are men, often involved in prostitution, pornography, or the adult entertainment business, who have undergone breast augmentation but have maintained their genitalia" (Brown and Rounsley, 1996, p. 16).

STDs: Sexually transmitted diseases. In men, STDs such as hepatitis, anal warts, gonorrhea, chlamydia, human papilloma virus, syphilis. Lesbians and bisexual women are vulnerable to the human papilloma virus, chlamydia, bacterial vaginosis, and trichomonas. If they have sexual intercourse with men, then they can contract STDs from them.

transgender: When a person's gender expression is different from what the culture deems appropriate for that gender, that person's identity is considered to be transgendered. When a person's culturally ascribed gender (which is assigned at birth according to the person's genital sex) conflicts with the person's internal, individual sense of his/her gender identity, then he or she identifies and expresses him or herself as transgender (Brown and Rounsley, 1996; Israel and Tarver, 1997; Marcel, 1998).

The word *transgender* is used as an umbrella term to refer to all people who in some way see and present themselves as the opposite gender. It is a "term used to describe the full range of individuals who have conflict with or question about their gender" (Brown and Rounsley, 1996, p. 18).

> Transgender has come through common usage in our community to mean any type of behavior that challenges dichotomous societal roles. It is an umbrella term that covers the occasional cross-dresser, someone who has need for sex reassignment surgery, a transgenderist, a post-operative transsexual, or any variation in between (Richards, 1997, p. 504).

transgenders or **transgendered people** (sometimes referred to as **transgenderists**): Those who make the choice to express themselves and live as a member of the gender opposite their anatomical sex. While some transgenders may use hormones or other cosmetic procedures, they do not alter their bodies via genital reassignment surgery. Transgenderists do "as little or as much as they wish to their physical bodies, but stopping short of genital surgery" (Denny, 1997, p. 39).

transphobia: The specific fear, revulsion, and hatred directed at those who "violate" the culture's gender rules, i.e., transgendered people.

transsexuals: People who are born with the biological characteristics of one sex but know themselves to be the opposite sex and gender. Some transsexuals are born *intersex* and grow up knowing they are not the sex they were assigned. Others grow up knowing that their bodies do not match their core gender identity. There are both female-to-male (FTM) and male-to-female (MTF) transsexuals, and many want to change their bodies to match their gender identity through hormones and, sometimes, through genital reassignment surgery. Transsexuals may be pre-operative or post-operative, but whatever stage they are in, once they make the transition they tend to live fully as the gender opposite their birth sex.

transvestites: *See* CROSS-DRESSERS (the more preferred term).

Appendix B

Organization Audit:
Evaluating Organizational Attitudes and Practices

Job Recruitment/Hiring/Promotion

- Are job announcements sent to lesbian, gay, bisexual, and transgender agencies and organizations such as NALGAP, LGBT community centers, and the LGBT newspapers and media?
- Are job candidates who are openly lesbian/gay/bi/trans, or presumed to be lesbian/gay/bi/trans, or who have experience working with sexual orientation and gender identity issues and concerns discriminated against in any way, at any level, with regard to hiring and promotion?
- Do informal guidelines exist regarding positions that openly lesbian/gay/bi/trans people would or would not be permitted to hold?
- When candidates are interviewed for jobs, does the agency attempt to identify and screen out persons who are homo/bi/transphobic or who are not committed to ending discrimination against all minority-status persons?
- Do the systems for recruiting board and staff members effectively recruit diverse members and, if not, what is being done to change the system?

The Organizational Environment for Employees

- Does the agency's/organization's nondiscrimination clause in its employment and service policies include protections related to sexual orientation (or sexual preference) and gender identity (as well as all of the groups identified by local, state, and federal civil rights agencies)? Are all of the employees aware of the non-discrimination policy?

Adapted version with input from Agency Checklist on Diversity by Anthony J. Silvestre, PhD, LSW, in D. Finnegan and E. McNally, *Dual Identities: Counseling Chemically Dependent Gay Men and Lesbians* (1987).

- If employees at the agency are unionized, does the union contract give equal protection to LGBT members?
- Is it generally accepted for LGBT employees to be honest about their gender identity and sexual orientation, both on the job and away from the job, without fear of sanctions or reprisals from management?
- Are LGBT staff ever formally or informally instructed to keep their sexual orientation or gender identity hidden or quiet?
- Is the agency environment such that some employees can safely choose to be "out of the closet" as lesbians, gay, bisexuals, or transgendered people on the job?
- Is the workplace generally supportive of diversity regarding gender and sexual orientation of staff members?
- Are "dyke," "fag," "ac/dc," "he/she" jokes tolerated? Are jokes about differences based on weight, appearance, and various types of non-conformity tolerated?
- Are gay men, lesbians, bisexuals, or unmarried staff more socially isolated?
- Does management defend LGBT-supportive stands if such stands are questioned?
- Have employee benefits and leave time policies been analyzed to determine if they are equitable for single and LGBT employees?
- Are LGBT individuals represented on the boards and on the advisory and community committees?
- Are LGBT issues ever discussed at meetings of boards and committees? Are these concerns seen as important for all members to deal with?
- What mechanism does the board have for ascertaining the needs of the LGBT communities and of LGBT clients?
- What advisory groups does the agency have in place? Are they diverse? Are many of their members LGBT people? How does the agency communicate with organizations that represent LGBT and other minority groups?
- Has the agency ensured the confidentiality of personnel records or other documents that contain information (whether implicit or explicit) about the sexual orientation and/or transgender identity of any staff members?

Professional Development

- Has the agency's staff, ranging from management to line staff to maintenance workers, received in-service training on sexual orientation and gender identity? Has the Board of Directors received training?

- Is the staff encouraged to participate in on-going diversity training on the issues relevant to sexual orientation, gender identity, ethnic, and cultural issues?
- Are there standards and methods for evaluating cultural competence?
- Does the agency enlist the help of professional consultants and supervisors knowledgeable about LGBT issues to assist staff with specific problems and issues when they arise with particular patients?

Provision of Services

- Are announcements of services routinely sent to LGBT agencies, organizations, and media?
- Do the intake forms, other forms (including medical, social, psychological, sexual histories), treatment plans, brochures, and consumer publications assume the heterosexuality and traditional gender categories of the staff, clients, and donors?
- Do the grant proposals and contracts for services show that the agency is serving a population that includes gay men, lesbians, bisexuals, and transgender people?
- Does the agency state that LGBT people are among the populations to be served?
- Are the agency's confidentiality procedures adequate for protecting LGBT clients?
- Do the agency's referral and resource lists include people and agencies with positive experience and expertise in working with lesbians, gay men, bisexuals, and transgendered people?
- Are gay/lesbian/bisexual/transgender meetings of AA and NA and Al-Anon listed as choices for clients?
- Are clients helped to attend these meetings if they choose to do so?
- Are sexual orientation and gender issues relevant to either clients or staff addressed in intakes, supervision, and/or staff meetings?
- Have the agency's programs and materials been analyzed and evaluated to identify areas where services/information do not adequately meet the needs of LGBT people? Have corrective steps been taken?
- When services are designed for family members or co-dependents, have the needs of same-sex couples been included? Have the needs of partners, friends, and family members of transgendered people been included?

- At public hearings and in meetings with governmental officials and other public or private service providers, has the agency supported better services for the sexual and transgender minority communities?
- Is the agency prepared to meet the diverse needs of LGBT people—including, and especially, youth; older people; physically challenged individuals; racial and ethnic populations of LGBTs?

Information Sharing and Community Relations

- Do the agency's bulletin boards and literature racks include brochures, newsletters, flyers with information about LGBT organizations, events, and services?
- Does the agency's library contain books and articles by and
- about LGBT people? Does it include books, articles, tapes by
- and about LGBT recovering alcoholics and substance abusers?
- Do films and audiotapes and lectures used in patient and community education include lesbians, gay men, bisexuals, and transgendered people and those who know about these individuals?
- Do LGBT groups of AA, NA, and Al-Anon bring meetings into the agency?
- Has the agency worked cooperatively and mutually with LGBT groups in education efforts, fundraising, and/or special community projects?

Appendix C

Resources

It is very important to know how, when, and where to refer clients for the help they may need with living their lives as LGBT persons and maintaining their recovery from substance abuse. In order to be able to do so, counselors need to develop a network of available referrals and resources for LGBT people and to keep updating these lists. Part of this network will consist of other agencies which offer particular assistance to LGBT individuals, such as medical treatment. Another part of the network should consist of personal and professional contacts that counselors have with sensitive and accepting members of AA and with therapists skilled at working with the LGBT populations. If there are colleges in the area, there may be LGBT groups on campus. There are LGBT switchboards, political groups or caucuses, and social groups in many areas of the country and within organizations and professionals groups (e.g., religious groups, social workers, lawyers, teachers, psychologists, medical students).

The Internet is an excellent resource for information about LGBT people and about substance abuse for both counselors and clients. Entering the words, *lesbian, gay, bisexual,* or *transgender* into search engines brings up thousands of Web sites with listings of international, national, regional and local groups, books, journals, chat groups, political and social groups, and organizations.

However, without access to the Internet, there are other ways to find valuable information. What follows is a list of the resources (both on and off the Internet) that we believe will be most helpful to counselors and clients.

Gayellow Pages

Renaissance House
P.O. Box 533 Village Station
New York, NY 10014-0533
(212) 674-0120
www.gayellowpages.com

Many resources are listed in this publication. The national (including Canada) edition and the regional editions are updated frequently and provide a wealth of information including therapists, counseling centers, church groups, social and political organizations, book stores, health groups, hotlines, some gay/lesbian meetings of AA.

Gay/Lesbian Newspapers and Bookstores

All major cities and many smaller cities have one or more LGBT newspapers and independently-owned bookstores that can provide information about local resources and gay/lesbian networks and activities. Many twelve step and support groups are listed in LGBT newspapers or posted on bulletin boards in local bookstores. Some of the local newspapers and bookstores may be found in local phone directories, in the Gayellow Pages, or online.

LGBT Switchboards

Most urban and some suburban areas of the country have switchboards which provide referral information for callers in need of help. Some of these switchboards may have lists of LGBT-sensitive therapists, support or social groups, and AA meetings. Counselors need to familiarize themselves with these resources and provide them to clients when needed. Many of the switchboards are also listed in the Gayellow Pages.

Specialized Groups

There are support groups in most large urban areas for just about every special issue and problem imaginable. A number of these groups have web sites and many of them are listed in the Gayellow Pages. In addition, they may be found through the local LGBT switchboard or the local Metropolitan Community Church (a church serving the LGBT communities). Surprisingly, many rural and suburban places outside of large metropolitan areas also have LGBT networks and support groups and many people drive long distances to attend meetings.

National Resources

National Association of Lesbian and Gay Addiction Professionals: Serving the LGBT Communities Since 1979

NALGAP
901 N. Washington Street #600

Alexandria, VA 22314
Phone: 703/465-0539
Fax: 703/741-6986
www.nalgap.org

NALGAP is a nonprofit membership organization founded in 1979 dedicated to the prevention and treatment of alcoholism, substance abuse, and other addictions in the lesbian/gay/bisexual/transgender communities. NALGAP's mission is to confront homophobia and heterosexism in the delivery of services to LGBT people and to advocate for LGBT-affirming programs and service. NALGAP provides information, training, networking and advocacy, and support for addiction professionals, individuals in recovery, and others concerned about LGBT health. The national NALGAP office also supplies information, consults with treatment and educational agencies, provides trainers, and makes referrals when appropriate for those who call or write. It is an excellent resource for people interested in providing quality care for clients, learning more about LGBT substance abuse, and becoming more involved in NALGAP's activities such as regional and national conferences and meetings. Both LGBT and non LGBT people can become members and receive a quarterly newsletter.

Prevline: LGBT Substance Abuse Web Site
www.health.org/features/lgbt/index.htm

An excellent governmental Web site developed with NALGAP and other LGBT community guidance, housed at Prevline, (www.health.org), the site for NCADI—The National Clearinghouse for Alcohol and Drug Information—a service of SAMHSA—The Substance Abuse Mental Health Services Administration operated by SAMHSA's Center for Substance Abuse Prevention (CSAP). The "Celebrating the pride and diversity . . . LGBT" PREVLINE section is one of the best and most comprehensive sources of information about LGBT substance abuse prevention, treatment, and rehabilitative services—including resources, links to other sites, questionnaires, and other features.

Society for the Psychological Study of Lesbian, Gay, and Bisexual
Concerns (Div.44) of The American Psychological Association (APA)
www.apa.org/divisions/div44

An excellent web site which includes Guidelines for Psychotherapy with Lesbian, Gay, and Bisexual Clients as well as Policy Statements on Gay and Lesbian Issues. Provides answers to questions about sexual orientation and homosexuality and web links to a number of other organizations. Also gives information and resources, such as the Committee on Lesbian, Gay, and Bisexual Concerns' five-part journal series, "Psychological Perspectives on Lesbian and Gay Issues."

www.iac-aa.org
International Advisory Council for Homosexual
Men and Women in Alcoholics Anonymous (IAC)
2101 Crystal Plaza Arcade
PMB 144
Arlington, VA 22202

The IAC publishes a *World Directory of Gay/Lesbian Groups of Alcoholics Anonymous* (available for a $6.00 donation) which is updated periodically. This directory of meetings includes places, days, and times of meetings, and in some cases contact persons. It also publishes a newsletter and a list of Gay/Lesbian Roundups, which are conferences put on by members of AA and Al-Anon in many different cities. For example: Omaha, April; Dallas, May; San Francisco, June; San Diego and Seattle, August. These roundups may be helpful to clients for contacts with other clean and sober people, information from workshops, and basic support. The IAC Web site includes a tape library, the Directory, Roundup information, and a newsletter.

Many of the following groups, although titled "gay" or "lesbian," now include information and services for bisexual and transgender people.

Parents, Families, and Friends of Lesbians and Gays (PFLAG)
http://www.pflag.org
1726 M Street, NW, Suite 400
Washington, DC 20036
202/467-8180 Fax: 202/467-8194

Gay and Lesbian Medical Association (GLMA)
www.glma.org
459 Fulton Street, Suite 107
San Francisco, CA 94102
Tel: 415/255-4547
Fax: 415/255-4784

Human Rights Campaign
www.hrc.org
919 18th Street NW, Suite 800
Washington, DC 20006
202/628-4160
Fax: 202/347-5323

A national organization working for lesbian and gay equal rights. Web site has many links to numerous other national and regional LGBT groups.

National Lesbian and Gay Task Force
www.nlgtf.org
1700 Kalorama Rd. NW
Washington, DC 20009-3509
202/332-6483
TTY: 202/332-6219
Fax: 202/332-0207

Al-Anon Family Groups
http://www.al-anon.alateen.org
1600 Corporate Landing Parkway
Virginia Beach, VA 23454-5617
888/425-2999

Religious Groups

Metropolitan Community Church
www.ufmcc.com

Dignity (Catholic)
www.dignityusa.org
1500 Massachusetts Avenue NW, Suite 11
Washington, DC 20005-1894
800/877-8797
202/861-0017

Presbyterian Parents Group
www.presbyterianparents.org
PPGL, Inc.
P.O. Box 600882
Dallas, TX 75360-0882

Integrity (Episcopal)
www.integrityusa.org

Jewish
www.jewish.com/search/Special Interests/Gay Lesbian/

Youth Groups

National Youth Advocacy Coalition
http://www.nyacyouth.org/
1638 R Street, NW
Suite 300
Washington, DC 20009
202/319-7596
Fax: 202-/319-7365

National Coalition for LGBT Youth
www.outproud.org
Guide to books, brochures, and other information for LGBT youth.

www.youthresource.com
LGBT forums, chats, and resource center.

Bisexuals

www.biresource.org
Bisexual Resource Center—serving the bisexual community since 1985—*Bisexual Resource Guide 2000,* which lists every known bisexual group worldwide, is available. Excellent site with links to many other sites. Bookstore, video store, music, and other products.

www.bisexual.org
Web site includes the Klein sexual orientation grid, information, books, conferences, search, and resources.

www.biNetUSA.org
Activist group since 1988, with conferences, information, organizing, educating, web site, leadership forums, resources—local, regional, and national.

Transgender/Transsexual

www.gender.org
Excellent gender education and advocacy, with many resources and links to other sites. Includes a library and archives.

www.symposion.com/ijt/
The International Journal of Transgenderism web site has all the issues of the journal and several helpful books available online.

www.amboyz.org
The American Boyz is an organization which aims to support people who were labeled female at birth but who feel that is not an accurate or complete description of who they are (FTMs) and their significant others, friends, families, and allies (SOFFAs). Provides education, support, social events, newsletters, publications, web sites, e-mail lists, local meetings, and the national True Spirit Conference.

www.hbigda.org
Harry Benjamin International Gender Dysphoria Association (HBIGDA) is a professional organization devoted to the understanding and treatment of gender identity disorders with 350 members throughout the world in psychiatry, endocrinology, surgery, law, psychology, sociology, and counseling. Web site has links to transgender organizations, information, resources; transsexual women's resources; and gender programs and service centers in Toronto, New York, Seattle, and University of Minnesota.

For further information, contact:
Bean Robinson, PhD, Exec. Dir.
1300 S. Second St., Suite 180
Minneapolis, MN 55454
612/625-1500
612/626-8311

www.ifge.org
The International Foundation for Gender Education includes gender news, events, *Tapestry Magazine,* movies, books, newsletter, etc.

IFGE
P.O. Box 540229
Waltham, MA 02454-0229
781/899-2212
Fax: 781/899-5703

www.isna.org
Intersex Society of North America is an organization devoted to ending the shame, secrecy, and unwanted genital surgeries for people born with atypical sex anatomy. Books, articles, newsletter, bibliography, FAQ, and links resources.

www.firelily.com/gender/gianna/
Web site for Gianna E. Israel, a therapist who provides counseling services for the transgender community. She also publishes articles on transgenderism issues, including a regular column in *Transgender Tapestry* and a series of Gender Articles.

www.annelawrence.com

Web site has a wealth of medical and other resources for transsexual women.

Libraries and Information Online

www.gerberhart.org

Gerber Hart Library has a lesbian, gay, and bisexual library and archives and Virtual Research Collections. Midwest's leading lesbian and gay archives with links to many other collections.

www.haworthpress.com
800/429-6784

Haworth Press publishes a number of journals and books on substance abuse, bisexuality, lesbians, gay men, and gender.

www.choicesconsulting.com
321 Washington Ave.
Albany, NY 12206

Web site for Arlene Istar Lev, MSW, a therapist from Albany, New York, includes information and articles about understanding and helping transgender people, lesbians, and parenting as well as extensive bibliographies, resource lists, and links to other helpful Web sites.

LGBT Substance Abuse Resources

In some areas there are LGBT community centers and other programs which address the health and social issues and needs of LGBT people. Ordinarily, these facilities and services can be located in the Gayellow Pages, on the Internet, through LGBT switchboards, or through NALGAP. Listed below are some of the established centers and facilities around the country that have knowledge, services, and direct support for LGBT substance abusers.

Regional/State/Community Resources

California

Alternatives, Inc.
2526 Hyperion Avenue, Suite 4
Los Angeles, CA 90027
323/671-1600
1-800-DIAL GAY (342-5429)
Fax: 323/671-1605
http://www.alternativesinc.com

Los Angeles Gay & Lesbian Center
Addiction Recovery Services
McDonald/Wright Building
1625 N Schrader Boulevard
Los Angeles, CA 90028-6213
323/993-7640
TDD 323/993-7698
www.laglc.org

Van Ness Recovery House
1919 North Beachwood Drive
Hollywood, CA 90068
323/463-4266

Progressive Research & Training for Action
2809 Telegraph Ave., Suite 208
Berkeley, CA 94705
510/705-8918
Fax: 510/705-8922
www.prta.com

The Stepping Stone
3425 Fifth Avenue
San Diego, CA 92103
619-295-3995
http://steppingstonecsd.org/

Lyon-Martin Women's Health Services
1748 Market Street
Suite 201
San Francisco, CA 94102
415/565-7667
Fax: 415/252-7490

New Leaf Services for Our Community
(Formerly Operation Concern 18th St. Services)
1853 Market Street
San Francisco, CA 94103
415/626-7000
Fax 415/626-5916
TDD 415/252-8376
http://www.NewLeafServices.org

District of Columbia

Whitman-Walker Clinic
1407 S Street, NW.
Washington. DC 20009
202/797-3500
www.wwc.org

Massachusetts

Fenway Community Health
Mental Health and Addiction Services
7 Haviland Street
Boston, MA 02115
617/267-0900
TTY 617/859-1256
En espanol 617/926-6460
www.fenwayhealth.org

The GLBT Health Access Project
Transgender Education Network
100 Boylston Street, Suite 860
Boston, MA
617/988-2605

Minnesota

Pride Institute
14400 Eden Martin Drive
Eden Prairie, MN 55344
612/934-7554
800/54-PRIDE
www.pride-institute.com

New York

Lesbian & Gay Community Services Center
Gender Identity Project
Project Connect (Alcohol and substance abuse services)
SpeakOUT: LGBT Recovering Community Support Project
208 West 13th Street
New York, NY 10011
212/620-7310
www.gaycenter.org

Lambda Treatment and Recovery Program
Human Service Centers
87-08 Justice Avenue
Suite 1G
Elmhurst, NY 11373
718/476-8480
www.human-service-centers.org

Gay Men's Health Crisis
The Tisch Building
119 West 24 Street
New York, NY 10011
212/807-6655
GMHC Hotline: 1-800-AIDS-NYC (1-800-243-7692)
TTY: 212/645-7470
Substance Use Counseling and Education: 212/367-1354
www.gmhc.org

Washington

Stonewall Recovery Services
430 Broadway St. East
Seattle, WA 98102
206/461-4546
Fax: 206/461-3749
www.stonewallrecovery.org

Appendix D

Suggested Readings

LGBT Substance Abuse Treatment

SAMHSA:CSAT Publication: *A provider's introduction to substance abuse treatment for lesbian, gay, bisexual, and transgender individuals.* NCADI Inventory #BKD392. To order a free copy: 1/800/729-6686 or www.health.org/features/lgbt/index.htm.

Lesbian and Gay

Bohan, J.S. (1996). *Psychology and sexual orientation: Coming to terms.* New York: Routledge. (Includes material on bisexuals)

D'Augelli, A.R. and Patterson, C.J. (Eds.) (1995). *Lesbian, gay, and bisexual identities over the lifespan: Psychological perspectives.* New York: Oxford University Press.

Glassgold, J.M. and Iasenza, S. (Eds.) (1995). *Lesbians and psychoanalysis: Revolutions in theory and practice.* New York: The Free Press.

Greene, B. and Herek, G.M. (Eds.) (1994). *Lesbian and gay psychology: Theory, research, and clinical applications: Psychological perspectives on lesbian and gay issues* (Vol. 1). Thousand Oaks, CA: Sage.

Howard, K. and Stevens, A. (Eds.) (2000). *Out and about campus: Personal accounts by lesbian, gay, bisexual, and transgendered college students.* Los Angeles: Alyson Books.

Kominars, S.B. and Kominars, K.D. (1996). *Accepting ourselves and others: A journey into recovery from addictive and compulsive behaviors for gays, lesbians, and bisexuals.* Center City, MN: Hazelden.

Munson, M. and Stelboum, J.P. (Eds.) (1999). *The lesbian polyamory reader: Open relationships, non-monogamy, and casual sex.* Binghamton, NY: The Haworth Press, Inc.

Bisexual

Firestein, B. (1997) *Bisexuality: The psychology and politics of an invisible minority.* Thousand Oaks, CA: Sage.

Klein, F. (1993). *The bisexual option*. (Second edition). Binghamton, NY: The Haworth Press, Inc.

Ochs, R. (1994). *The international directory of bisexual groups* (Eleventh edition). Cambridge, MA: Bisexual Resource Center.

Storr, M. (Ed.). (1999). *Bisexuality: A critical reader*. New York: Routledge.

Swan, W.K. (Ed.). (1997). *Gay/lesbian/bisexual/transgender public policy issues: A citizen's and administrator's guide to the new cultural struggle*. Binghamton, NY: Harrington Park Press.

Weinberg, M., Williams, S., and Pryor, D. (1994). *Dual attraction: Understanding bisexuality*. New York: Oxford University Press.

Transgender/Transsexual

Bornstein, K. (1994) *Gender outlaw: On men, women, and the rest of us*. New York: Vintage Books.

Brown, M.L. and Rounsley, C.A. (1996). *True selves: Understanding transsexualism*. San Francisco: Jossey-Bass.

Bullough, B., Bullough, V.L., and Elias, J. (Eds.) (1997). *Gender blending*. Amherst, NY: Prometheus Books.

Ettner, R. (1999). *Gender loving care: A guide to counseling gender-variant clients*. New York: W.W. Norton and Co.

Feinberg, L. (1998) *Transliberation: Beyond pink or blue*. Boston: Beacon Press.

Israel, G.E. and Tarver, D.E. (1997). *Transgender care: Recommended guidelines, practical information, and personal accounts*. Philadelphia: Temple University Press.

Lev, A. I. (in press). *Transgender emergence: Counseling gender variant people and their families*. Binghamton, NY: The Haworth Press, Inc.

Stuart, K.E. (1991). *The uninvited dilemma: A question of gender*. Portland, Oregon: Metamorphous Press.

Wilchins, R.A. (1997). *Read my lips: Sexual subversion and the end of gender*. Ithaca, NY: Firebrand Books.

References

Allen, M.P. (1997). The changing face of the transgender community. In B. Bullough, V.L. Bullough, and J. Elias (Eds.), *Gender blending* (pp. 311-315). Amherst, NY: Prometheus Books.

Alvarez, W. (1994). *Sanctioned bias: Homophobia and its impact upon the therapeutic process.* Paper presented at the Meeting of the New York State Society for Clinical Social Work, Metropolitan Chapter, New York, March.

American Psychiatric Association (1968). *Diagnostic and statistical manual of mental disorders* (DSM-II) (Second edition). Washington, DC: Author.

American Psychiatric Association (1980). *Diagnostic and statistical manual of mental disorders* (DSM-III) (Third edition). Washington, DC: Author.

American Psychiatric Association (1994). *Diagnostic and statistical manual of mental disorders* (DSM-IV) (Fourth edition). Washington. DC: Author.

Bachman, J. (2000). Ignorance about AIDS still widespread, survey finds. *Los Angeles Times,* December 4. Internet: *The Los Angeles Times* Archives.

Bailey, J.M. (1995). Biological perspectives on sexual orientation. In A.R. D'Augelli and C.J. Patterson (Eds.), *Lesbian, gay, and bisexual identities over the lifespan: Psychological perspectives* (pp. 102-135). New York: Oxford University Press.

Basgara, O. and Pomerantz, R.J. (1993). Human immunodeficiency virus type I replication in peripheral blood mononuclear cells in the presence of cocaine. *Journal of Infectious Diseases, 168.* 1157-1164.

Bean, M. H. (1981). Denial and the psychological complications of alcoholism. In M.H. Bean, E.J. Khantzian, J.E. Mack, G.E. Vaillant, and N.E. Zinberg (Eds.), *Dynamic approaches to the understanding and treatment of alcoholism* (pp. 55-96). New York: Free Press.

Beatty, R. (1983). *Alcoholism and the adult gay male population of Pennsylvania.* Unpublished master's thesis, The Pennsylvania State University.

Bell, A. and Weinberg, M. (1978). *Homosexualities: A study of diversity among men and women.* New York: Simon and Shuster.

Berger, J. (1994). The psychotherapeutic treatment of male homosexuality. *American Journal of Psychotherapy, 48*(2), 251-261.

Billy, J.O.G., Tanfer, K., Grady, W.R., and Klepinger, D H. (1993). The sexual behavior of men in the United States. *Family Planning Perspectives, 25*(2), 52-60.

Bloomfield, K.A. (1993). A comparison of alcohol consumption between lesbians and heterosexual women in an urban population. *Drug and Alcohol Dependence, 33,* 257-269.

Blumenstein, R. (2001). Private conversation with R. Blumenstein, MSW, Director, Gender Identity Project, Gay and Lesbian Community Center, New York, January 25.

Blumstein, P.W. and Schwartz, P. (1977). Bisexuality: Some social psychological issues. *Journal of Social Issues, 33*(2), 30-45.

Bockting, W.O. (1997). Transgender coming out: Implications for the clinical management of gender dysphoria. In B. Bullough, V.L. Bullough, and J. Elias (Eds.), *Gender blending* (pp. 48-52). Amherst, NY: Prometheus Books.

Bockting, W.O., Robinson, B.E., and Rosser, B.R.S. (1998). Transgender HIV prevention: A qualitative needs assessment. *AIDS Care, 10,* 505-526.

Bohan, J.S. (1996). *Psychology and sexual orientation: Coming to terms.* New York: Routledge.

Bolin, A. (1997). Transforming transvestitism and transsexualism: Polarity, politics, and gender. In B. Bullough, V.L. Bullough, and J. Elias (Eds.), *Gender blending* (pp. 25-32). Amherst, NY: Prometheus Books.

Booth, L. (1995). A new understanding of spirituality: The effects of alcoholism and recovery on spirituality. In R. J. Kus (Ed.), *Spirituality and chemical dependency* (pp. 5-17). Binghamton, NY: The Haworth Press, Inc.

Bornstein, K. (1994). *Gender outlaw: On men, women, and the rest of us.* New York: Vintage Books.

Boswell, H. (1997). The transgender paradigm shift toward free expression. In B. Bullough, V.L. Bullough, and J. Elias (Eds.), *Gender blending* (pp. 53-57). Amherst, NY: Prometheus Books.

Bradford, J., Plumb, M., White, J., and Ryan, C. (1994). Information transfer strategies to support lesbian research. In *Psychological and behavioral factors in women's health: Creating an agenda for the 21st century—American Psychological Association conference proceedings,* May. Washington, DC: American Psychological Association.

Bradford, J. and Ryan, C. (1987). *National lesbian health care survey: Implications for mental health care.* Washington, DC: National Lesbian and Gay Health Foundation.

Bradford, J., Ryan, C., and Rothblum, E.D. (1994). National lesbian health care survey: Implications for mental health care. *Journal of Consulting and Clinical Psychology, 62,* 228-242.

Breakwell, G.M. (1986). *Coping with threatened identities.* New York: Methuen.

Brown, L.S. (1995). Lesbian identities: Concepts and issues. In A.R. D'Augelli and C.J. Patterson (Eds.), *Lesbian, gay, and bisexual identities over the lifespan: Psychological perspectives* (pp. 3-23). New York: Oxford University Press.

Brown, M.L. and Rounsley, C.A. (1996). *True selves: Understanding transsexualism.* San Francisco: Jossey-Bass.

Brown, S. (1998). *Addiction, trauma, and developmental arrest.* Paper presented at the Addiction and Trauma Conference, New York, February.

Bullough, B., Bullough, V.L., and Elias, J. (Eds.), (1997). *Gender blending.* Amherst, NY: Prometheus Books.

Bux, D.A. (1996). The epidemiology of problem drinking in gay men and lesbians: A critical review. *Clinical Psychology Review, 16*(4), 277-298.

Cabaj, R.P. (2001). Clinical issues with gay male clients. In SAMHSA:CSAT (Ed.), *A provider's introduction to substance abuse treatment for lesbian, gay, bisexual, and transgender individuals* (pp. 79-86). Washington, DC: Substance

Abuse Mental Health Services Administration: Center for Substance Abuse Treatment (SAMHSA:CSAT).

Cass, V. C. (1979). Homosexual identity formation: A theoretical model. *Journal of Homosexuality, 4*(3), 219-235.

Cass, V. C. (1984). Homosexual identity: A concept in need of definition. *Journal of Homosexuality, 9*(2/3), 105-126.

Cass, V.C. (1990). The implications of homosexual identity formation for the Kinsey model and scale of sexual preference. In D.P. McWhirter, S.A. Sanders, and J. Reinisch (Eds.), *Homosexuality/heterosexuality: Concepts of sexual orientation* (pp. 239-266). New York: Oxford University Press.

Cass, V.C. (1992). Lesbian/gay identity formation and coming out. Paper presented at Seminar on Lesbian and Gay Health Issues, Sydney, Australia, September.

Center for Disease Control (CDC): National Center for HIV, STD and TB Prevention (NCHSTP). (2000, January 13). HIV/AIDS cases among gay and bisexual men of color now exceed cases among white gay and bisexual men. CDC: NCHSTP: Internet. http://www.cdc.gov/nchstp/od/nchstp.html

Center for Disease Control (CDC): National Center for HIV, STD and TB Prevention (NCHSTP). (2001, January 31). Need for sustained HIV prevention among men who have sex with men. CDC: NCHSTP: Internet. http://www.cdc.gov/nchstp/od/nchstp.html

Centers for Disease Control and Prevention (CDC). (1994). Cigarette smoking among adults—United States, 1992, and changes in the definition of current cigarette smoking. *MMWR, 43*(9), 342-346.

Centers for Disease Control and Prevention. (1999). USPHS/IDSA guidelines for prevention of opportunistic infections in persons infected with human immunodeficiency virus. *MMWR, 48* (RR10: 1).

Cerbone, A.R. (1997). Symbol of privilege, object of derision: Dissonance and contradictions. In B. Greene (Ed.), *Ethnic and cultural diversity among lesbians and gay men: Psychological perspectives on lesbian and gay issues* (Vol. 3), (pp. 117-131). Thousand Oaks, CA: Sage.

Chan, C.S. (1995). Issues of sexual identity in an ethnic minority: The case of Chinese American lesbians, gay men, and bisexual people. In A.R. D'Augelli and C.J. Patterson (Eds.), *Lesbian, gay, and bisexual identities over the lifespan: Psychological perspectives* (pp. 87-101). New York: Oxford University Press.

Chan, C.S. (1997). Don't ask, don't tell, don't know: The formation of a homosexual identity and sexual expression among Asian American lesbians. In B. Greene (Ed.), *Ethnic and cultural diversity among lesbians and gay men: Psychological perspectives on lesbian and gay issues* (Vol. 3), (pp. 240-248). Thousand Oaks, CA: Sage.

Choi, K-H., Salazar, N., Lew, S., and Coates, T.J. (1995). AIDS risk, dual identity, and community response among gay Asian Pacific Islander men in San Francisco. In G.M. Herek and B. Greene (Eds.), *Lesbian and gay psychology: Theory, research, and clinical applications: Psychological perspectives on lesbian and gay issues,* Vol. 2. (pp. 19-31). Thousand Oaks, CA: Sage.

Clark, D.H. (1997). *Loving someone gay.* Berkeley, CA: Ten Speed Press.

Clements, K. (1999). *The transgender community health project: Descriptive results.* San Francisco: San Francisco Department of Public Health.

Cochran, S.D., Bybee, D., Gage, S., and Mays, V.M. (1996). Prevalence of self-reported sexual behaviors, sexually transmitted diseases, and problems with drugs and alcohol in three large surveys of lesbian and bisexual women. *Women's Health: Research on Gender, Behavior, and Policy, 2*, 11-34.

Cochran, S.D. and Mays, V.M. (2000). Relation between psychiatric syndromes and behaviorally defined sexual orientation in a sample of the U.S. population. *Epidemiology. 151*(5), 516-523.

Cohen, J. (1993). HIV risk among women who have sex with women. *San Francisco Epidemiologic Bulletin, 9*, 25-29.

Coleman, E. (1987). Assessment of sexual orientation. *Journal of Homosexuality, 14*(1/2), 9-24.

Cross, W. E. (1971). Discovering the black referent: The psychology of black liberation. In V. J. Dixon and B. G. Foster (Eds.). *Beyond black or white: An alternate America* (pp. 95-110). Boston, MA: Little, Brown.

D'Augelli, A.R. (1994). Lesbian and gay male development: Steps toward an analysis of lesbians' and gay men's lives. In B. Greene and G.M. Herek (Eds.), *Lesbian and gay psychology: Theory, research, and clinical applications: Psychological perspectives on lesbian and gay issues* (Vol. 1) (pp. 118-132). Thousand Oaks, CA: Sage.

D'Augelli, A.R. and Garnets, L.D. (1995). Lesbian, gay, and bisexual communities. In A.R. D'Augelli and C.J. Patterson (Eds.), *Lesbian, gay, and bisexual identities over the lifespan: Psychological perspectives* (pp. 293-320). New York: Oxford University Press.

D'Augelli, A.R. and Hershberger, S.L. (1993). Lesbian, gay, and bisexual youths in community settings: Personal challenges and mental health problems. *American Journal of Community Psychology, 21*, 421-448.

Dean, L., Meyer, H.H., Robinson, K., Sell, R.L., Sember, R., Silenzio, V.M.B., Bowen, D.J., Bradford, J., Rothblum, E., Scout, D., White, J., Dunn, P., Lawrence, A., Wolfe, D., and Xavier, J. (2000). Lesbian, gay, bisexual, and transgender health: Findings and concerns. *Journal of the Gay and Lesbian Medical Association, 4*(3), 101-151.

Denny, D. (1991). Dealing with your feelings. *The AEGIS Transition Series.* Decatur, GA: Aegis.

Denny, D. (1994). *Identity management in transsexualism: A practical guide to managing identity on paper.* King of Prussia. PA: Creative Design Services.

Denny, D. (1997). Transgender: Some historical, cross-cultural, and contemporary models and methods of coping and treatment. In B. Bullough. V.L. Bullough, and J. Elias (Eds.), *Gender blending* (pp. 33-47). Amherst, NY: Prometheus Books.

Denny, D and Green, J. (1996). Gender identity and bisexuality. In B.A. Firestein (Ed.), *Bisexuality: The psychology and politics of an invisible minority* (pp. 84-102). Thousand Oaks, CA: Sage.

Denzin, N. (1987). *The recovering alcoholic.* Beverly Hills, CA: Sage.

Dillon, C. (1993). Developing self and voice in therapy with lesbians. *Developments: The Newsletter of the Center for Women's Development at HRI Hospital, 2*(3), 1, 5.

Du Rant, R.H., Krowchuck, D.P., and Sinal. S.H. (1998). Victimization, use of violence, and drug use at school among male adolescents who engage in same-sex behavior. *Journal of Pediatrics, 133*(1), 113-118.

Eadie, J. (1993). Activating bisexuality: Towards a bi/sexual politics. In M. Storr (Ed.). (1999), *Bisexuality: A critical reader* (pp. 119-137). New York: Routledge.

Eigen. M. (1996). *Psychic deadness*. Northvale. NJ: Jason Aronson, Inc.

Eminem (2000). "Remember Me." *Marshall Mathers LP*. Los Angeles: Interscope Pearl Records.

EMT Group, Inc. (1992). *The research symposium on alcohol and other drug problem prevention among lesbians, gay, and bisexual men*. (October). Sacramento, CA: Author.

Etscovitz. L. (1997). The inner dimensions of gender transformation. In B. Bullough. V.L. Bullough, and J. Elias (Eds.), *Gender blending* (pp. 485-489). Amherst, NY: Prometheus Books.

Evans, N. and D'Augelli, A.R. (1996). Lesbians, gay men, and bisexual people in college. In R. Savin-Williams and K. Cohen (Eds.), *The lives of lesbians, gays, and bisexuals: Children to adults* (pp. 201-226). Fort Worth, TX: Harcourt Brace.

Faderman, L. (1991). *Odd girls and twilight lovers: A history of lesbian life in twentieth-century America*. New York: Columbia University Press.

Faulkner, A.H. and Cranston. K. (1998). Correlates of same-sex sexual behavior in a random sample of Massachusetts high school students. *American Journal of Public Health, 88*(2). 262-266.

Feinberg, L. (1998). *Trans liberation: Beyond pink or blue*. Boston, MA: Beacon Press.

Fifield, L., DeCresenzo, T.A., and Latham, J.D. (1975). *On my way to nowhere: Alienated, isolated. drunk*. Los Angeles, CA: Gay Community Services Center.

Finke. G. and Northway, R. (1997). Patterns in and treatments for gender dysphoria. In B. Bullough. V.L. Bullough, and J. Elias (Eds.), *Gender blending* (pp. 383-389). Amherst, NY: Prometheus Books.

Finnegan, D.G. and McNally, E.B. (1996). Chemically dependent lesbians and bisexual women: Recovery from many traumas. *Journal of Chemical Dependency Treatment, 6*(1/2). 87-107.

Firestein, B.A. (Ed.) (1996). *Bisexuality: The psychology and politics of an invisible minority*. Thousand Oaks, CA: Sage.

Flores, P. J. (1988). *Group psychotherapy with addicted populations*. Binghamton. NY: The Haworth Press, Inc.

Fox, R.C. (1995). Bisexual identities. In A.R. D'Augelli and C.J. Patterson (Eds.), *Lesbian, gay, and bisexual identities over the lifespan: Psychological perspectives* (pp. 48-86). New York: Oxford University Press.

Fox, R.C. (1996). Bisexuality: An examination of theory and research. In Cabaj, R.P. and Stein. T.S. (Eds.). *Homosexuality and mental health* (pp. 159-184). Washington, DC: American Psychiatric Press.

Fox, R.C. (2000). Therapy with bisexuals: An interview with Ron Fox. *In the Family, 6*(4). 6-9, 21.

France, D. (2000). Tuning out Dr. Laura. *Newsweek*, September 18, p. 80.

Frosch, D.. Shoptaw. S., Hubber, A., Rawson, R.A., and Ling. W. (1996). Sexual HIV risk among gay and bisexual male methamphetamine abusers. *Journal of Substance Abuse Treatment, 13,*.483-486.

Gainor, K. (2000). Including transgender issues in lesbian, gay. and bisexual psychology: Implications for clinical practice and training. In B. Greene and G.L. Croom (Eds.), *Education, research, and practice in lesbian, gay, bisexual, and transgendered psychology: A resource manual: Psychological perspectives on lesbian and gay issues* (Vol. 5). Thousand Oaks, CA: Sage.

Garber. M. (1999). Vice versa: Bisexuality and the eroticism of everyday life. In M. Storr (Ed.) *Bisexuality: A critical reader* (pp. 138-143). New York: Routledge.

Garnets, L.. Hancock, K., Cochran, S., Goodchilds, J., and Peplau, A. (1991). Issues in psychotherapy with lesbians and gay men: A survey of psychologists. *American Psychologist, 46*(9), 964-972.

Gartner, R.B. (1999). *Betrayed as boys: Psychodynamic treatment of sexually abused men*. New York: Guilford Press.

George. S. (1993). Women and bisexuality. In M. Storr (Ed.) (1999), *Bisexuality: A critical reader* (pp. 100-106). New York: Routledge.

Ghindia, D.J.. Hart, S., Gochros, H.. and Pellicio, W.J. (2001). Related health issues. In SAMHSA:CSAT (Ed.). *A provider's introduction to substance abuse treatment for lesbian, gay, bisexual, and transgender individuals* (pp. 105-113). Washington. DC: Substance Abuse Mental Health Services Administration: Center for Substance Abuse Treatment (SAMHSA:CSAT).

Glassgold, J.M. and Iasenza. S. (1995). *Lesbians and psychoanalysis: Revolutions in theory and practice*. New York: Simon and Shuster.

Glionna, J.M. (2001). HIV rate rising among gay men in S.F. *The Los Angeles Times*, 25 January. Home Edition: Part A.

Goffman. E. (1963). *Stigma: Notes on the management of spoiled identity*. Englewood Cliffs, NJ: Prentice-Hall.

Gomez. C.A. (1995). Lesbians at risk for HIV: The unresolved debate. In G.M. Herek and B. Greene (Eds.), *Lesbian and gay psychology: Theory, research, and clinical applications: Psychological perspectives on lesbian and gay issues* (Vol. 2) (pp. 19-31). Thousand Oaks. CA: Sage.

Gonsiorek, J.C. (1995). Gay male identities: Concepts and issues. In A.R. D'Augelli and C.J. Patterson (Eds.), *Lesbian, gay, and bisexual identities over the lifespan: Psychological perspectives* (pp. 24-47). New York: Oxford University Press.

Goodrum, A.J. (2000). *Gender identity 101: A transgender primer*. <www.users. qwest.net/~ajgoodrum/gender101.htm>.

Greene, B. (2000). Beyond heterosexism and across the cultural divide: Developing an inclusive lesbian, gay, and bisexual psychology: A look to the future. In B. Greene and G. L. Croom (Eds.), *Education, research, and practice in lesbian, gay, bisexual, and transgendered psychology: A resource manual: Psychological perspectives on lesbian and gay issues* (Vol. 5) (pp. 1-45). Thousand Oaks. CA: Sage.

Grube, J. (1991). Natives and settlers: An ethnographic note on early interaction of older homosexual men with younger gay liberationists. *Journal of Homosexuality, 20*, 119-135.

Hall, J.M. (1992). An exploration of lesbian's images of recovery from alcohol problems. In J. Kelly (Ed.), *The research symposium on alcohol and other drug problem prevention among lesbians, gay and men* (pp. 91-109), October. Sacramento. CA: EMT Group, Inc.

Harris, L.E. (1997). A legal path of androgyny. In B. Bullough, V.L. Bullough, and J. Elias (Eds.), *Gender blending* (pp. 495-502). Amherst, NY: Prometheus Books.

Hemmings, C. (1995). Locating bisexual identities: Discourses of bisexuality and contemporary feminist theory. In M. Storr (Ed.), (1999). *Bisexuality: A critical reader* (pp. 193-200). New York: Routledge.

Herek, G.M. (1995). Psychological heterosexism in the United States. In A.R. D'Augelli and C.J. Patterson (Eds.), *Lesbian, gay, and bisexual identities over the lifespan: Psychological perspectives* (pp. 321-346). New York: Oxford University Press.

Herman, J. L. (1992). *Trauma and recovery: The aftermath of violence—from domestic abuse to political terror.* New York: Basic Books.

Hughes, T.L., Haas, A.P., Razzano, L., Cassidy, R., and Matthews, A. (2000). Comparing lesbians' and heterosexual women's mental health: A multi-site survey. *Journal of Gay and Lesbian Social Services, 11*(1), 57-76.

Human Rights Campaign Foundation (2000). *The state of the workplace for lesbian, gay, bisexual, and transgendered Americans.* Washington, DC: Human Rights Campaign Foundation.

Hutchins, L. (1996). Bisexuality: Politics and community. In B.A. Firestein (Ed.), *Bisexuality: The psychology and politics of an invisible minority* (pp. 240-262). Thousand Oaks, CA: Sage.

Imhof, J., Hirsch, R., and Terenzi, R.E. (1984). Countertranferential and attitudinal considerations in the treatment of drug abuse and addiction. *Journal of Substance Abuse Treatment, 1,* 21-30.

Israel, G.E. and Tarver, D.E. (1997). *Transgender care: Recommended guidelines, practical information, and personal accounts.* Philadelphia: Temple University Press.

Jones. F. (1997). Eloquent anonymity. [Review of the book *Lush life: A biography of Billy Strayhorn*]. *Readings: A Journal of Reviews and Commentary in Mental Health,* March, *12*(1), 10-14.

Josselson, R. (1987). *Finding herself: Pathways to identity development in women.* New York: Jossey-Bass.

JSI Research and Training Institute. Inc. (2000). *Access to health care for transgendered persons in Greater Boston.* Boston: Gay, Lesbian, Bisexual and Transgender Health Access Project.

Kammerer, N., Mason, T., and Connors, M. (1999). Transgender health and social service needs in the context of HIV risk. *International Journal of Transgenderism, 3,* 1-2.

Katz, J. (1976). *Gay American history: Lesbians and gay men in the U. S. A.* New York: Avon Books/Thomas Y. Crowell Co., Inc.

Kelly, J. (Ed.). (1995). *Preventing alcohol and other drug problems in the lesbian and gay community,* May. Sacramento. CA: EMT Group, Inc.

Khantzian, E.J. (1981). Some treatment implications of the ego and self distur-
bances in alcoholism. In M.H. Bean, E.J. Khantzian, J.E. Mack, G.E. Vaillant,
and N.E. Zinberg (Eds.), *Dynamic approaches to the understanding and treatment of alcoholism* (pp. 163-188). New York: Free Press.

Khantzian, E.J. (1998). *Addiction, trauma, and self-medication*. Paper presented at
the Addiction and Trauma Conference, February, New York.

Kinsey, A.C., Pomeroy, W.B., and Martin, C.E. (1948). *Sexual behavior in the human male*. Philadelphia: W. B. Saunders Co.

Kinsey, A.C., Pomeroy, W.B., Martin, C.E., and Gebhard, P.H. (1953). *Sexual behavior in the human female*. Philadelphia: W. B. Saunders Co.

Klein, F. (1978). *The bisexual option: A concept of one hundred percent intimacy*.
New York: Arbor House.

Klein, F. (1993). *The bisexual option*. (Second edition). Binghamton, NY: The
Haworth Press, Inc.

Kominars, S.B. and Kominars, K.D. (1996). *Accepting ourselves and others: A
journal in recovery from addictive and compulsive behavior for gays, lesbians,
bisexuals, and their therapists*. Center City, MN: Hazelden.

Kroll, K.F. (1997). Transsexuality and religion: A personal journey. In B. Bullough,
V.L. Bullough, and J. Elias (Eds.), *Gender blending* (pp 490-494). Amherst,
NY: Prometheus Books.

Krystal, H. (1988). *Integration and self-healing*. Hillsdale, NJ: Analytic Press.

Kus, R.J. (1987). Alcoholics Anonymous and gay American men. *Journal of Homosexuality, 14*(1/2), 253-276.

Kus, R.J. (1988). Alcoholism and non-acceptance of gay self: The critical link.
Journal of Homosexuality, 15(1/2), 25-41.

Kus, R.J. (1990). Coming out: Its nature, stages, and health concerns. In R.J. Kus
(Ed.), *Keys to caring: Assisting your gay and lesbian clients* (pp. 30-44). Boston:
Alyson.

Kus, R.J. (1995). Self-examination in addiction recovery: Notes on Steps 4 and 10.
In R.J. Kus (Ed.), *Spirituality and chemical dependency* (pp. 65-77). Binghamton, NY: The Haworth Press, Inc.

Lev, A.I. (1998). Invisible gender. *In the Family. 4*(2), 8-11.

Lev, A.I. (in press). *Transgender emergence—A developmental process*.
Binghamton, NY: The Haworth Press, Inc.

Levin. J.D. (1998). *Case presentation*. Paper presented at the Addiction and Trauma
Conference, New York.

Lohrenz, L., Connely, J., Coyne, L., and Spare, L. (1978). Alcohol problems in several midwest homosexual populations. *Journal of Studies on Alcohol, 39*, 1959-
1963.

Lombardi, E. L. and van Servellen, G. (2000). Building culturally sensitive substance use programs for transgendered populations. *Journal of Substance Abuse
Treatment, 19*, 291-296.

Lombardi, E. L., Wilchins, R.A., Priesing, D., and Malouf, D. (1998). *Gender violence: Transgender experiences with violence and discrimination*. Manuscript
submitted for publication.

Loris, M. (1994). Countertransference love, hate, and empathy. *Developments: The Newsletter of the Center of Women's Development at HRI Hospital*, Winter 3(1). 1, 4.

Marcel, A.D. (1998). *Determining barriers to treatment for transsexuals and transgenders in substance abuse programs.* Boston: Transgender Education Network. Justice Resource Institute Health.

Marcel, A.D. (2000). Transgender issues and care. Presentation to CSAT LGBT Work Group, Washington, DC. October.

Markowitz, L. (1995). Bisexuality: Challenging our thinking. *In the Family, 1*(1), 6-11, 23.

Markowitz, L. (1997). Editor's note. *In the Family, 2*(4), 2.

Markowitz, L. (2000). Editor's note: "Queerly named." *In the Family, 6*(1), 2.

Maugh, T.M. (2001). Researchers raise concerns on HIV rate. *The Los Angeles Times*, February 6. *The Los Angeles Times* Archives: Internet.

McCann, L. and Pearlman, L.A. (1990a). *Psychological trauma and the adult survivor: Theory, therapy, and transformation.* New York: Brunner/Mazel.

McCann, L. and Pearlman, L.A. (1990b). Vicarious traumatization: A framework for understanding the psychological effects of working with victims. *Journal of Traumatic Stress, 3*(1), 131-149.

McCrady, B.S. and Epstein, E.E. (1999). *Addictions: A comprehensive guidebook.* New York: Oxford University Press.

McGowan, C.K. (1999). *Transgender needs assessment:* (For the HIV Prevention Planning Unit). New York: New York City Department of Health.

McKirnan, D.J. and Peterson, P.L. (1989a). Psychosocial and social factors in alcohol and drug abuse: Epidemiology and population characteristics. *Addictive Behaviors, 14*, 545-553.

McKirnan, D.J. and Peterson, P.L. (1989b). Psychosocial and social factors in alcohol and drug abuse: An analysis of a homosexual community. *Addictive Behaviors, 14*, 555-563.

McKirnan, D.J. and Peterson, P.L. (1992). *Gay and lesbian alcohol use: Epidemiological and psychological perspective.* Paper presented at the Research Symposium on Alcohol and Other Drug Problems among Lesbians and Gay Men, Los Angeles.

McNally, E.B. (1989). *Lesbian recovering alcoholics in Alcoholics Anonymous: A qualitative study of identity transformation.* Unpublished doctoral dissertation, New York University, New York.

McNally, E.B. and Finnegan, D.G. (1992). Lesbian recovering alcoholics: A qualitative study of identity transformation—A report on research and applications for treatment. In D.L. Weinstein (Ed.), *Lesbians and gay men: Chemical dependency treatment issues* (93-103). Binghamton, NY: The Haworth Press, Inc.

Milton, A. (1995). *Lavender light: Daily meditations for gay men in recovery.* New York: Perigree Books.

Mitchell, S.A. (1997). *Influence and autonomy in psychoanalysis.* Hillsdale, NJ: The Analytic Press.

Moran, N. (1996). Lesbian health care needs. *Canada Family Physician, 42*, 879-884.

Mulry, G., Kalichman, S.C., and Kelly, J.A. (1994). Substance use and unsafe sex among gay men: Global versus situational use of substances. *Journal of Sex Education and Therapy, 20,* 175-184.

Munson, M., and Stelboum, J.P. (Eds.). (1999). *The lesbian polyamory reader: Open relationships, non-monogamy, and casual sex.* Binghamton, NY: The Haworth Press, Inc.

Nealy, E. (1995). *Amazon spirit: Daily meditations for lesbians in recovery.* New York: Perigree Books.

Neisen, J.H. (1994a). *Counseling lesbian, gay, and bisexual persons with alcohol and drug abuse problems.* Alexandria, VA: NAADAC Education and Research Foundation.

Neisen, J.H. (1994b). *Reclaiming pride: Daily reflections on gay and lesbian life.* Deerfield Beach, FL: Health Communications.

Nemoto, T., Keatley, J., Cauley, V., Fernandez, A., Rivera, M., Mathew, A., Operario, D., Tamar-Mattis, S., and Tran, J. (1998). *MTF transgender of color study: Preliminary summary from focus groups.* San Francisco: Health Studies for People of Color, Center for AIDS Prevention Studies, UCSF.

The New York Times (1999). Interview. *The New York Times,* p. A27.

Ochs, R. (1994). *The international directory of bisexual groups* (Eleventh edition). Cambridge, MA: Bisexual Resource Center.

Ostrow, D.G. and Kessler, R.C. (1993). *Methodological issues in AIDS behavioral research.* New York: Plenum Press.

Paul, J.P., Hays, R.B., and Coates, T.J. (1995) The impact of the HIV epidemic on U. S. gay male communities. In A.R. D'Augelli and C.J. Patterson (Eds.), *Lesbian, gay, and bisexual identities over the lifespan: Psychological perspectives* (pp. 347-397). New York: Oxford University Press.

Perina, B.A. (2000). Clinical issues in the treatment of chemical dependency with individuals of transgender experience. Workshop presented at NALGAP/NAADAC Conference, July, Denver.

Ponse, B. (1978). *Identities in the lesbian world: The social construction of self.* Westport, CT: Greenwood Press.

Pramaggiore, M. (1996). Sex, power, and pleasure. In M. Storr (Ed.), (1999). *Bisexuality: A critical reader* (pp. 144-149). New York: Routledge.

Prince, V. (1997). Seventy years in the trenches of the gender wars. In B. Bullough, V.L. Bullough, and J. Elias (Eds.), *Gender blending* (pp. 469-476). Amherst, NY: Prometheus Books.

Ratner, E.F. (1993). Treatment issues of chemically dependent lesbians and gay men. In L.D. Garnets and D.C. Kimmel (Eds.), *Psychological perspectives on lesbians and gay male experiences* (pp. 567-578). New York: Columbia University Press.

Reback, C.J. and Lombardi, E.L. (1999). HIV-risk behaviors of male-to-female transgenders in a community-based harm reduction program. *International Journal of Transgenderism, 3,* 1-2.

Reinisch, J.M., Ziemba-Davis, M., and Sanders, S.A. (1990). Sexual behavior and AIDS: Lessons from art and sex research. In B. Voeller, J.M. Reinisch, and M. Gottlieb (Eds.), *AIDS and Sex: An integrated biomedical and biobehavioral approach* (pp. 37-80). New York: Oxford University Press.

Richards. K. (1997). What is a transgenderist? In B. Bullough. V.L. Bullough, and J. Elias (Eds.), *Gender blending* (pp. 503-504). Amherst. NY: Prometheus Books.

Rosario, M., Hunter, J., and Gwadz, M. (1997). Exploration of substance abuse among lesbian, gay, and bisexual youth: Prevalence and correlates. *Journal of Adolescent Research. 12*(4), 454-476.

Royce. J.E. (1995). The effects of alcoholism and recovery on spirituality. In R.J. Kus (Ed.), *Spirituality and chemical dependency* (pp. 19-37). Binghamton, NY: The Haworth Press. Inc.

Rudy, D. (1986). *Becoming alcoholic: Alcoholics Anonymous and the reality of alcoholism*. Carbondale. IL: Southern Illinois University Press.

Rust. P.C. (1996). In B.A. Firestein (Ed.), *Bisexuality: The psychology and politics of an invisible minority* (pp. 127-148). Thousand Oaks, CA: Sage.

Ryan. C.C., Bradford, J.B., and Honnold. J.A. (1999). Social workers' and counselors' understanding of lesbians. *Journal of Gay and Lesbian Social Services, 9*(4), 1-26.

Ryan, C.M.. Huggins. J., and Beatty. R. (1999). Substance use disorders and the risk of HIV infection in gay men. *Journal of Studies on Alcohol, 60*(1), 70-77.

Saghir, M.T. and Robins, E. (1973). *Male and female homosexuality: A comprehensive investigation*. Baltimore: Williams and Wilkins.

SAMHSA. (1996). National Household Survey on Drug Abuse, Main Findings of 1996. Rockville. MD: SAMHSA.

SAMHSA:CSAT (Ed.) (1999). *Cultural issues in substance abuse treatment*. Washington, DC: Substance Abuse Mental Health Services Administration: Center for Substance Abuse Treatment (SAMHSA:CSAT).

SAMHSA:CSAT (Ed.) (2000). *Substance abuse treatment for persons with HIV/AIDS*. Washington. DC: Substance Abuse Mental Health Services Administration: Center for Substance Abuse Treatment (SAMHSA:CSAT).

SAMHSA:CSAT (Ed.) (2001). *A provider's introduction to substance abuse treatment for lesbian, gay, bisexual, and transgender individuals*. Washington, DC: Substance Abuse Mental Health Services Administration: Center for Substance Abuse Treatment (SAMHSA: CSAT).

San Francisco Department of Public Health (SFDPH) (1991). *HIV Seroprevalence Report, 2,* 21.

San Francisco Department of Public Health (SFDPH) (1993a). *Health behaviors among lesbian and bisexual women: A community-based women's health survey*. San Francisco: Author, AIDS Office. Prevention Services Branch.

San Francisco Department of Public Health (SFDPH) (1993b). *HIV Seroprevalence and risk behaviors among lesbians and bisexual women: The 1993 San Francisco/Berkeley women's survey*. San Francisco: Author. AIDS Office. Surveillance Branch.

San Francisco Department of Public Health, AIDS Office (SFDPH) (1997). *HIV prevention and health service needs of the transgender community in San Francisco: Results from eleven focus groups*. San Francisco: Author.

Savin-Williams, R.C. (1994). Verbal and physical abuse as stressors in the lives of lesbian, gay male, and bisexual youths: Associations with school problems, running away, substance abuse, prostitution, and suicide. *Journal of Consulting and Clinical Psychology, 62,* 261-269.

Savin-Williams, R.C. (1995). Lesbian, gay male, and bisexual adolescents. In A.R. D'Augelli and C.J. Patterson (Eds.). *Lesbian, gay, and bisexual identities over the lifespan: Psychological perspectives* (pp. 165-189). New York: Oxford University Press.

Schrang, E.A. (1997). In G.E. Israel and D.E. Tarver. (1997). *Transgender care: Recommended guidelines, practical information, and personal accounts* (pp. 236-240). Philadelphia: Temple University Press.

Seage. G.R.. Mayer, K.H., Horsburgh, C.R., Holmgerg, S.D.. Moon, M.W., and Lamb, G.A. (1992). The relation between nitrite inhalants, unprotected receptive anal intercourse, and the risk of human immuno-deficiency virus infection. *American Journal of Epidemiology, 135,* 1-11.

Shernoff. M. (1997). Conclusion: Mental health considerations of gay widowers. In M. Shernoff (Ed.) (1997), *Gay widowers: Life after the death of a partner* (pp. 137-155). Binghamton, NY: Harrington Park Press.

Skinner, W.F. (1994). The prevalence and demographic predictors of illicit and licit drug use among lesbians and gay men. *American Journal of Public Health, 89,* 1307-1310.

Skinner, W.F. and Otis, M.D. (1992). Drug use among lesbians and gay people: Findings, research, design. insights, and policy issues from the Trilogy Project. *Proceedings of the research symposium on alcohol and other drug problem prevention among lesbians and gay men.* Sacramento, CA: EMT Group, Inc.

Skinner, W.F. and Otis. M.D. (1996). Drug and alcohol use among lesbians and gay people in a southern U. S. sample: Epidemiological. comparative, and methodological findings from the Trilogy Project. *Journal of Homosexuality, 30*(3). 59-92.

Smith. A. (1997). Cultural diversity and the coming-out process: Implications for clinical practice. In B. Greene (Ed.), *Ethnic and cultural diversity among lesbians and gay men: Psychological perspectives on lesbian and gay issues* (Vol. 3), (pp. 279-300). Thousand Oaks. CA: Sage.

Stall, R.D. Greenwood, G.L., Acree, M., Paul, J., and Coates, T.J. (1999). Cigarette smoking among gay and bisexual men. *American Journal of Public Health,* 89(12), 1875-1878.

Stall, R.D., McKusick. L., Wiley. J., Coates, T.J., and Ostrow, D.G. (1986). Alcohol and drug use during sexual activity and compliance with safe sex guidelines for AIDS: The AIDS behavioral research project. *Health Education Quarterly, 13,* 359-371.

Stall, R.D., Paul, J.P., Barrett, D.C., Crosby, G.M., and Bein, E. (1999). An outcome evaluation to measure changes in sexual risk-taking among gay men undergoing substance use disorder treatment. *Journal of Studies of Alcohol, 60*(6), 837-845.

Stall. R.D. and Wiley, J. (1988). A comparison of alcohol and drug use patterns of homosexual and heterosexual men: The San Francisco Men's Health Study. *Drug and Alcohol Dependence, 22,* 63-73.

Stevens. P. (1993). Lesbians and HIV: Clinical, research. and policy issues. *American Journal of Orthopsychiatry, 63,* 289-294.

Stuart, K.E. (1991). *The uninvited dilemma: A question of gender.* Portland, OR: Metamorphous Press.

Surrey, J. (1992, December 5). *Women, addictions, and codependency: A relational perspective.* Paper presented at the Stone Center Seminar, New York City.

Swan, W.K. (1997). The agenda for justice. In W.K. Swan (Ed.), *Gay/lesbian/bisexual/transgender public policy issues: A citizen's and administrator's guide to the new cultural struggle* (pp. 123-129). Binghamton, NY: Harrington Park Press.

The Transgender Substance Abuse Treatment Policy Group of the San Francisco Lesbian, Gay, Bisexual, and Transgender Substance Abuse Task Force. (1995). *Transgender protocol: Treatment services guidelines for substance abuse treatment providers.* San Francisco: Author.

Tilleraas, P. (1988). *The color of light.* Center City, MN: Hazelden.

Troiden, R.R. (1988). *Gay and lesbian identity: A sociological analysis.* Dix Hills, NY: General Hall.

Valentine, D. (1998). *Gender identity project: Report on intake statistics, 1989-April 1997.* New York: Lesbian and Gay Community Services Center.

Valverde, M. (1985). Sex, power, and pleasure. In M. Storr (Ed.). (1999). *Bisexuality: A critical reader* (pp. 112-116). New York: Routledge.

Vannicelli, M. (1989). *Group psychotherapy with adult children of alcoholics: Treatment techniques and countertransference considerations.* New York: Guilford.

Warren, B.E. (1999). Sex, truth and videotape: HIV Prevention at the Gender Identity Project in New York City. *International Journal of Transgenderism, 3,* 1-2.

Watkins, C.E. (1985). Countertransference: Its impact on the counseling situation. *Journal of Counseling and Development, 63*(6), 356-64.

Weinberg, G. (1972). *Society and the healthy homosexual.* Garden City, NY: Anchor Press/ Doubleday.

Weinberg, M. S. and Williams, C. J. (1974). *Male homosexuals: Their problems and adaptations.* New York: Oxford University Press.

Weinberg, M., Williams, S., and Pryor, D. (1994). *Dual attraction: Understanding bisexuality.* New York: Oxford University Press.

Weiss, S.H. (1993). *Risk of HIV and other sexually transmitted diseases (STD) among (high risk bisexual and heterosexual) women in Urban Northern New Jersey.* Paper presented at the Ninth International Conference on AIDS, Berlin, Germany, June.

White, J.C. and Dull, V.T. (1997). Health risk factors and health seeking behaviors in lesbians. *Journal of Women's Health, 6*(1), 103-112.

Wilchins, R.A. (1997). *Read my lips: Sexual subversion and the end of gender.* Ithaca, NY: Firebrand Books.

Wolfe, D. (2000). *Men like us: The GMHC complete guide to gay men's sexual, physical and emotional well-being.* New York: Ballantine Books.

Woll, C.H. (1996). What difference does culture make? Providing treatment to women different from you. In B.L. Underhill and D.G. Finnegan (Eds.), *Chemical dependency: Women at risk* (pp. 67-86). Binghamton, NY: The Haworth Press, Inc.

Wright, E.M., Shelton, C., Browning, M., Orduna, J.M.G., Martinez, V., and Wong, F.Y. (2001). Cultural issues in working with LGBT individuals. In SAMHSA: CSAT (Ed.), *A provider's introduction to substance abuse treatment for lesbian, gay, bisexual, and transgender individuals* (pp.15-27). Washington, DC: Substance Abuse and Mental Health Services Administration: Center for Substance Abuse Treatment (SAMHSA:CSAT).

Xavier, J.M. (2000). *The Washington, DC transgender needs assessment survey: Final report for phase two.* Washington, DC: Administration for HIV/AIDS, Department of Health of the District of Columbia Government.

Index

Page numbers followed by the letter "f" indicate figures.

Harris, Eric, 54
Harry Benjamin International Gender
    Dysphoria Association
    (HBIGDA), SOC, 32-33
Hate crimes, 2, 84
Health care, transgendered person, 205
Health care professionals
    and LGBs, 79
    transphobia, 81, 82-83
Health problems, LGBT, 160
Heroin, transgendered persons, 55, 153,
    203
Heterosexism
    concept of, 13, 14, 73-74
    negative force of, 4, 13-14, 19, 60
    public attitudes, 2
Heterosexual, sexual orientation, 33-34
"Heterosexual privilege," 37, 190
Heterosexual-Leaning Type, bisexual
    type, 36
Heterosexuals, alcohol abuse, 51-52
Hip-hop, homophobic "lyrics," 87
Hispanics, 71, 156
HIV/AIDS
    gay men, 150
    prevention education, 157-158
    prevention of, 154-157
    and self-care, 154
    staff training, 159
    treatment of, 149
HIV/AIDS tests, and confidentiality,
    149
"Homo-cidalism," 13
"Homo-cide," 13
Homophobia
    against transgendered, 200
    concept of, 10-11, 12-13, 14, 73
    institutionalized, 76-79
    internalized, 91, 94, 96, 174
    negative force of, 4, 19, 60
    public attitudes, 2, 75
"Homosexual" culture, 134
Homosexual identity, model
    development, 164
"Homosexual panic," 170

Homosexuality
    and "conversions" of, 78
    etiology of, 49-50
    misguided treatment, 79-80
    as sexual orientation, 33
Homosexual-Leaning Type, bisexual
    type, 36
Hormones, 160, 205, 206
Hostility/anger
    counselor strategies, 106-107
    countertransference, 62
    LGBT defense mechanism, 100,
        105-106
Housing, transgendered substance
    abusers, 32, 58, 124
Housing discrimination, LGBT, 84
Hudson, Rock, 85

Identities, dual, 18-19
Identity
    definition of, 15
    development of, 15
    multiplicity of, 15
    stigmatized, 17-18
    structural views, 16
    threats to, 15-16
    trauma impact, 19-20
Identity acceptance, LG, 183-187
Identity comparison, LG, 172-177
Identity confusion
    bisexual, 191
    LG, 168-172
Identity emersion, LG, 178, 182-183
Identity immersion, LG, 178-181
Identity internalization, bisexual, 192
Identity label formation, bisexual, 191
Identity model, LGBT, 163-165, 167
Identity synthesis, LG 187-188
Identity uncertainty, bisexual, 192-193
Immaturity, bisexual stereotype, 37
Immersion stage, LG identity, 178-181,
    211
Information seeking, transgender stage,
    210